AUSSIE GRIT

Mark Webber is a former Formula One driver who raced for Minardi, Jaguar, Williams and Red Bull. He was twice winner of the Monaco Grand Prix, as well as the British and Brazilian Grands Prix. In 2010 he controversially missed out on the World Championship to team mate Sebastian Vettel. In June 2013 Webber announced his retirement from Formula One and subsequently joined Porsche on a long-term deal, racing in the premier LMP1 sportscar category of the FIA World Endurance Championship. His aim is to win the legendary Le Mans 24 Hour race.

Also by Mark Webber

Up Front

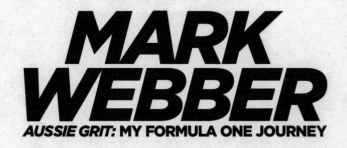

MARK WEBBER

AUSSIE GRIT: MY FORMULA ONE JOURNEY

PAN BOOKS

First published 2015 by Pan Macmillan Australia Pty Ltd

First published in the UK 2015 by Macmillan

First published in paperback 2016 by Pan Books
an imprint of Pan Macmillan
20 New Wharf Road, London N1 9RR
Associated companies throughout the world
www.panmacmillan.com

ISBN 978-1-5098-1354-4

A CIP catalogue record for this book is available from the British Library.

Printed and bound by CPI Group (UK) Ltd, Croydon, CR0 4YY

Visit **www.panmacmillan.com** to read more about all our books
and to buy them. You will also find features, author interviews and
news of any author events, and you can sign up for e-newsletters
so that you're always first to hear about our new releases.

Contents

Foreword

BY SIR JACKIE STEWART

MARK WEBBER HAS HAD A WONDERFUL CAREER AS A TOP-line racing driver. The first time I ever heard his name was from Ann Neal, his long-term partner, who was trying to get Mark to drive in Britain for the British Formula Three Championship. I was running Paul Stewart Racing with my son Paul at that time, and we were regular winners. Ann thought that Mark would be an ideal young, up-and-coming driver for us to take on. Yet, unfortunately we had committed to our drivers by the time Ann called and, therefore, we were unable to add Mark to our team.

However, I then took an interest in following his career and was enormously impressed, like an awful lot of other folk, when he came fifth in the Australian Grand Prix, in Melbourne, driving a Minardi. In fact, Mark's fifth-place finish, in a car that had never appeared so high on the leader's board, got a bigger ovation than the winner of the race that year. It was a tremendous achievement by a young Australian, in what was not expected to be a World

Championship points collector car. All of the Formula One folk were mightily impressed and, from that time on, Mark was high on the list of any Formula One Team; which, of course, was the start of a very successful and impressive career at the highest levels of motorsport for Mark.

For me, Mark Webber is one of my really good friends. He's very enjoyable company, has a great sense of humour and we spend quite a lot of time together, either at my house, on the telephone, or in our travels around the world. His mum and dad are wonderful people too, and you can see where Mark has got his charm from. In addition to which, all the girls fancy Mark Webber! He's a good conversationalist, he is certainly a good-looking man, with a great physique, which has not gone unnoticed among his female admirers. But he's very unspoiled by it, which is a rare commodity. He is extremely unassuming, very loyal and dependable.

Mark has had huge success as a racing driver and could easily have won the World Championship, in my opinion, under different circumstances. The occasion when he came closest to achieving this was when he followed Alonso, at very close proximity, all the way through the Abu Dhabi Grand Prix, which was the last race of the season. The modern Grand Prix tracks allow drivers to make mistakes, run wide, so when Alonso made such errors and previously all Mark would have needed to do was to finish ahead of him to secure the World Championship that year, Fernando used as much road as he needed, therefore not allowing Mark to overtake him.

In years past, nobody could have done that, because going wide on a corner would have meant getting on the grass with little or no traction and maybe even having an accident. However, because of the modern tracks being so forgiving, Mark, in my opinion, was robbed that year of becoming World Champion.

My most enjoyable times with Mark have always been away from the track. His casual approach to dress code is somewhat contrary to my philosophy and, of course, it's something that we still joke about often. My funniest experience was when I was somewhat in awe of Mark winning the Monaco Grand Prix for the first time and we were in attendance at the glamorous gala which takes place at the Sporting Club in Monte Carlo on the Sunday night of the race weekend. The visiting dignitaries and the past winners, in the case of myself and Helen, were seated at the table of Their Serene Highnesses, all dressed in black tie and the ladies in long dresses, and all their finest jewellery.

When Mark arrived as the winner, he was wearing a pair of jeans, a T-shirt and running trainers! Most of us were taken aback, to say the least, but not our Mark; he was comfortable, he was at ease, and it had never occurred to him – or I fear Ann – when packing to come to the Riviera for the Grand Prix that he might win the race and, under such circumstances, would be expected to be in black tie and evening wear; not to mention sitting with Their Serene Highnesses. I, of course, took best advantage of giving him a hard time, but he handled the whole thing with great style and, indeed, elegance. Nevertheless, when he won the Grand Prix for the second time, he was fully prepared to be in black tie and looking a million dollars.

He's now living a life out of Formula One and driving for one of the great brands of the world, Porsche, in the World Endurance Championship. He is also venturing into the arena of media and public speaking, where he's learning that presentation skills and dress code are sometimes just as important as knowing the right people, saying the right things and driving the right cars.

This book is indeed well overdue because of what Mark has achieved in motor racing. Most people would be extremely proud of what he has accomplished. He has carried himself in a very dignified fashion and has remained a true Australian, in the fullest sense, and is much loved because of that. There are no sides and no airs and graces to Mark Webber. What you see is what you get, and what you get is great value and, if you are me, great friendship.

Prologue

'MULTI 21': A RAG TO
A RED BULL

WHEN THE TELEPHONE CALL CAME, MY FIRST REACTION WAS one of surprise.

'Wow,' I thought, 'that's a pretty big statement with 12 laps to go, given we're running this way round!'

'Telephone call' is the expression we use to describe radio communication from the pit wall to the cockpit. The statement being made over the radio was 'Multi 21'. Even in a sport where mixed messages are the order of the day, 'Multi 21' was the clearest order we could have been given. Both Sebastian Vettel and I, in Red Bull Renaults #1 and #2 respectively, knew exactly what it meant: that our cars should finish the Malaysian Grand Prix, second round of the 2013 Formula One World Championship, in that order, #2 followed by #1, with me first and Sebastian second. That's how we were running at the time, with me leading my teammate late in the race and no threat from anyone else.

Why was I surprised? Rarely had the call come when it was in my favour, that's why. But this time the circumstances were very much in my favour: I had timed my crossover – the moment at which to make the mandatory tyre change from one Pirelli compound to the other – perfectly. Seb had got tangled up with the pursuing Mercedes and I found myself in clear air, so I was out in front.

I was a lot less surprised by Sebastian's reaction to the 'Multi 21' message.

After the final stops, when he was cruising up behind me, I could see the 'letter-box' opening on the rear wing of his car: he was using its Drag Reduction System (DRS) to increase his top speed. Straightaway I knew he was going against what the team had asked us to do. He was going to make it hard for me.

Not for the first time another thought followed: 'How the f#*k are we, as a team, in this situation?'

In hindsight I should have turned my engine back up and got into the fight, but there was so much going on in my head that it never occurred to me to do so. We came home first and second, but instead of finishing with the cars in #2 and #1 order, Vettel took the victory.

The incident was the final nail in the coffin of my relationship with Red Bull Racing at management level. 'Multi 21' was just one flashpoint in a sequence that began as far back as Istanbul in 2010. It was an important stage on my journey, but it's not the whole story.

This book is.

IN THE COCKPIT:
A MARATHON IN SHOES
TWO SIZES TOO SMALL

IT'S A CLOSED WORLD.

All your senses are either severely limited or under unremitting assault. The space you occupy is small and bloody hot.

The helmet is tight-fitting. Your view is confined to what you can see through the 'mailbox' opening in your helmet and in two postage-stamp-sized rear mirrors.

And you are in this minor hell, all going well, for two hours. You're in isolation, but it's far from splendid.

The cockpit gradually becomes a lonely place as the clock ticks down to race start. In many ways it's similar to sitting in any racing car – except it's a lot more claustrophobic.

A Grand Prix car is built for speed, not comfort. The driver doesn't get into his car, he inserts himself into the cockpit as a living component of the machine. The cockpit is a compact place, especially for a driver of my dimensions. At around 184 centimetres and a fighting weight of 75 kilos

I was never the ideal size or weight for a Grand Prix driver. There have been tall F1 drivers – men like Dan Gurney in the old days, Gerhard Berger more recently, Jenson Button today – but they are the exceptions who prove the rule. Better to be a jockey than a Michael Jordan.

The space is really tight around your knees – it's like sitting in an old-fashioned bathtub with your feet higher than your backside. The pedals are actually moulded around your racing boot, both for comfort and to counter excessive vibration: the last thing you want is for your foot to slip off the pedal at high speed in the middle of a race. The boots are thin-soled so you can feel everything and they are the one item I'm very fussy about – once I break a pair in nicely they generally last me for a season.

Helmets are different: I go through between four and seven. The exterior takes a bit of a hammering, especially if you are coming through from the back of the grid as the 'marbles' (small pieces of rubber coming off other cars' tyres) come pinging at you on the way through. I used to push my head back into the headrest a lot because that way I could move my head around in the helmet a bit. The interior is customised for each driver, although not the straps, and I found they used to sit a little too far rearwards for me. At fast tracks like Monza, Red Bull Chief Technical Officer Adrian Newey used to hate running any little windscreens in front of the cockpit because of the aerodynamic effect, and I had to open my mouth to counteract the helmet lift from the onrushing air. I would end up with two bruises under my neck.

I had only one superstition: I always got into my car from the left, a hangover from my karting days – if you got in on the right side of one of those you ended up with burns on your arm from the engine!

But I did have a race-day routine. It began with a last visit to the treatment couch to have my hips and pelvis loosened up a little and my shoulders and neck rubbed.

In F1 the pit lane opens to let the cars out on track for their final warm-up procedures half an hour before race start. At that stage I was always happy to talk to my partner, Ann, or Dad but people I didn't know were kept well away.

Then it was time to hop in. Or, more accurately, step, slither and bump into your seat, which has been almost literally tailor-made to your unique dimensions. The driver is the biggest component in that cockpit: they make the seat up around him, starting from behind. It couldn't fit more snugly if it came from Savile Row.

The seatbelts intensify that feeling. They come together in a six-pointed star at your centre: two of them come up through the groin area on either side of your manhood; and there are two lap straps and two shoulder straps, all designed to the nearest millimetre around your size. What most people don't realise is that if you're not careful the edges of the belts can fold or 'pinch' and when they do those edges can be quite sharp, especially around the more sensitive areas of a bloke's anatomy.

With the help of one of your pit crew, the belts are pulled extremely tight, for two reasons: the first, obviously, is to hold you in place in the event of what we call a 'shunt'; the second, less obviously, is to help eliminate the muscle fatigue that would come from trying to keep yourself properly in the seat without belts. You need to be a fixed component of the machine.

How tight are the belts? Back in 2001, when I won the F3000 race at Imola, I was on painkillers to counter the effects of a broken rib caused by the extreme cornering loads in a recent F1 test in the Benetton-Renault.

With less than 15 minutes to race start, I sometimes hop out again – the reverse of bump-slither-step – and attend to the physical necessities or, putting it another way, go for a pee at the last possible moment; and stretch the lower back and glutes one last time because they are going to be immobilised for the next couple of hours. Hop back in, check the belts and HANS device, the one that looks after the head and neck, get as comfortable as the car allows, connect the drink bottle.

So: you are strapped into a space barely big enough to contain you in the first place. You can scarcely move, except for your feet, arms, hands. The headrest comes in pretty snugly around you; down goes the visor, the radio sits about 3 millimetres off your lips, earplugs in, drink tube coming in beside the radio . . . and the sensation of enclosure is heightened even more. With that comes stress and elevated heart rate, which goes up because of the pressure on your ribcage; you can't breathe normally as you would standing or running or riding a bike, you're in a quite different position.

Don't focus too far ahead, just concentrate on getting the immediate things right. Talk to your race engineer: how strong is the wind out on the circuit? What's the track temperature? Have we got our plan right for controlling the first part of the race?

As the countdown intensifies, all the people begin to melt away. Just moments before the start of the warm-up lap may be the first time this weekend I have seen, 'live' as it were, the Ferrari or Mercedes alongside me on our row of the grid.

A practice start at the end of pit lane was part of the pre-race routine; so was a full throttle check, always insisted on by engine-supplier Renault; then a radio check and an electronics check on the clutch. Coming through the grid was like threading the needle, manoeuvring the car through the literally hundreds of people – pit crew, media, race officials, VIPs and countless hangers-on – who manage to find their way out there.

The warm-up lap is broken down into three sectors. Sector 1 is all about getting the engine cooled after sitting, sometimes for an alarmingly long time, waiting for the signal to go. Use high gears, say up to seventh, and sit at around 6000 revs if possible. I'm working the tyres, veering sharply from side to side to get them warm, but not overdoing the zig-zag stuff. 'Engine temp fine,' crackles through my earplugs, so it's time to focus on the brakes. Now I can open the throttle and hit the brake pedal to warm them up without worrying about the effects of any overheating on the engine behind me. In Sector 3 I'm off the leash to do whatever I like on the engine front; now it's all about making sure brakes and tyres are up around their ideal working temperatures.

F1 fans will be familiar with those sudden bursts of pace – burn-outs – from the drivers midway through their warm-up lap, and that's another little bit of information to be retained. We used to be given documents telling us where we could start those burn-outs on the circuit in relation to visual cues like sponsor hoardings – all very well if you could remember the right sponsor!

Another factor in the equation: fuel. Is this a circuit where our fuel consumption is critical? Or, just as importantly, someone else's? In my latter F1 days the Mercedes cars were known to be fuel-sensitive: if the two Red Bulls were on the front row we sometimes debated whether we should do an unusually fast formation lap to help set their nerves on edge, though in practice we never did. Pull up in my grid slot, select neutral . . . and wait for the moment of truth.

I used to get a call from pit wall when the 17th of the 22 cars had reached its grid slot. That's when I selected first gear. Then I built the engine revs from the moment when the second of the five red lights on the gantry came on. Waiting for the lights to go out, the drivers feel their heart rate rise. Mine was less dramatic than many: with a resting heart rate in the low 40s when I was at peak fitness, it would climb to around 120 at a Grand Prix start and the maximum I ever recorded was 182. A big part of it is simple adrenaline; I could sound perfectly normal in conversation with my crew but my heart rate would be noticeably higher than before.

The simple truth of a Grand Prix start is that you must react to the lights as best you can. People probably think you're trying to get a jump on everyone else by anticipating that moment – but that's a reasonably good way to get yourself penalised for a jump start. It's hard to anticipate in any case because there is a random 'window' of 3–5 seconds in which the lights will go out. You'll be doing 100 kilometres an hour in less than three seconds and it's risky to get ahead of yourself.

Raw acceleration, braking, cornering – everything is on an extreme level. Even people who are used to racing at a high level in other categories struggle to totally calibrate with what a Formula 1 car can do. The more experience you gain, the slower things get, but the inputs – the movements the driver makes on steering-wheel, throttle and so on – are unbelievably fine.

If the two Red Bulls were on the front row of the grid I would regularly lose 3 or 4 metres to Sebastian in the first couple of seconds of a race. We tried various techniques to help reaction time; I did a warm-up routine before getting into the car but I binned that idea because my reaction times were actually better on a lower heart-rate, not higher. That's to do with your unique physical make-up. In the days when they were teammates at Ferrari, Eddie Irvine's reaction times were markedly superior to Michael Schumacher's, and another Ferrari favourite, Felipe Massa, was always very quick. But bear in mind that we are talking about a range of around only two-hundredths of a second . . .

Part of my perceived problem with race starts in the later stages of my F1 career was not, as a lot of people probably thought, down to age, but my sensitivity to rubber! At any race start the driver wants to be as sensitive as he can to what happens when he drops the clutch and begins to feel the wheels move under him. It's essential to eliminate or at least minimise wheel-spin – and after the change of rules on F1 tyre supply I just couldn't 'feel' the Pirellis to the degree I should have done.

So much information to process as the crucial moment approaches. Do we know the tyre temperatures? What's the grip level from the track like? It can vary dramatically depending on whether a driver's starting position is on the left or right side of the track. One will have had more rubber laid down on it during race weekend than the other as the cars follow the correct line, and that rubber will interact with your tyres to help 'launch' the car into motion.

What's the clutch's 'bite' point, the moment at which the car comes alive? Back in my Formula Ford days it was pretty straightforward: 8000 revs, dump the clutch, bang, go! The technical sophistication of a Grand Prix car is light years away from that, but the reactions from the components governed by technology were never entirely predictable – a bit like the driver's!

And what about the track itself? They can be worlds apart: at Interlagos in Brazil, the start is uphill so the driver has to keep his foot on the brakes to stop rolling backwards; at Suzuka in Japan it's the exact opposite as the circuit plunges immediately downhill to that thrilling first corner and the car wants to start rolling forward.

Then all hell is let loose on your eardrums, first by the sound of your engine screaming into racing mode. The first few seconds of a race – often so crucial to what happens at the other end – also depend on the track. Take Monaco: the run to the first corner, Ste Dévote, is short, tense and incredibly tight; Monza is the opposite, with that long, long run down to the right–left chicane at the end of the straight. Getting the gear-shift points is vital: lights on the wheel and, if you have asked for it, a 'beep' will remind you to shift.

A driver goes through so many emotions during the course of a race – all your sensations are heightened – so if someone goes off the track you can actually smell the cut grass before you go past the scene. It's just as well, really:

your eyes are not telling you all that much. The driver's eye-line is at knee level so the sensation of speed is greatly increased from where he is sitting, and the trajectory can be a little hard to pick out.

Our vision – already fairly tightly defined by our helmets – is further reduced by the high sides of the cockpit with the padded insert to protect the driver's head in case of impact. Believe it or not, but when I'm in the cockpit I can't see my own front wing. And it only gets worse when it rains.

Your visibility then is virtually nil, so you are making micro-decisions the whole time. I can't think of any sport, motorcycle racing excepted, where such focus is required, where your visibility is so severely tested at such speed. Every now and again you get a break in the level of spray, you catch a glimpse of a braking board or something else that will give you a context.

You're looking for hoardings or signs as markers to where exactly you might be on a 5-kilometre circuit. Your default vision has been pulled back so much closer to where you are sitting and believe me, pulling information from the side of the car rather than the front, working out to within 20 metres where you actually are, is mentally very draining. The racing lines change in the wet, too. More than ever, in these conditions, composure is what's called for.

Mental strength is certainly what you need when it comes to racing at a place like Monaco. But then there is no place remotely like Monaco. When I was leading there it was constant resetting, lap by lap: copy and paste what you did last time round, nudge your confidence level up over a two-to-three lap stretch; don't try to grab too much round there. At Mirabeau, for example, the downhill run followed by the right-hander that takes you towards the hairpin, you have to fight against the feeling that you're on the brakes too early. Jenson Button once asked me if I felt, as he said he did, that as the race went on the Monaco barriers actually closed in on you even more. My answer was a firm 'No': those barriers don't move; it's always about you, your car and the track you are on.

Our job is to keep the car on the absolute limit and get it through the corners as quickly as possible. Every F1 corner is a tightrope, with the driver working as hard as he can to balance the car and get a bit more out of it – yet this animal underneath us is trying to pull our arms out of our sockets and our head off our shoulders.

Corner entry is the crucial thing: hit the brakes at the right moment, hit them hard and ignore the deceleration forces – up to five times your own body weight – going through you.

Next: turn into the corner itself. Some turn in early, others 'go deeper', then turn in later and more violently. Keep the car in line: don't put too much lock on, don't slide – stay on that tightrope. Get to the apex, the real change of direction, and start thinking about getting out of the corner. Keep the beast in line before you release it . . . use all of the road and then some on exit . . . then get on the throttle. Focus, feeling and concentration, corner after corner, lap after lap.

In fact you can get into that trance-like state that sporting people call 'the zone'. For a racing driver it's about flow and rhythm, your inputs allowing the car to weave its way around a circuit smoothly and consistently – something you can gauge by your lap times. When I was 'in the zone'

I found myself thinking like a chess-player, several moves ahead; when the car was going through Casino Square I was already mentally at Mirabeau. There was that feeling of easy repeatability: every lap would be timed to within a tenth of a second of the one before or after. Rhythm . . . repetition.

It's so hard to shut down after a Grand Prix. Your ears feel as if you've just got out of an aeroplane but then these things are fighter jets that stay on the ground, so in a sense you have. You've been fixed for so long at the centre of a storm of sound and vibration, your concentration levels have been phenomenally high as you process information coming at you and changing virtually with every metre of ground you have been covering. All you want to do is get out of there.

What's it like to be in the cockpit of an F1 car?

It's like running a marathon in shoes two sizes too small.

1

No Wings, Learning to Fly: 1976–94

I WAS AN ADDICT BEFORE I WAS 10.

I simply couldn't get enough: I'd have my fix on a Sunday night, or Monday morning, and I'd keep coming back for another hit, and another one after that. It started in 1984, when I was just seven years old. That was the year Nigel Mansell should have won the Monaco Grand Prix for Lotus but crashed in the wet on the hill going up towards Casino Square. His accident left a young bloke called Ayrton Senna in with a great shout of winning his first Grand Prix in a Toleman Hart, of all things, but the race was stopped because of the rain and Alain Prost was declared the winner for McLaren on count-back instead. I remember it like yesterday. My drug, of course, was Formula 1.

I was born on 27 August, 1976, midway through the memorable year when Britain's James Hunt and Austrian Niki Lauda went head-to-head for the world title. Their season-long duel, including Lauda's near-fatal crash in Germany, was the subject of the highly successful 2013 movie *Rush*. When I came on the scene the Webber clan was living in Queanbeyan (from the Aboriginal 'Quinbean', meaning 'clear waters') in the Southern Tablelands of New South Wales, hard up against the border with the Australian Capital Territory. It's best known for producing people who excelled in sport, like cricketer Brad Haddin, squash star Heather McKay and Rugby Union great David Campese.

Queanbeyan had been the stamping ground for the Webber family for a couple of generations by the time I arrived. My paternal grandfather, Clive, was born in Balmain in Sydney and my grandmother on that side, Tryphosa – Dad tells me it's a Biblical name but he's never come across it in his reading – was from Cessnock in the Hunter region of New South Wales. Both of them moved to the Queanbeyan area early in life, before they knew each other. They married in Queanbeyan in 1941. My dad, Alan, came along in 1947 and he has one sister, Gwen.

Clive was originally a wood merchant, back in the days when there was good business to be done delivering firewood. He delivered wood to Hotel Currajong, where then Prime Minister Ben Chifley spent a lot of time, and also supplied wood to Parliament House. When war broke out Clive went down to Sydney to enlist but was sent home when they realised they needed to hang on to the bloke who delivered wood to such important addresses. He continued as a wood carter until 1955, when he bought what became the family business, Bridge Motors, a Leyland dealership with two petrol bowsers on the footpath on the main street of Queanbeyan.

My dad and mum met in the early sixties. My mum, Diane, was from a well-known local family, the Blewitts. Her dad, David George Blewitt – 'DG' for short – and her mum, Marie, were married in 1947, but Marie died of cancer at the age of 48 so my sister Leanne and I never knew her. Dad tells me Marie was a wonderful lady: they got along famously and she worked for him at one stage. DG had 2000 acres which my mother's sister Pam still owns and runs. Mum was at school with Dad's sister and often used to spend time at their home. Mum likes to say she couldn't stand Dad at first, but he insists that was only because he used to like watching the ABC, all the old English comedy shows he still enjoys, and she thought he was being a bit of a smartie-bum, as he puts it. She must have got over that because they started going out in 1968 and were married in 1971, on Dad's 24th birthday. As he likes to say, he 'Blewitt' when he married her! My sister, Leanne, came along in 1974 and in 1976 I followed. I share the same birthday with cricketer Sir Donald Bradman and, coincidentally, with two Grand Prix drivers from the not-so-distant past, Derek Warwick and Gerhard Berger.

Dad built our family home in Irene Avenue, an awesome place that for me was filled with good memories. I went to Isabella Street Primary and then Karabar High, both close to home. I represented the school in athletics and Rugby League, I played Aussie Rules and I was quite keen on cricket and swimming. I was a jack of all trades and legend of none! Perhaps surprisingly it was my mum who encouraged me to get involved in as many different sports as I could. 'Having a go' was how she put it, and I was only too happy to take her advice.

Beyond the normal schoolboy activities, Dad was all over motor sport. As a youngster he used to hitchhike to Warwick Farm, which was then a popular Sydney motor-racing venue. Naturally, with Clive running a mechanical repairs business, there were always motorbikes around so it's no surprise that I grew up with an interest in motor sport myself.

I often think of my grandfather Clive. He was a really special person – incredibly popular, always had a smile on his face, a hell of a man for a practical joke. He was unique and definitely important to what I've stood for, the legacy left to his own son and to me. Dad's pretty similar. He likes to say every day is a birthday for him, he doesn't want to have any enemies, just wants to have a good time. Clivey was a legend and many of Dad's traits – and some of mine as well – have come from him.

Mum's dad, DG, loved us to bits, but he was a farmer and always busy. I remember him worrying incessantly about me either injuring myself on the motorbike at the farm or starting bushfires. Over the years I did both, so perhaps he had every reason to be worried! It's fair to say, too, that I was never going to be a farmer. I was always at the workshop tinkering away with Clive. The business grew, so they moved it out of town, and Dad took it on from there.

It wasn't the showiest joint around but it was always a popular spot – the same guys were always around the place. Opposite our house in Irene Avenue in Mark Place lived a family called the Zardos. Both their lads used to work at Dad's petrol station and Gino Zardo went on to become one of the best photographers in New York. He calls me 'Sparky' whenever I see him, and that's all down to Clive. When

I was born Clive said, 'He's a little Champion spark plug!' and the name just stuck.

Clive died of cancer at 78 when I was 15. The day he died, I was staying with one of my best mates, Peter Woods, and his mum came down and said, 'Your granddad passed away.' I was a mess. Seeing what he'd had to go through for the past three years of his illness had been extremely painful for our family. Clive hadn't even seen me go-karting, which I started when I was 13. I would love for all my grand-parents to have seen what I've achieved, for Mum and Dad's sake. You always want those sorts of relationships to go on forever, but of course they can't. Dad's a big, solid man, as you would expect an ex-Rugby player to be, whereas Clive was like me, lean and tall. Mum often says in some of the photos when he was young he's just a dead ringer for me when I was that age. Tryphosa died around the time of the first Melbourne Grand Prix in 1996. I remember Dad getting the phone call just as we were leaving the hotel and being totally blown away by how strong he was. I think of them often and when I've raced, although they never saw me turn a wheel, they've always been with me. Cancer and its impact on so many lives means something specific and very painful to me.

Queanbeyan wasn't a big town by any stretch of the imagination, but Leanne and I quickly built our own separate group of friends as we were growing up. My earliest memories of Leanne are of being on the farm on our motor-bikes and tailing lambs. She was always into animals and had a far more natural instinct for the farm than I ever did. We had massive family times together on the farm in the evenings, my grandfather DG, Aunty Pam, Uncle Nigel and their two boys, Adam and Johnny, Mum, Dad, Leanne and me. There were lots of summer holidays to Mollymook on the New South Wales south coast where Dad's sister Gwen had a holiday home. Leanne and I would both take a couple of friends so there were always lots of kids running amok or hitting the surf.

In school term Leanne and I were always on a different program. I was always late to bed and late to school, she was the complete opposite. Mum used to take us both to the Queanbeyan swimming club on Wednesday nights and I remember how freezing cold it was. Leanne and I did a bit of recreational stuff together but that stopped when racing took over.

Dad had played Rugby Union through school and on weekends until he was in his thirties. He was pretty good, too: he represented New South Wales as a junior, played first grade in the local competition and he likes to boast that he played for Queanbeyan alongside Australian great David Campese in 1981.

Thanks to Mum and Dad, sport certainly played a large part in my own upbringing. Dad still remembers very fondly the day I was picked above my age group for a Rugby League final: I scored two intercepted tries and helped us win the local shield. I played full-forward in Aussie Rules and kicked quite a few goals, and I had a crack at tennis as well. I wasn't a gun at any of it, but the mentality in the Webber household was to have a crack.

Queanbeyan was a small enough town with plenty of competitive families who loved sport. There was always that natural sort of comparison going on. 'Were you in the newspaper?' was a frequent question among the people I grew up with. But it was always very friendly: it wasn't a contest between parents as to whose son had done what, it was always just a question of wanting to do well, because that's what we were encouraged to do.

I did enjoy sport, and I'm pretty sure that's where my competitive nature grew. Whether it was a football match or a computer game, I always liked to win. My only problem was that I wouldn't put in the practice and the discipline to improve. It wasn't till I was much older that my focus sharpened and I could see the benefits of applying myself.

I got a privileged insight into the need for discipline and dedication in sport at a pretty early age. When I was 13 I 'worked' for a year as a ball-boy for the Canberra Raiders, a little job that came about because Dad knew the Raiders' Under-21 coach, Mick Doyle. Ball-boy for Mal Meninga and those blokes for a year – what an opportunity! Ten dollars a game was big bucks in those days, and I even travelled to all the away games, which meant hotel rooms in places as far afield as Brisbane. Phenomenal experience for a kid in his early teens!

To see those guys play, to hear the legendary coach Tim Sheens firing them up – I didn't fully realise how lucky I was to have that experience. At that stage I simply didn't understand how important motivation was. Those players did whatever it took to get them out on the paddock week in, week out, because that's what competing and winning is all about: turning up and having a real go.

Sport apart, school and I didn't really connect. Depending on which of my teachers you asked, they would tell you: 'Mark Webber? He was loud . . . he was popular . . .

he was articulate . . . he was a bit arrogant . . . he was lazy and unmotivated . . . he drove his car like a maniac!'

Most of those descriptions were true, I suppose, but the negative stuff didn't come about because I didn't like being at school in the first place. Far from it: I loved school, I rarely missed a day. But I was mischievous and disruptive in the classroom, no question about it. It used to frustrate Mum quite a lot and she threatened me with boarding school on a number of occasions. Dad didn't help matters because if the school hauled him and Mum in when I was in trouble he'd laugh when he heard what I'd been getting up to. He even went so far as to tell them that he wished he had thought up some of my pranks when he was at school. Actually he had: one of them was stuffing potatoes up the exhaust pipes of the teachers' cars and he confessed he had done that in his own youth. On another memorable occasion I was in an agriculture class and I buried all the shovels. Next day the teacher couldn't find them; I got a telephone call and told them they were right there beneath their feet!

My last year at school was when I had the biggest fun I've had in my life, because I got my driving licence. I was never one for studying but when there was something I was interested in, like getting my licence, it seemed to come more easily. I got the book you needed to study to go for your licence one day and passed it the next! I had just one lesson from a friend of Dad's who ran a driving school, but Dad had let me sit on his lap when I was eight or so on the way out to the farm, and I'd had plenty of chances to drive tractors and other farm vehicles before I was 10, so the licence was never a problem. My first car was a 1969

Toyota Corona, two on the tree, $500, and you can imagine the stuff we got up to.

At school lunchtimes I would load up the car with mates and head for the nearby rally stages or fire trails. Sometimes I'd go and recce them on my own then put the wind up my passengers later by spearing off the tarmac road straight onto dirt tracks, safe in the knowledge that I knew exactly what I was doing. They weren't massively impressed! Nor was the teacher who hopped in with me one day to go and buy some ice. He said later I had two speeds, Fast and Stop, and swore he would never get in a car with me again.

On our muck-up day – the final day of Year 12 when the students virtually take over the school – the boys filmed an on-board lap of me driving around Queanbeyan which involved several near-misses with parked cars and plenty of handbrake turns. My trademark move was to stop at pedestrian crossings with the handbrake; somehow I never managed to convince Dad that the square rear tyres with wire hanging out were a standard tyre defect!

Speaking of tyres, all four of mine were let down one day – by one of my teachers. Mr Walker taught science and I was never in any of his classes, but he clearly took exception to the fact that I used to park in the staff car park. Well, it was convenient – much closer to roll-call. Once we got to the bottom of it, some mates and I went round to his house one night about a week later to get a bit of our own back. Nothing serious: just some flour and eggs, or maybe a couple of those potatoes stuffed up the exhaust pipe. That plan had to be abandoned – Mr Walker was sitting in his car even though it was 10.30 at night!

I also used my Toyota to deliver pizzas around the Quean-beyan and Canberra area. I soon found out there was a skill to learning house names and numbers and finding flats and units, after countless episodes of knocking on doors with a pizza in hand only to be told, 'Nah mate, you've got the wrong house.' Delivering to parties was always the worst: I'd always get the piss taken out of me in my horrendous uniform with a little leather pouch which I would rifle through trying to give back the right change.

Dad says now that he was worried I might turn out a bit of a devil, but every now and again I would knuckle down to school work. The most important thing for me was to have a relationship with the teacher. If there was a bit of friction between us, that meant I never had the motivation to pay attention. But a few teachers along the way worked out how I ticked, things clicked and I made a half-decent stab at their subjects. A lot of the people I knew did well at Karabar High, but I used it mainly for socialising, playing sport and having meals at the canteen!

*

When my love of Formula 1 emerged Dad was as happy as a sand-boy. Australia had started getting television coverage of Grand Prix racing in the aftermath of Alan Jones's World Championship year in 1980, although races weren't always shown as they happened because of the time difference, and I think Dad was delighted that I had caught the bug. He was particularly impressed by Jack Brabham, long before 'Black Jack', as he was later known, became the first knight of motor racing. Jack had made a name for himself on speedway circuits that weren't all that far from where we lived. His was certainly the biggest name in the Webber household, and my story as a racing driver really begins with how inspirational Jack was both to Dad and then to me.

Dad was a huge open-wheeler fan. He loved going to watch Jackie Stewart and other international drivers racing at Warwick Farm against our local heroes in the Tasman Series. Touring cars, which are so popular in Australia, just never cut it as far as we were concerned – it was the Indianapolis 500 and Formula 1 for us! The best drivers in the world were in single-seaters and Dad loved the precision and accuracy of that kind of racing. I guess most young boys follow what their dads love, and that's what I did.

Mum could hardly get me off to school on Monday mornings after a Grand Prix; I'd tape every race, watch it 'live', then watch it again when I got home from school. Mum and Dad used to have friends round, parents of other kids I knew and while they sat there I'd be watching a Grand Prix for probably the eighth or ninth time, the same race over and over again, with a bowl of my favourite ice-cream.

The Australian Grand Prix was staged in Adelaide starting in November 1985, when I was nine years old. It was televised by Channel 9 in those days. I needed eight video tapes just for that one race weekend alone! It was always the final race of the season, so after Adelaide I'd be in mourning for four months before F1 came round again, the first race usually broadcast from Brazil, to see the new drivers in their different helmets, and all the different teams. It was just brilliant, I loved it. Dad and I couldn't wait for each new season to start.

The first year Dad took me to the Grand Prix was 1987, when I was 11. The drive took us 14 hours and I got the sulks when Alain Prost, who was my hero in those days, retired after 53 laps with a brake disc failure. At that stage Alain had won two of his eventual four World Championships; he had also recently overtaken Jackie Stewart's long-standing record of 27 Grand Prix victories.

How could I possibly have dreamt that 25 years later Alain Prost and a kid from Queanbeyan would go cycling together on one of the most famous stages of the Tour de France and be on first-name terms?

But I will never forget the first impression these cars made on me in Adelaide. Our seats were on the front straight; Martin Brundle, now a popular television analyst of the sport, was first round in his Zakspeed and I nearly lost my breakfast! It went past us so fast I just couldn't believe there was a driver at the wheel. To me, these guys were absolutely bloody awesome – I even climbed trees trying to get a better view. That's when F1 started to become religious for me.

But for all the passion I put into it, I never thought for a moment at that stage that I would get any closer to Formula 1 than hanging off a tree in Adelaide to watch those great names rip past me. These drivers were a million miles away from the kind of racing I had first been exposed to, which revolved around dirt-bikes, sprint cars – brilliant little rockets designed for high-speed racing on short oval tracks – and midget cars.

For several years, starting when I was just eight and going through to my early teens, Dad took me to our nearest speedway at Tralee, in the Queanbeyan suburbs, where I perched on his shoulders to watch the exploits of local blokes like George Tatnell and Garry Rush, a 10-time national sprint car champion. Some of the big American names came over as well. I remember Dad being blown away by seeing Johnny Rutherford, the multiple Indianapolis 500 winner from Texas who was nicknamed 'Lone Star JR', out here in a sprint car and behaving as if he was just a normal bloke.

A particular favourite of ours was another American called Steve Kinser. It was mesmerising to watch him – he seemed to be able to put his car wherever he liked, he could pass anywhere at all. Dad had never raced but he was what you would call a petrol-head and I was delighted to go along with him. But even later, when the idea of racing in my own right first began to take hold in my mind, the question remained: 'How the f#*k are *you* going to get to F1, coming from Queanbeyan?' It was a legitimate enough question. You can count the number of Australians who have achieved anything significant in Formula 1 on the fingers of one hand. When I was a boy F1 was in the air because of Alan Jones, and before that because of Jack Brabham, but as far as we were concerned it was a game for Europeans, Americans and Brazilians, not for people like us.

*

I'd been riding motorbikes since I was a little tacker of about four or five when I had the run of DG's farm at weekends. Dad would set up little tracks for me and I'd race around for hours on end on my Pee Wee 50. One day I had a massive shunt which knocked the stuffing out of me. I would have been eight at the time and I was covered in blood and black and blue all over. Dad wasn't too keen to take me back to the farmhouse for fear of incurring the wrath of Disey – my mum. Instead he drove me straight home to

Queanbeyan and cleaned me up the best he could. I also had a decent stack with my auntie Pam: I was sitting on the tank, grabbed full throttle and if I remember rightly the two of us cleaned up a fence.

Dad had the Yamaha dealership in Queanbeyan for 16 years, but he never encouraged me to get into bikes in a serious way. He once sold a road bike to a fellow who was killed on it a few months later. Dad had felt misgivings about the sale at the time and he took it badly – he felt very sorry for the family. He and I never did anything competitive with bikes, but Bridge Motors did have a little team in motocross and speedway. Dad used to say those kids would ride over the top of each other to win, never mind what the other competitors might do!

But it wasn't until I got to 12 or 13 that I put my foot on the first rung of the motor-racing ladder. One of my schoolmates' father was doing some racing of his own in midgets, but he also had a go-kart and I was pretty keen to have a go at that. Dad reminded me that the whole Webber family had had a crack at go-karting one time at a fun park up in Surfers Paradise. He wasn't particularly impressed by my skills on that occasion!

But as most motor-racing people will tell you, karting is the perfect way for a budding racing driver to get started. You can drive them as young as seven, or even earlier, and it was through karting that some of F1's biggest names – men like Ayrton Senna and Michael Schumacher – were introduced to the sport they would eventually dominate.

Karting trains the young driver in precision, car control, basic setting-up of the kart, and the hustle and bustle of racing wheel-to-wheel. I will admit I found it quite intimidating. Those things are pretty quick when you're only 13 and they don't have bodywork to protect you – but once you get the hang of it and relax, it's brilliant.

To help me develop my fledgling skills, before delivering pizzas to the wrong addresses I worked at the local indoor go-kart centre, where Mum or Dad had to come and get me, often at two or three in the morning – and I had school the next day. The other boys and I used to finish up there at midnight, then we'd drive the karts for two hours ourselves. There would only be three or four of us but we'd switch the tyre barriers around to make much more advanced tracks than the punters would use. We also used fire extinguishers to wet certain corners on the braking points, the apexes or exits, really mixing up our skill sets and our feel for grip from the tyres.

Dare I say it, there were even nights when we'd take the karts out onto the road! The centre was on an industrial estate and at two in the morning it was a very quiet place. The only other traffic we might see would be the cars visiting the nearby red-light district!

I guess the karting bug bit me, but at first I was still doing my ball-boy duties for the Raiders and I couldn't attend all the meetings. By the time I was 15 Dad had bought me a second-hand kart, which we used in 1990 and 1991. On the karting scene there was a meeting roughly once a month out at the Canberra Go-Kart Club.

There were six meetings in 1991, the year in which I turned 15, and there would be four heats at each. Dad didn't actually come to my early races! He was busy building the new service station so I went with my schoolmate Matthew Hinton and John, his dad.

In 1990–91 in that second-hand kart we were doing pretty well at meetings in and around Canberra. Then Andy Lawson, who ran the Queanbeyan Kart Centre, custom-built a frame to fit me. Andy was a plant engineer but Dad reckons he could easily have made a living as a race-car engineer in Formula 1. He fabricated his own go-karts, did all the engine preparation and he was able to coax the last ounce of power out of them. Dad insists we owe a great debt to Andy, one of those brilliant backyard engineering blokes that Australia and New Zealand seem to produce who can put something in the lathe and 10 minutes later the component is made. Dad had known of him for quite a while without getting to know him well. Andy also prepared karts for a family called the Dukes. The boy, Ryan, had already won an Australian title; Dad thought he could learn from his father, Ray, and I certainly learned quickly from Ryan. They were what Dad likes to call 'decent people': no helmet-throwing, no tantrums, just good, down-to-earth sporting types, the kind of people he was more than happy to be associated with.

Around this time Dad made a business decision that had a big impact on both our lives. 'I never forced Mark into racing,' he will tell you. 'He just wanted to do it, he had a natural aptitude for it and he was able to run at the front pretty quickly. It's also fair to say that the racing was a means to a short-term end: it allowed me to spend more time with Mark than I had been doing. I invested long hours in Bridge Motors, time that took me away from family life, so I decided to lease the service station to Caltex. It was probably the best goal I ever kicked because it gave me two things: money, as it left us comfortably off, and that even more precious commodity, time. It allowed me and Mark to go racing together – and it gave him a privilege I never enjoyed because he was given Fridays off school to travel with me to his next race meeting!'

Through '93 we kept the Lawson kart and also ran a Clubman with a bigger, more powerful engine. Dad decided we should try our hand in places like Melbourne and Sydney – he loved to see me winning all those races close to home but he had the bigger picture in mind and he felt he needed to throw me in at the deep end. The idea was for me to learn, to improve my racecraft, and competing at Oran Park or down at Corio in Geelong was a good way to do it.

I won quite a few races and the 1993 NSW Junior National Heavy title. I wasn't the right size or weight for karting; I wasn't an absolute gun but I probably could have done better if Dad had put in the resources others were putting in. On the other hand he was probably aiming a bit higher already.

*

Halfway through 1993 a well-known face in Australian motor-racing circles, 'Peewee' Siddle, ran a Formula Ford trials day at Oran Park. Greg, to give him his real name, was the Australian importer, in partnership with Steve Knott, of the famous and internationally successful Van Diemen race-car brand from the UK. For many decades, Formula Ford was the worldwide entry-level category for aspiring racing drivers. It kicked off in the UK in 1967 and soon spread through Europe and across to the States. It reached Australia in 1970.

The idea behind Formula Ford was to provide a basic single-seater car, each with the same engine – they started with Ford Cortina GT power units – and without wings in order to keep the design as simple as possible. The essence of Formula Ford is learning how to handle yourself in 'traffic', as we call it, because the lack of wings means the cars can run in close formation and the racing is often spectacular, wheel-to-wheel stuff.

The day at Oran Park cost $5000. Ten drivers from Canberra and Queanbeyan – or their families – tipped in $500 each. They made two cars available, one set up for smaller drivers, the other for us taller blokes. I had a go in both and at the end of the day I was 1.6 seconds quicker than anybody else. That was the first time I'd driven a Formula Ford and I thought they were shit-boxes compared to the sharpness and agility of a go-kart!

But I enjoyed being in a car with a gearbox, sliding it around, and what I really liked was being on a big track – checking the kerbs, using big lines, coming right out wide through the corners and nearly touching those walls at Oran Park.

Dad reckons that day was when the penny dropped: 'Over a second and a half – that's light years in motor-racing terms. I couldn't get my head around the fact that he was going so well, but I figured it couldn't all be down to the engine because everybody had the same one. I thought, "Maybe he *has* got some ability after all."' As for me, I was still very young and I believed Formula Vee, an open-wheeler class a step below Formula Ford, was as far as I was ever going to go. Dad was thinking about the path ahead: Formula Ford, on to Formula 3 – the first acquaintance with cars with wings and aerodynamic characteristics – then on to one of several possible stepping-stones to the pinnacle of Formula 1. But that never crossed my mind.

Through Peewee (who probably knew more about my ability than Dad did, given his long experience in motor racing) we learned that Craig Lowndes's 1993 Australian Formula Ford Championship-winning car was available. Dad had a careful look at it, thought it had been pretty well maintained and we bought it, but we did struggle a bit with it in our first year. It was Andy Lawson who set the car up; he'd never worked on a Formula Ford and it was a hard first year for us, especially as we jumped straight into the national series. I didn't really have much of a clue about setting a race car up. I was still at school; some of my mates and I used to play computer games, but of course they were of limited use when it came to the real thing and there wasn't a lot of spare time to go and learn on-track rather than on-screen. It's fair to say that in year one in Formula Ford my feedback to my team was useless, and it hadn't improved a lot by the time we went into our second season either.

That first year Dad and I put about 100,000 kilometres on the old Landcruiser as we criss-crossed this huge country on our way to and from race meetings. The trip from home to Adelaide in South Australia, across the endless Nullarbor Plain to Wanneroo in Western Australia and back to Queanbeyan was 10,000 kilometres on its own.

The 1994 Australian Formula Ford Championship consisted of eight rounds, crammed into a six-month schedule from February to July. Our three-man team – Michael Foreman, my go-kart buddy and mechanic, Andy

Lawson, my engineer, and me, the driver – had absolutely no experience of the category so we didn't set the world on fire that first year, but we were up there some of the time: third at Phillip Island was my best result and 30 points meant I finished 14th overall.

I also got the chance to compete on the track where my addiction to racing had begun. We went to Adelaide to take part in the non-championship Formula Ford races on the undercard at the Australian Grand Prix. Before we set out I had a monster shunt in the final championship round at Oran Park. I lost control at the dog-leg at the bottom end of the circuit, got on the grass, hit the wall and destroyed the car. It was my first big crash and it hurt! It was a rela- tively small injury, but a massive wake-up call. Dad had to spend money, and Andy had to spend so much time putting everything back together as best he could – and I spent plenty of cold winter nights in the workshop helping him and Michael to rebuild the car. I remember thinking that this could be the end of the road for me; the shunt had dented my confidence and serious doubts had set in: was I cut out for the job of being a racing driver?

Earlier that year the death of three-time Formula 1 World Champion Ayrton Senna in the San Marino Grand Prix had also weighed on me. After watching that Imola race I went to bed expecting that Senna would be okay. When Mum woke me with the terrible news I cried into my cornflakes. Dad sat at the other end of the house because he didn't want to watch the news reports confirming Senna's death with me. I didn't go to school that day; Dad granted me a rare day off. Next day even friends who didn't follow motor racing tip-toed around me because even they knew what had happened and what it meant to me. It was a nightmare: Ayrton Senna wasn't supposed to be killed in a racing car, he was invincible. I was shattered.

But ultimately neither Senna's death nor my own Oran Park mishap affected my determination to keep racing. F1 and Ayrton Senna were a long way away from where I was, after all. But by the time we went to Adelaide we were really at the Last Chance Saloon. If we got blown away in these races, with no results to speak of and no cash, we would probably have to pull the pin on the whole thing. But I fell in love with the street track straightaway, and we were quick the whole weekend.

So much so that we were on the front row alongside that year's champion, Steven Richards – and then the bloody battery failed. Once I got going I drove through the whole field on the formation lap to take up my position, which you are not supposed to do. The stewards black-flagged me – the sign that a driver has been disqualified. I was livid, but all I could do was complete the first part of the race and then dutifully pull in. We returned to Queanbeyan spitting chips, but happy that our first crack at Adelaide had gone well despite that final disappointment.

2

Wingless Wonders: 1995–96

THE END OF 1994 WAS A CROSSROADS FOR DAD. HE HAD TO decide whether to put up the money for us to go round again or not. In that first year he had funded me himself and he couldn't commit to another year without finding some sponsorship support and seeing some results.

At the first round of the 1994 Australian Formula Ford Championship at Amaroo Park in Sydney in February, everyone – Dad and me included – was being introduced to the category's new media and PR officer.

I remember saying to her, 'You must be important, then!'

Little did I realise just how important Ann Neal was going to become, not only in my racing career, but in my life. She thought I was a bit of a smart-arse when we first met. 'But I liked how bold and cheeky he was,' she says, 'and how mature he seemed. When I asked someone how old he was, I was shocked when they said 17 – he was confident beyond his years.'

Ann was born in England; she got into motor-sport journalism by writing for a magazine and local newspapers about oval racing. She took a passing interest in the exploits of Derek Warwick, whom she'd seen in Superstox racing on the ovals and who became one of the few drivers to graduate from there to car racing. When Ann met Derek at a function years later she was introduced to his brother Paul, who was 10 at the time. Paul wanted to emulate his big brother and when he moved up to Formula Ford, she followed, handling his press and PR work. One thing led to another: she was introduced to Mike Thompson, the founder of Quest Formula Ford cars, who asked her to look after the media for a young driver, Johnny Herbert, in 1986. Johnny had just won the prestigious Formula Ford Festival.

Ann married Australian Rod Barrett in November '87. He had gone to the UK to seek his own fame and fortune as a saloon-car driver and was working at the famous Jim Russell School for up-and-coming racing drivers. Rod lived at Carlton House in Attleborough in Norfolk, a bed-and-breakfast that was home away from home for many young international racing drivers. Every young Aussie was beating a path to their door at that time too, guys like Paul Stokell, Russell Ingall – they always had a nucleus of Australians around them. After they married they bought a house in Kent and Rod became Media Director at Brands Hatch. Ann was providing copy for all the Brands Hatch programs, which meant four race circuits in the group as a whole, and was part of the press team at the British Grand

Prix when it was staged at Brands. Even so, she wasn't a big F1 fan, preferring grassroots racing.

Ann's next position was with a public relations company where she looked after the motor-sport interests of the big oil firm Duckhams. She also worked on behalf of Ford and one of their projects was Formula Ford. 'By 1989,' she says, 'the formula was failing to attract young drivers because there were so many other forms of racing springing up which had better prize funds and offered more opportunities. I produced a report for Ford which they took on board; they got serious about it and I took over the media/PR role on their behalf in 1991.'

That was the good news.

'The unbearably bad news,' Ann recalls, 'was that '91 was also the year when Paul Warwick lost his life in a big accident at Oulton Park, a famous racing circuit up in Cheshire in England's north-west. I was at Cadwell Park that day on Formula Ford duty – six months pregnant with my son Luke – and wasn't able to attend Paul's race, as I often did. A week later Rod rolled a production saloon at Brands Hatch and we decided we didn't want any more to do with motor racing.'

Rod couldn't get out of his contract so Ann worked the '92 season and they emigrated to Australia after her last day, which was that year's Formula Ford Festival. It was won by the young Danish driver Jan Magnussen, whose manager called Ann the next day to ask if she would be interested in handling Jan's media! She told him she was on a plane out of the UK – and those who follow F1 will recall that Jan's son Kevin made his F1 debut for McLaren in 2014 at Albert Park and finished on the podium. A familiar name through my own F1 career has been Jenson Button; at that same stage Ann was contacted by John Button, Jenson's father, about playing the same media role for his son.

After six months Rod was going back to his old employer, Coca-Cola, as State Manager. The trouble was that the state in question was Western Australia, which Ann found too remote. Luke was coming up to his first birthday and they knew no one. Then Coke took Rod to Sydney, and hey presto, work opportunities began to open up for her. She hadn't lost the motor-racing bug despite Paul's death; she accepted an offer to become press and PR coordinator for the Australian Formula Ford Championship. She also began working for Wayne Gardner's new V8 touring car team in Sydney's western suburbs, but no sooner had they started settling in Sydney than Coca-Cola offered Rod a job in Malaysia, which was too good for him to refuse.

Looking back, Ann says, 'I didn't want to give up my career yet again. I hadn't migrated to Australia to end up living in Kuala Lumpur. We tried to keep the relationship alive by commuting back and forth but it was never going to work out and I was also getting into my stride with my work, which I loved. Rod and I separated and ultimately divorced; it was difficult for a while but we've been good friends for years now and Rod even joined Mark and me at some Grands Prix.'

Ann remembers our first meeting and my opening remark about her being so important. She can even remember what I was wearing – a stripey green and red top, one of those United Colors of Benetton things – so that was pretty prophetic, as things turned out! After that first meeting we kept in touch. My family sometimes met up with Ann and

Luke for weekend get-togethers, and I ensured she got her motor-sport fixes by dragging all my old F1 tapes out. By way of revenge she would bring down all her British Formula Ford tapes for me.

In those early days Ann and Luke hadn't been in Australia for very long. Luke was an only child with no cousins or anyone remotely close to his age in Australia, so it was a great experience for him to see life in rural Australia, particularly on the family farm, and to meet everyone – it was a family lifestyle he didn't have. Something a lot of kids in Australia would take for granted, no doubt, but Luke had been parachuted into life Down Under and it was great that we were able to show him a snapshot of what we were all about.

Late in 1994 Dad asked Ann if she could help us find some sponsorship. It wasn't the kind of work she enjoyed most, but she had been keeping an eye on this family trying to find their way in the big wide world of motor racing and she must have seen something she liked, because eventually she agreed.

'When I met Mark it struck me that maybe this was the driver I could try and manage,' she says. 'That was the challenge for me: having worked for Johnny Herbert's management as he made his way up from Formula Ford to F1, I wanted to see if I could step up to the plate. When I got to know Mark I could see we had a lot in common and we both had a burning desire to be successful. One October day at Bathurst, where we had gone to watch the "Great Race", he said, "I want to do something with my life." He already knew he didn't want to spend his whole life in Queanbeyan – he wanted something more and he was hungry, which stuck in my mind. I don't think he particularly knew what he wanted out of life and he certainly didn't know how to carve out a career in motor sport, but the fact he wanted *something* gave me a great foundation to work with.'

*

By this stage both my parents were putting a bit of heat on me. Mum insisted that I finish my Higher School Certificate, which I did, although my results might not have been what she was hoping for. In Dad's eyes getting results on track was the priority if I was to keep doing what I really wanted to do. Otherwise I would have had to get a 'real' job, and I knew how fortunate I was – I could work with Dad, I had that safety net and I think inside I believed I would use it at some stage.

But I was keen by now to make racing my focus, and that meant taking the first major step on my journey: getting out of Queanbeyan. So I did something that horrified Disey: I went to live in Sydney. We'd met Spencer Martin in 1994 when his son Matt was racing with me in Formula Ford. When we went to that first Amaroo Park meeting Dad and I were driving in to the circuit when he spotted Spencer and said to me, 'Mark, I'll tell you a bit about this fellow in a minute but right now we're going to pitch camp alongside him.'

He was well aware of Spencer's background and thought he was one of the best drivers Australia had produced. Spencer had won the Gold Star as Australia's outstanding racing driver in 1966 and 1967, he had taken a break from the track to marry and start a family, and then returned to

excel in Historic racing and Porsches. Among other claims
to fame, Spencer drove for well-known Australian racing
identity David McKay's Scuderia Veloce team, worked as a
mechanic to Graham Hill in the Tasman Series, and generally knew everything there was to know about starting a
career as a racing driver. Dad and Spencer hit it off from
the start. He felt it was like our relationship with the
Dukes family: good people, and in the end we are still great
friends to this day. 'Another good decision by old Al!' as Dad
likes to remind me. When I moved to Sydney, it was the
Martin family who took me in and I stayed with them up
until the time I first travelled to the UK late in 1995 to go
and see the Formula Ford Festival.

I earned my keep as a driving instructor at the Oran Park
circuit. Meanwhile Ann and I put together six sponsorship
proposals, though we didn't have a huge amount to put into
the document because I hadn't achieved much in 1994. But
she put me in a professional studio to get some decent shots
done and we had the proposals ready just before Christmas.
It had to be done then because by the time everybody strag-
gled back to work in February it would be far too late.

One of the proposals landed on the desk of Bob Copp
at Yellow Pages. He called us up straightaway. So Ann flew
down to Melbourne, where Bob was based, the following week – and she flew solo because my services weren't
required at that stage.

That's how Ann started working with us. As a woman
working in a very male-dominated industry in Australia
I think Ann has always felt she had to make her point a bit
harder or more strongly to be taken seriously, something
she never had to do back in the UK. But when she secured

that Yellow Pages sponsorship she had something she was in charge of. She took ownership of it, and it was down to her – and me – to show Yellow Pages we could make it work.

Bob Copp got it from the start: he understood the need to rejuvenate the company image for the internet era. He knew that a third and more of the Yellow Pages client base was in the automotive business sector, they had already had some involvement at Bathurst and he knew the way forward wasn't with touring cars, so Ann's proposal had turned up just at the right time. I had youth on my side, while innovation and technology – key parts of the Yellow Pages profile – were crucial ingredients of single-seater racing. Bob Copp was looking for emerging talent; Ann was fervently hoping that I was it.

For that second Formula Ford year I ran a new car in full Yellow Pages livery, which looked great. For the small Team Webber, as we began to call ourselves, it *was* great, and the start of a terrific relationship with the company.

When I tell you I scored 158 points and finished fourth overall that year – 128 points better than in 1994 – you can see how much work went into getting there. But while fourth was a fair improvement from my first campaign, it also shows that I simply wasn't consistent enough. It was the same old story: we had no set-up on the car at all. We had started out working with a bloke who was recommended to Dad by Peewee. But at our first meeting at Sandown in Melbourne in early February 1995, things went wrong from the start. We couldn't even get out for the warm-up at the first of the two races there because the car was too low! That same afternoon Dad was on the phone to Peewee again.

Despite all the drama I kick-started the year with a pretty good win in the first Sandown race. I took the lead on the opening lap in tricky wet conditions and increased it all the way to beat Jason Bright and Monaghan by a country mile. The second race at that meeting was wet as well, but I was spun round by someone on the second lap; I fought my way back up to second but then had an even worse spin and that was that. Still, Dad was reassured by my efforts. Peewee came back to him with an alternative and the next name to crop up belonged to Harry Galloway.

Harry was one of the first men in Australia to grasp the importance of aerodynamics when it came to racing cars. Like Andy Lawson he was a brilliant fabricator, although he hadn't worked for a little operation like ours. We enjoyed a terrific relationship with Harry and he was a big help as things started to pick up out on the track.

Phillip Island was another wet race – and I used to love it when it rained! I couldn't believe the lines other drivers would use, and I'm talking about the big guns. You would cruise up on some of the guys you were fighting with and they just weren't being creative, they didn't have the trust in the car in those conditions. The heavier the rain, the less the visibility, the more I enjoyed it. It was so heavy at Phillip Island that they cancelled the Supercars – but they put the Formula Fords out there! We had a misfire in qualifying so I started from eighth and I was leading after the first lap. Mind you, we nearly didn't make it out in the first place. Someone put the Channel 7 on-board camera and film on the car and it caught fire: Dad had to put it out before it took hold! Then we got out there and I put 20 seconds into the rest of the field in eight laps . . .

But poor scores in the next couple of rounds cost me dearly. No consistency: I was either winning by 20 seconds or crashing; the Brights and Monaghans were experienced, good Formula Ford drivers who were not only quick, but also knew what they needed to do to win. I didn't.

There was one particular lesson I still needed to learn, and that was the importance of feedback and setting the car up properly. The direction came mainly from the people in my corner: both Harry and Peewee's partner, Steve Knott, were experienced and had worked with some good drivers. Steve enjoyed a fine reputation as an engine-builder in Australia and he seemed to take a shine to this young bloke from Queanbeyan.

But I was very shallow at that stage – I was a late developer in that respect and I must have been frustrating to work for. I never pushed for any changes to the car, I just got in and drove it. I thought I could drive fast enough without worrying about all the little details. I had more poles in 1995 than anyone else but found it hard to convert them into wins on race days. Formula Ford was renowned for its rough-and-tumble style of racing and I'd get involved in scraps, lose a few spots, regain them and then knock a corner off the car. The end of the 1995 Australian Formula Ford Championship was a fairly typical Webber weekend, at Oran Park: I was on pole, but I had a big crash and, as they say in the Eurovision Song Contest, it was *nul points* once more.

I once read something by Stirling Moss saying that his first aim was always to win whatever race he was in, and that's why he never won a championship. I could relate to that: back then I was never concerned about trying to build up for a championship; I never felt particularly rewarded by playing the percentage game – I always wanted to try to win the race I was in at the time. If it didn't come off, I would come back and try again next time. But time showed that to be a strategy that didn't really work in terms of trying to put championships together.

But Ann had a plan . . .

By the end of 1995 Annie told me, in no uncertain terms, that – and I quote – I had to get my arse out of there. She didn't just mean Australian Formula Ford, either: she meant Australia. She thought it was time for me to go and have a crack at some of the big guys, and she proposed to help me go about it in a serious, business-like way.

'How the f#*k are *you* going to get to Formula 1 coming from Queanbeyan?' Anyone who wants to trace my journey should start with a piece of paper that Ann drew up on 6 July 1995. According to 'Mark Webber Career Path Options', I would be in Formula 1 within seven years. What was she on? She had it all mapped out: a move to the UK, graduation through the racing classes, and the ultimate target, a seat in a Benetton Grand Prix car at the turn of the century. It was all there in black and white: whether I started in Europe, Asia or the United States, all roads led to a Formula 1 cockpit.

Looking back, we were pretty naïve. We weren't short of people telling us we were crazy even to entertain the idea of making it to F1. In fact if we'd known back then what we know now I doubt we would even have contemplated it. But now Ann and I had a plan and our assumption was that if we worked hard and refused to take no for an answer we would succeed. It never occurred to us that things beyond our control might stand in our way, but then perhaps our naïveté worked in our favour. And anyone who expressed doubts was doing us a favour as well: they simply made us all the more determined to show them what we could do.

We were thinking along the same lines in one way: I was quite keen to go to England and check out the racing over there. Formula Ford enjoyed a worldwide reputation as the stepping-stone from karts to single-seater, open-wheeler racing, and it had been the bridge to racing success for some very famous names over the years. As Ann well knew, the Formula Ford Festival, staged each year at Brands Hatch, was the unofficial World Championship of the category: do well in that and you would attract the attention of some very important people on the European motor-racing scene.

The original idea for '95 was just to go over and see this festival for myself. Ann arranged a meeting with Ralph Firman, the founder and boss of Van Diemen race cars, perhaps the biggest name in Formula Ford. Ann, Luke and I went over and stayed with Ann's mum, Bettine. Here was I, thinking, 'Wow, Van Diemen, this is going to be awesome, stuff of legends, Ayrton Senna drove for these guys . . .' I was a little taken aback by the look and feel of the place when I actually went there in early October 1995.

But what I quickly realised was that Van Diemen epitomised the British motor-sport industry as it had developed over the years since the Second World War. The history of it all is very special, moving from one-man bands in lock-up garages – which some of my future F1 employers had been! – through to the internationally significant industry that thrives in the UK today. Look beyond the gleaming, state-of-the-art premises we see today: the British motor-racing industry's beginnings were far more humble, in fact it all began very much as a cottage industry. Once I got my head round that, I still knew I was in a special place.

That impression was reinforced by the photographs on the walls, by seeing more brand-new Formula Ford cars together in one place than I had ever seen before, and especially by seeing one of Ayrton Senna's Van Diemens sitting under wraps in the workshop. When he came to the UK from Brazil at the start of the 1980s he won Formula Ford 1600 and 2000 titles in Van Diemens; in those days the Brazilian superstar lived just up the road in a humble bungalow in Norwich.

Annie had already pulled off a coup of sorts by organising that first meeting, because it meant my sights could be set higher than just going to the festival as a spectator. My goals were still so modest then: I just wanted to try to race in the UK to see how I would go. The category had been founded on Ford's famous 1600cc Kent engine in the sixties; by the early nineties Ford had made its 1800cc Zetec power units available, so there was something of a two-tier system in operation, although in Australia we were all still in the less powerful cars. When we started to think about taking part in the Formula Ford Festival in October 1995 I had a 'second-tier' 1600 car in mind. The 1800 was the plant to have, as all the big names were in that division.

Ralph was very straight with me about my prospects on track, especially as he knew I would be ring-rusty after the early end to our own national series back in Australia.

'Look, mate,' he said, 'you're actually going to get creamed, you haven't raced for four months, these guys are festival specialists.'

Annie and I spoke about it and felt we couldn't go home without having done anything. The whole idea was at least to get out on track among these so-called big guns of the Formula Ford world and see where I stacked up. What was the point in trailing back to Australia without doing that? Ralph had left the door ajar by offering me a test in a Formula Ford 1600 over at Snetterton in Norfolk. On the day, though, the test was actually in an 1800cc car; I matched the number-one driver, the guy they planned to try to win the festival with, on the first day. I was a dog with two dicks! I thought I was World Champion already and all I'd done was a little test at Snetterton. But I was thinking, 'I can go home happy, it's good, these guys have got two legs, two arms, I can race them.'

It was just as well I did feel that way, because Ralph rang up a week later and said, 'Do you want to do the festival in the 1800?' As the offer began to sink in the doubts started creeping in, too. Ralph was right – I hadn't raced for four months, and now I had to do the festival for the first time, and in the main category.

I needed to fork out five grand – pounds, not dollars – for the week, and Yellow Pages again stepped up. All week I tried to focus on keeping it straight and learning as I went; when I reached the semi-finals and finished fifth in mine, that meant I was in the top 10 overall and through to the final itself.

In the end the only two drivers who beat me were the front-runners from the main Formula Ford series, Kevin McGarrity of Ireland and Brazilian Mario Haberfeld, and it was only when Haberfeld got a tow near the end that he managed to pip me for second place. In point of fact he and

I were third and fourth on the road but the guy between us
and McGarrity, Giorgio Vinella, was disqualified.

Unbeknown to Ann and me there were two interested
spectators in the grandstand that cold winter afternoon.
When we returned to the paddock we found Dad and his
old mate Bruce Greentree had made a split-second decision
to fly over from Australia. They were on the ground in the
UK for 46 hours, and in the air for 49, but they had a ball!
As Dad says, 'It was marvellous to see Mark thrown in at
the deep end again, this time by someone other than his
father, and coming out with third place. There had been
a fair chance that he wouldn't even make the final but he
did, and it was a great job on his part.'

My introduction to the famous festival was good enough
for Ralph Firman to say, 'Come back next year, you've got
a works drive,' and that was how my international racing
career really started.

There was only the small matter of the finance to put
in place: it may have been a works drive with Van Diemen
but we still had to find the money to pay for and run a
car. Back we went to Australia to have our second crack at
the support race at the Australian Grand Prix in Adelaide
in November – the last Formula 1 weekend to be staged in
the South Australian capital, as it turned out. My car was
entirely yellow for the Yellow Pages sponsorship but it was
like a red rag to a bull: I could imagine the other Aussie
guys thinking, 'Webber's been over there to the festival, he
thinks he's pretty special, we're going to kick his arse.'

I qualified on pole by a big chunk; in the first race a front
roll-bar broke and I was getting chucked around a lot through
the corners, then I got punted out of the lead and had to

retire. But I won the second race, my final outing in Australia in Formula Ford, and I was happy with that. People used to say all the decision-makers in the F1 teams were watching you, but they were forgetting one small thing: we were on the track at 7.30 at night! So you believed in your own mind it was a big deal, but you might as well have been racing in front of five people for all the difference it made.

Still, it meant enough for me to be introduced to Gordon Message, who was then team manager at Benetton, and I had my photograph taken with a driver by the name of Michael Schumacher.

Before Ann and I left Australia again to head over to England for the 1996 Formula Ford season with Van Diemen, on the weekend of 8–10 March I had the chance to race again, this time in a Formula Holden, on the supporting program at the Australian Grand Prix. It was only four months since my Adelaide win because a man by the name of Ron Walker, a former lord mayor of Melbourne, had pulled off something of a coup by snatching the jewel in the Australian motor-racing calendar away from its 11-year home in Adelaide and bringing it back to the picturesque setting of Albert Park, where there had been Australian Grand Prix meetings in 1953 and 1956. The race would be the first one on the 1996 F1 calendar.

I wasn't aware at the time how important Ron's influence would become in my own developing career. I just wanted to show what I could do in Formula Holden, a class introduced in Australia in 1989 to emulate the F3000 category that was taking hold in Europe as the feeder formula to F1. Unlike Formula Fords, these cars were brutal: they weighed in at 675 kilograms, their V6 engines pushed out 300 horsepower, and with stiff suspension and a low ride height they were very physical cars for the drivers to handle.

I had already tried one out at Mallala in South Australia, thanks to a generous offer from the man who was largely responsible for the series in its early days, Malcolm Ramsay. Curiously enough, at that Mallala test day north of Adelaide Dad spoke to the great Australian-based New Zealand all-round driver Jim Richards, who confirmed Dad's suspicion that there was something to build on in my case. But he also told Dad, 'You've got to get him out of here!' So Annie wasn't the only one thinking along those lines.

I didn't have a great start to the Formula Holden support race program in Melbourne that weekend: in the opening race I went straight on at Turn 3, which F1 driver Martin Brundle would make instantly world-famous when his Jordan flew through the air at the same spot, but I won the second six-lapper when Paul Stokell slowed on the opening lap, and I passed him and led all the way home.

Television analyst Geoff Brabham – Sir Jack's eldest son and a brilliant racer in his own right – said this Mark Webber bloke was very talented and trying very hard to head overseas to further his career. How right he was, on the second count at least!

So at the ripe old age of 19 I was heading back to England. Earlier in the year Ann and I had put together a raffle for places in the Yellow Pages corporate suite at the Australian Grand Prix and raised $3000 in Queanbeyan and Canberra! Annie, my family and friends all pitched in and for a week we hit all the local shops and industrial estates flogging raffle tickets, the proceeds from which went towards helping me set up home in the UK. Not everyone was happy to see me go: Mum had thought it was bad enough when I left Queanbeyan for Sydney, and in those days the other side of the world still seemed a lot further away than it does now.

When I first left Australia in late 1995, I was desperate to see for myself some of the tracks like Brands Hatch, which I'd only ever seen in photos in *Autosport*. 'What's it going to be like?' I asked myself. 'How amazing it's going to be even to see it, and then to do the race and the festival, have that first little bit of exposure to the European scene, knowing that I'm over here racing . . .'

Now Ann and I were going back, not only for a second crack at the festival but to contest the British Formula Ford Championship that preceded it. Who knew what lay ahead?

3

A Wing and a Prayer

RACING IN EUROPE WAS A REAL EYE-OPENER. IN THE FIRST race over there, the yellow flags were out to warn drivers not to overtake and guys were still trying to punt each other off at the next corner! Talk about uncharted waters – we were pushing off in our little boat out into big seas, and the waves kept getting bigger the further we went!

The good thing about 1996 was that Dad didn't have to put in much money at all; Annie was working too, and together we just chipped away. Everything had to be done the cheapest and fastest way possible because we didn't have the luxury of hanging around. I was already nearly 20 and couldn't worry about winning Australian titles as some people like Peewee wanted me to, or do two years in Formula Ford and then another two years in F3 before I had a crack at F1. Stalling would have cost money we didn't have – a lot more money. We had some momentum behind us and just had to take advantage of it while it lasted.

For those first few months in England, we stayed with Ann's mum at Hainault in Essex, which isn't exactly the leafiest suburb in England. I was in a box room – a very small box room – which was absolutely freezing and very different to what I had grown up with. The room was so small that when I lay down in bed my head touched the wall at one end, my feet the other. I missed my family and my mates and the comforts of home.

There was a gym nearby so I used to get the tube there, but I had no idea what I was doing, I was just tootling around and believing I was getting fit. At that time Michael Schumacher was starting to win World Championships and everybody was saying what a super-fit guy he was, so off I went to the gym. I'd never been in a gym in my life!

I earned some money by buzzing up and down to work as a driving instructor at the circuits at Brands Hatch, Snetterton and anywhere else that would have me. I had an old B-registration Ford Fiesta (thanks to that raffle money), which I used to drive round the M25, jumping the Dartford Toll to save a couple of quid here and there. I was doing big mileage in my B-reg and I remember only being able to put £10 worth of petrol in at times. My wages were £43 for almost a 12-hour day, but I had a ball. Most of my fellow instructors were aspiring young drivers like me, so we would all go off in our different directions at the weekend to race and then come back on Monday morning with colourful stories of what had happened. We were all trying to forge a career, trying to keep the dream alive. I always had to work and all the guys I was instructing with at Brands Hatch were in the same boat. It was a struggle for all of us.

In stark contrast to this were the Brazilians, most of whom would rock in with a full racing budget and turn up at race meetings driving flash BMWs or Mercedes. They were semi-professional drivers, even at Formula Ford level. I never let it get to me, in fact I turned it into a positive and used it as motivation. I was turning up in my B-reg on a wing and a prayer, hoping it wouldn't fail me.

One of my fellow instructors was Dan Wheldon, the talented British driver who would be tragically killed in the States in 2011. The other instructors were a bit older than us; they'd tried to make a go of their careers too but had either run out of money or simply hadn't made it, though they were still good enough to teach other people how to drive around a racetrack.

Ann and I rented a partly furnished house in Attleborough. We were stretched financially on a personal level but Ann was freelancing in PR and earning enough money so we could pay our way, and I was contributing where I could. A lot of our money would go on rent – not just the house we were living in but a TV and video player as well! It didn't come with either but we couldn't afford to buy luxuries like that. The house was a few miles south-west of the cathedral city of Norwich, so I could be close to the Van Diemen factory. Any racing driver will tell you how valuable it is to forge close links with the team you are racing for, getting to know the people, being a part of the team as fully as you can.

Because many of the junior racing teams were based there, Norfolk was a hub for young racers from all over the world. I remember coming home after being at the pub with the Van Diemen mechanics and excitedly telling Ann that Jan Magnussen had been there too. He had just graduated to F1 at that stage and had popped in to catch up with his old mates. I couldn't believe that I was actually moving in the same circles.

I spent a lot of time at the Van Diemen factory. I have vivid memories of Ralph Firman himself, a chain-smoker, always with a cigarette in his mouth, even when he stuck his head into the cockpit to ask for some driver feedback, so the ash fell off around your feet . . . Ralph single-handedly bringing a testing session at the Snetterton circuit to a stop when his old Merc clipped the bridge over the track and knocked an advertising hoarding into our path . . . Me in my B-reg Ford waiting to cross a junction near the factory and Ralph in his old tank of a Merc sneaking up behind me, sitting there behind the wheel in his trademark Coke-bottle glasses and deliberately pushing me out across the very busy A11 . . . Me picking up the odd extra £90 to drop his mum off at Gatwick Airport in that same battered old Merc of his!

The 1996 season started well enough for me and my teammate, Kristian Kolby from Denmark. I won the second race of the series at Brands Hatch and led the championship for a while, then had a run of absolute rubbish results. I spun out of the lead at Oulton Park; I threw Thruxton away because I was way out in front and cruising and thinking about other things rather than concentrating on the race, and all in front of Alan Docking, an expatriate Australian who enjoyed a very big reputation as a successful team owner. Docko, who was eyeing me up for F3 the next year, went ballistic at me. He was a patriotic, passionate Aussie who knew I had thrown an easy win away. I couldn't afford to make those mistakes.

I decided then that I wanted to go home. I was homesick; I wasn't sure what I was doing so far away from my family and friends. Was it all worth it? Was I missing out on what was happening back home? I figured I'd head back Down Under for two or three weeks and have a break, but as soon as I arrived in Australia I saw that everyone was still doing exactly the same thing, nothing had changed. Within two or three days I realised that I was kidding myself; I'd been given a tremendous opportunity over in England and I needed to get my arse back over there again and take that opportunity seriously.

It's hard to explain just how tough leaving Australia had been, how difficult it was to raise the cash to fly home – always economy, always exhausting. But we were determined to make this work. As Mick Doohan had said to me, it's a long way to go home with your tail between your legs.

Back in England, Ann and I moved house to Aylesbury in Buckinghamshire, on the edge of motor sport's equivalent of Silicon Valley. We had started out as teammates and friends on a mission but over time our friendship had deepened into something else. I enjoyed spending time with her and we felt entirely comfortable in each other's company. Moving to England was a huge step for me and I think it was a case of us needing one another and that's how the relationship was formed. I had a lot of trust in her as she was in my corner from day one. She fought so hard for me and it was amazing to have a great companion who shared my passion for motor sport. From the beginning, Ann was the only one on my level (my dad to a lesser degree) who believed that my dream to race in F1 could happen. When you're sharing that kind of belief with someone, that person lifts you.

In the beginning, Ann and I decided to keep our relationship quiet because in a professional sense it wasn't going to help my cause if Ann was seen to be extolling the virtues/ talents of her boyfriend to heavy-hitters and decision-makers. We didn't want to risk not being taken seriously, so we always believed it was better for Ann to be seen negotiating as an independent third party. Over the first few years some people may have had their suspicions but certainly up until my first year in F1, we kept the relationship pretty much under wraps.

Being in a relationship with Ann, there was also her son, Luke, to consider. I had spent a lot of time with Luke back in Australia and by the time we were all living together in England, I was already like a big brother to him. To be honest, he was on the sidelines for me in the early days in the UK. He was too young to take to race weekends and I was so focused on what I was trying to do. That's why, later on in my career, I liked to involve him in some of the opportunities that came my way. I wasn't a hero to him, though: of course he liked seeing me do well, but he enjoyed other sports more, especially soccer and cricket, and he had his own heroes up on pedestals.

Living in Aylesbury also put me within shouting distance of Silverstone and Alan Docking Racing, even though I was nowhere near close to finalising a deal with him for 1997.

Once I got my head together I had a strong finish to the 1996 championship: four race wins made me the championship runner-up to Kolby. I was in with a chance of winning the European championship too: I had tasted pole position and victory at what would become one of my favourite circuits, Spa-Francorchamps in Belgium. However, Ralph didn't let me compete in the last rounds of the championship because he wanted me to focus on the Formula Ford Festival. The European Championship was on the same weekend at Brands so we could have entered but we didn't want to risk the car – or me – before my second tilt at the festival.

Take it from me, that's a hard meeting to win, even when you have enjoyed a successful first crack at it, as I had the year before: it's a lot easier to lose than to come out on top. Michael Schumacher and Kimi Räikkönen rocked up once upon a time and did nothing – that's the Formula Ford Festival for you.

There were some very fast Formula Ford drivers there and some had been testing on the track for a full week, up to 500 laps in preparation for the racing itself. The track is only a couple of kilometres long, and to get an advantage round there is very, very difficult. It's Chinese whispers all week about set-ups, tyres, pressures, so you simply try to keep it tight in your own team and figure out what you're going to use, your gear ratios, your engine. You can't go there thinking it's going to be a walk in the park.

Still, I was confident. There were five or six key rivals, the guys to keep an eye on in the heats and semis; I made sure I stayed with them and didn't give away any grid positions to them. It isn't a race where you want to be doing too much passing because you only expose yourself to the dreaded DNFs (Did Not Finish), so I wanted to start as far up as possible. There were, as always, a few hotshots from

Europe to contend with, but I qualified on pole position for my heat, and I won that. My race was dry – during the other race there was a bit of a sprinkle so their times were slower – and I found myself on pole for the final.

Pretty soon after the start it was back to normal service: Webber makes a terrible start, drops back to second, it's a wet race . . . Yet I knew everything was going to turn out well because it was all happening in slow motion. That feeling comes when you are so in control of the car and yourself that there are no surprises. You really are ahead of every scenario: everything is in hand, as if you've been here before. You act instinctively; it's a matter of muscle memory and reflex. I knew I had the other guys covered, all I had to do was make sure I didn't stuff it up.

I made it safely through the first lap and I was just starting to line up the race leader. I got a good run out of Clearways on to the straight; he went out wide, I covered that move as well, then thought, 'I'm going to go round you.' I got to the middle of the corner – and there were yellow flags everywhere. Someone's gone off. No! Why has the old bloke upstairs done that to me? So I had to let my man back through again. I put my hand up, let him past, slotted back in behind him, passed him again, built up a lead of more than two seconds – and the red flag came out to signal that the race had been stopped. Restart!

We pulled up on the grid again, I lined up on pole, Jacky van der Ende from Holland was second, Vítor Meira from Brazil fourth or thereabouts. This time, surprise, surprise, I didn't make such a bad start, but Vítor made an awesome one. So Meira was now leading – but not on aggregate over the two starts, so I was cool with that. I was happy just to stay in touch. We were quicker than anyone else and I knew that if I stayed there the win was mine. I wasn't going to go anywhere near Meira, there was no point. I'd done the hard work and I was leading the race overall. On the second or third lap after the restart, Vítor outbraked himself and crashed. After that I was on a test run, happily driving around in the wet . . . and not going off! I was wide awake and I wasn't going to let it go.

It was an important victory for me. There were 120 guys from different countries having a crack, and only 25–30 made the final, so to win it was a bit of a statement. But it was an early reminder of something I would remember throughout my career, namely that talent is no guarantee of success. There was a lot of quality in that Brands Hatch field but a lot of it was never realised because most of those young racers didn't have the iron self-belief and determination that makes you keep going.

A win like that is important because it leads nicely into Formula 3. People realise you've got the head to win the festival, and the pace; drivers who have done well there must be doing something right. Of course there was still a lot I needed to be tested on, but that win gave me some confidence and, more importantly, it gave people around me some confidence as well. As Ann says, you can do so much off the track but you've still got to go and get the results, and if I had crashed and burned in that final, who knows where we might have ended up.

Opportunities certainly opened up after that half-hour race. I was given a free test in a Formula 3 car, and that was to have enormous consequences later on. In fact I drove just about every car known to motor-racing man in the month after my festival win. Formula Opel at Zandvoort in Holland was an enjoyable experience; I did a Redgrave Racing Formula Renault test at Snetterton and one for Hayward Racing at Mallory Park, but our thoughts were already turning quite firmly towards F3.

As a footnote to that Brands Hatch weekend, I remember a juicy little confrontation that took place long after the track action was done and dusted. Fans may remember a Grand Prix driver called Martin Donnelly, whose F1 career was ended by a brutal accident in his Lotus at Jerez in Spain in September 1990. Well, Martin's dad was at Brands that weekend. The Kentagon's a famous pub at the circuit; everyone goes there to eat and drink after the race, win, lose or draw. It was pretty special to have the festival trophy presented to me a second time there in the pub, but Donnelly Senior had had a bit too much to drink. My parents had come over to watch me race – in fact Dad spent a fair amount of time with us in England during 1996 – and this bloke said or did something that left my mum less than impressed. My mechanic was a guy called Micky Galter, and Micky was not a man to be messed with – his hands were the size of shovels. Dad can usually take care of any nonsense, but he was in the background at this point, so Micky went up to Donnelly's dad, grabbed hold of him so that his little toes were dangling off the floor, and said, 'If you f#*k up this young boy's night . . .' We had a few lemonades after that and I drove home a happy man!

*

With the festival win under my belt, Team Webber was ready to take on the world. First we were going back to Australia to find lots of money, and that was our first mistake: there wasn't any to be found. Corporate Australia was convinced that Craig Lowndes was Australia's next F1 driver, because he had just embarked on a career in F3000 after winning in V8 touring cars at home. This was so frustrating to hear: no disrespect to Craig, he's a great driver, but there was no way in the world anyone could pitch up in Europe to race F3000 without doing the junior categories first. They'd get eaten alive.

One group of people in Australia who showed faith in me and did their best to keep the Webber name in people's minds were the guys at Channel 9, who in the early days of my motor-racing career were the F1 broadcasters in Australia. Whenever I came back home, they would ask me into their Sydney studios to offer my own comments on their F1 telecasts alongside Alan Jones and their larger-than-life host, Darrell Eastlake. They also invited me on to their popular weekend program *Wide World of Sports*, where skilled presenters like Ken Sutcliffe and Tim Sheridan worked very hard to get stories about me on air – Tim even brought a crew to Snetterton as early as 1995 to watch me in a Formula Ford race. But once again – and understandably so – there were just so many people asking me that familiar question: 'How the f#*k is a boy from Queanbeyan going to get into Formula 1?'

Once again it was Yellow Pages that helped us fan the flames. Bob Copp and his colleagues were particularly keen on seeing progress. They didn't want to see me in Formula Vauxhall, Formula Renault or any of those other categories that were starting to flourish back then. 'Formula 3 or nothing' was their attitude, and they were prepared to support us to get there because it's a category that people can understand, especially in Europe. Double F1 World Champion Mika Häkkinen had won the title in 1990, and the man who later put together the longest career in F1 history, Rubens Barrichello, succeeded him in 1991.

There weren't many drivers going from Formula Ford straight to F3 at that time. A few had done that in the past, Ayrton Senna for one, but in the mid-nineties a lot of younger drivers were going to the middle categories to get a bit more experience before they moved into Formula 3. We didn't have the time or money to do that: we had to skip a year at university, you might say, missing out part of the apprenticeship to catch up.

The overall cost for the UK F3 season was £245,000. Yellow Pages and Dad put a hundred grand in between them – Dad had had 15 months to recover from the shock of 1995 and there was also some inheritance money from my grandfather. We put it all together to buy a Formula 3 car. We were going to do the season with Alan Docking – the man who had given me the F3 test on the back of my Brands Hatch performance. 'We'll just go with the flow, mate, and see how we go,' was Docko's approach. Typical Australian way . . .

So we bought a brand-new Dallara race car with a Mugen Honda engine, which was the best engine-chassis combination available. The way it works is that the driver brings a racing budget with him in exchange for the structure, the technical support and the experience of the team that signs him up. After four races we were fourth in the British F3 championship. I started with two sixth places at Donington Park and Silverstone, finished the Thruxton weekend without adding to my total, but then I won the fourth race at Brands Hatch on the full Grand Prix circuit, not the shorter layout used for the Formula Ford Festival, starting from pole position and setting fastest race lap as well. We were taking some big scalps like the works Renault team, or Paul Stewart Racing, the title-winning team set up by Jackie Stewart and his son. We were up against some pretty reasonable outfits and we certainly didn't get the same Honda engines as PSR! That was the only race I won that year, but I was consistent and quick everywhere else.

But after the fourth or fifth race we were out of cash. The money from Yellow Pages and Dad had stretched only as far as acquiring the car and getting going. We hadn't paid Docko the money to continue racing for him and his patience was being stretched pretty thin.

Then, not for the first time, Annie had a brainwave.

By that time David Campese, the winger Dad once played with in the same Queanbeyan Rugby XV, had become one of Australia's greatest-ever players. Peter Windsor, a fellow Aussie and all-round sports fan who was team manager at Williams before becoming a respected motor-sport journalist, had been following my progress and suggested that I try to get in front of Campo somehow. The best chance would be while David was in the UK on his final Wallabies tour before he retired to set up a sports management company back in Sydney. Peter gave Campo a quick snapshot of who I was and what I was doing. He also found out when David was flying back to Australia, so he gave me the heads-up and off I went in my B-reg with a copy of my CV and sponsorship proposal tucked under my arm to stalk David at Heathrow. I handed the documents over to him and said if he was feeling bored on the 24-hour trip back to Australia he might like to read my proposal. When he got back he said he would be interested in managing my commercial affairs in Australia, and that's how our association started.

But what Ann was proposing in early 1997 went way beyond that. Some months after David agreed to represent me, she picked up the telephone in the middle of the English night, rang Campo and put our future in his hands. I had gone to bed that night destroyed, convinced we had reached the end of our journey. David's response – as an individual, not as a businessman – was phenomenal: overnight he sent the money we needed to cover what was owing to Docko and enough to get us through the next couple of races. While it was not enough to keep us going for long, it was an extraordinary gesture that let us battle on. It was also a lesson I have never forgotten about hunger, determination – and the need to lend an occasional hand.

*

While Ann and I were going cap in hand to Campo, a quite different avenue was beginning to open up for us. At the Australian Grand Prix in March 1997 I introduced myself to Norbert Haug at the official Grand Prix Ball where Yellow Pages always took a table, not only to entertain their own guests but also as an opportunity for me to network with F1 names. I'm not sure where I summoned up the courage to approach Norbert, but I seem to remember Ann pushing me towards him!

Norbert was the man in charge of the Mercedes racing program, which at that time supplied F1 engines to the mighty McLaren team, and his influence spread far and wide through the Mercedes-Benz empire. This 20-year-old Aussie gave him his card and said, 'Hi, I'm Mark Webber, I won the Formula Ford Festival last year, I'm doing Formula 3 this year and I wondered if you would mind if I kept you in touch with my results.'

To my surprise he said, 'Thanks, no problem,' and Ann was good about making sure we kept him informed of my progress. We weren't totally ripping up trees but we were getting good results, and she was determined to make people aware of what we were trying to do. In those pre-internet days that meant getting the results out – good, bad or indifferent – by the now antiquated method of faxing them. We sent them to Norbert and anyone who might be half-interested in following a young Aussie's journey as he tried to come up through the ranks. It was a team effort: Ann and I would come home from a race meeting on Sunday evening shattered, but both of us would still be at the fax machine in the early hours of Monday morning, punching in more than 30 individual numbers! I was always reminding Annie to make sure her release didn't run on to two pages because it then took twice as long to feed the sheets into the machine.

As things turned out, the fax mill worked. One morning – 15 May 1997, to be precise, just as I was getting ready for the sixth round of the F3 series at Croft up in North Yorkshire – I'd just jumped out of the shower to answer the phone at the top of the stairs. Luckily I sat down to take the call, otherwise I might have fallen down the bloody stairs.

It was Norbert Haug himself on the other end of the line. It seemed Gerhard Berger, who was then driving for

Benetton in what would turn out to be his last season as a Grand Prix driver, was unwell. Regular Mercedes sports-car driver Alex Wurz, an Austrian like Berger, was going to stand in for him.

'Alex drives with Bernd Schneider for us,' said Norbert. 'Do you want to come and do the Nürburgring sports-car race in his place?'

It blew me away, being asked to race at one of the most famous circuits in the world, up there in the Eifel Mountains in Germany, for one of the most famous teams in the world.

That was one of the biggest phone calls I've ever had in my career. I told Norbert I was absolutely thrilled to be considered but asked him to let me think about it. I wanted to ask Annie what she thought: it was only six months since I had been driving in Formula Ford, let's not forget, and here were Mercedes asking me to go to a track I had never seen, to try out a car, the CLK-GTR, that would take me to a whole new level. When Norbert rang back I suggested that it would be a good idea for me to do a preliminary test in the car, and he agreed.

To make it a truly representative test they were going to call in a guy by the name of Roberto Moreno from Brazil. F1 fans will remember that Moreno never really got the breaks he deserved in his career, but he did take part in 42 Grands Prix and he was second in a Benetton one–two finish behind Nelson Piquet at Suzuka in 1990. So here's Roberto Moreno, whom I used to watch over and over again in those Formula 1 races I used to tape as a kid, and they were going to compare me to him. Bloody hell!

The test took place in Austria at the A1-Ring, just days before my F3 race at the 1997 British Grand Prix. Alex Wurz was present and he was so helpful, telling me what I needed to do, what I needed to be careful of. I needed all the help I could get. Bear in mind the size of the teams I had been racing for, and the categories I was racing in. Then switch your mind to a highly prestigious international sports-car-racing class featuring many of the biggest players in the business. It would have been easy to feel overwhelmed.

This was my first exposure to the German way of doing things. You can imagine the garage, how professional everything was. They had everything laid out for me, the suit, the boots, the helmet – it was incredible. When I rocked up to the circuit at the start of the big day the first thing I saw was all the transporters: there were five trucks there just for the testing, and a Bridgestone tyre truck to boot. It was very nerve-racking because I knew how much rested on the next eight hours. I could have made a complete fool of myself – never been to Austria before, never been to this track before, never driven this car, don't know any people here. All I could do was put on my gear, jump in the car and get on with it.

Mercedes weren't just going to sign me without seeing what I could do: they knew I was doing solidly in F3, but naturally they wanted to make sure I could hold my own in a very different racing environment to anything I was used to. In situations like that you draw confidence from the people around you, and especially from the people who have been there before you. When I was in Formula Ford and Formula 3 I often thought of Jack Brabham and Alan Jones, and even my two-wheeled heroes, Mick Doohan and Wayne Gardner. They were a constant reminder to me: 'It is possible, Mark. Apply yourself, mate, this will be fine.' Of course there were lots of little demons on my shoulders saying this was going to be tough, but I ignored them and listened to the voice that was telling me to back myself instead.

So, a completely different environment for me: sports car, a windscreen, left-hand drive, not in the middle of the car but a little bit off-centre. I knew I was a reasonable racing driver but this was another challenge entirely. I remember slamming the door shut and firing the thing up – this was a V12 7.2-litre engine, an absolute rocket capable of doing 330 kilometres per hour.

My first reaction was sheer disbelief. I could not get my head around how much power the car had and how hard it would pull in fourth, fifth and sixth gears – the acceleration was something I'd never experienced in my life. The braking was similar to a Formula 3 car but obviously you're arriving so much faster at the corners. The car was absolutely beautiful to drive, and I knew that I had to put it on the limit.

I had one early spin and thought I'd blown it, but they were fine with that. They weren't telling me much at that stage, but I figured they felt the odd spin was normal for a young charger like me, bright-eyed, bushy-tailed and ready to go. It was a day of so many firsts for me, and I was absolutely on my own. Ann had said, 'They don't want anyone else there, Mark, they're interested in you, so get your backside over there and do it.' So as usual I took her advice!

After 10 or 15 laps I started getting used to the power and the brutal nature of the car. I remembered Dad talking about a racing car's power-to-weight ratio (he meant how light F1 cars were but how much power they had relative to that weight), and telling me this thing would also have plenty, but until you actually experience it you just can't imagine what it feels like.

As usual the hardest part was getting it off the corner, accelerating away when you're trying to feed that amount of power progressively onto the racetrack. A typical Formula 3 car is underpowered and overgripped; this car was overpowered and undergripped. And the track – we were using the shorter one – was a bit undulating, with a couple of blind corners on it, so that was more information to process and file away. It was challenging, but I can think of worse venues to go to for an initiation like the one they were putting me through. It was an averagely difficult venue for my first time, if not one of the more forgiving ones, and they probably did that deliberately. Of course I didn't think of that at the time, but they didn't take me somewhere like Jarama in Spain, where the run-off areas are very limited, meaning you have a high chance of having a big shunt there. So they did look after me to start with, but not for long – soon afterward they took me to other, less forgiving tracks, Jarama included.

Understandably enough I've had fond memories of the A1-Ring ever since. It was a defining day for me. There was a lot riding on those eight hours, not only for Ann and me. Alan Docking wanted me to land the Mercedes drive as well. While I was driving from the test back to the airport Docko rang me and said, 'How do you think you went, mate?' He was as anxious as we were: the funds from Campo had run out, and Alan wanted his money.

I said yeah, I thought it had gone all right. I didn't say much, just told him I hoped I had done enough.

As it turned out, I had.

Pushing me into Norbert Haug's path was another fantastic decision of Ann's. After my Austrian test, Norbert offered me a contract to race with the AMG Mercedes team in the FIA GT Championship in 1998. This would mean a major deviation from the course plotted in Ann's original career-path plan. The options she had drawn up were all based on a progression through single-seater racing categories. But there was nothing left in the fighting fund; if we didn't take this, we'd be going home. So you can imagine what Mercedes-Benz's offer meant to me at that stage: to have a manufacturer like that behind me was an incredible stroke of luck.

I asked Norbert if he would also take care of my F3 budget for the rest of the season, so that I could keep my racing edge, and he agreed. So AMG Mercedes paid for me to complete the British season, to the tune of £145,000. Negotiations began in earnest in June and the contract was in place by the end of September.

From that point on I pretty much turned professional.

As that realisation began to sink in, I went back to the UK and almost immediately pulled out what I thought was a reasonably good performance to finish second in the F3 race at the British Grand Prix meeting. It's funny what that little bit of reassurance can do for your confidence. After that I accumulated mainly top-four finishes and ended the season in fourth place overall behind Paul Stewart Racing's Jonny Kane, Frenchman Nicolas Minassian (who might have won the title but for a bizarre suspension when he took out his temper on a back-marker who had baulked him) and Peter Dumbreck.

I often wondered why Norbert picked me, an Australian. Eventually I found out. There was a man at AMG, the specialist race preparation arm of Mercedes-Benz, called Gerhard Ungar, and he was the one who took a liking to me. Gerhard, who had been in the Mercedes fold since 1987, was quite a powerful player at AMG; he had been watching my career from a distance, and he liked what he saw. I think he could understand the sheer tenacity behind what I was trying to achieve. I wasn't the only guy trying hard to make it, of course, but there was something in me that Gerhard saw and liked, and he was the one who put pressure on Norbert.

The end of 1997 was bizarre in a way: sports-car racing was not exactly the category we wanted to be competing in for 1998, but it was a very good alternative. Most of all, it took away the massive pressure of constantly needing to find the next dollar, having to explain to people that young drivers had to bring money to the team, not the other way round. It was a significant turning point for me: I was now being paid to drive a car. But very, very quickly I learned that responsibilities came with the money. It was by no means the first time I had felt a responsibility to other people – my parents, Ann, the Bob Copps and David Campeses of this world – but I now realised that, as my employers, Mercedes-Benz were at liberty to tell me exactly what they thought and expected of me. I was learning what the word 'professional' is all about. They're employing you to do a job and you have to demonstrate the right attitude, the right commitment: you're going to develop this car for them, you're racing this machine for them and on top of all that it just happens to be one of the most famous racing marques in the world.

4

Getting Ready for Take-off

I WENT INTO 1998 WITH ONE OF THE MOST SOUGHT-AFTER contracts a driver could have in his pocket outside of F1, but I knew there were hard yards ahead. Alan Docking had made a telling comment at the tail-end of 1997 when he explained why he had taken me on board for that F3 season.

'The young fellow's pointing a rocket at the moon,' Docko said, 'and the chances of hitting it are real slim.'

Alan was a seasoned motor-sport professional and he wasn't wrong. But at the start of 1998 I was already beginning to figure out ways of making the target easier to hit – and the target was success in sports-car racing, then a move to F1. There were two areas I needed to address: my knowledge of my car's behaviour and how my own decisions could affect it, and my personal fitness.

The key player in the first part of that learning process was the man who would be my 1998 teammate. Bernd

Schneider was 12 years older than me. As a kid he was a karting star, winning the world junior title before moving up to single-seaters in the German F3 series. He took that title as well in his second year, 1987, and that earned him the big call-up to Formula 1 with Germany's Zakspeed team. It was a difficult period for him, trying to qualify in a car that was always going to be at the back of the field – especially when they made the disastrous switch to Yamaha engines. After two seasons with Zakspeed he took part in the opening round of the 1990 World Championship for Arrows and did well to bring that car home in 12th place.

Bernd then found his niche in touring cars and sports cars. He raced with the well-known Joest team in a Porsche but by 1992 he was a Mercedes man, with several seasons in the DTM (the German Touring Car series) before he moved into the GT arena. By the time we got together in '98 Bernd Schneider was the reigning GT World Champion so he knew a thing or two about handling racing cars.

Why did they partner me with Bernd? Norbert Haug explained later that there had been some other options, like putting two young guys up against a pairing of the regular Mercedes drivers, but they were always in favour of putting young blood and experience together. That had already happened when Bernd and Dario Franchitti raced together, and Norbert had confidence in Bernd because he was very open, a great team player and one who would do what he could to help the inexperienced drivers.

Bernd Schneider was the first man to drive home to me how important car set-up was. Until I worked with him I had been pretty arrogant when it came to finding ways to improve the car. I'd always thought it was an excuse or a weakness if you couldn't drive around a problem or if you had to look at the telemetry, compare your teammate's lap times with your own and work out how he was achieving them. I always wanted to learn for myself and not show any weaknesses – and suggesting that I needed things changed on the car seemed like a weakness to me. I felt that I should be able to get the job done with whatever equipment I had been given. I was so bloody pig-headed.

That attitude didn't last long at Mercedes. They taught me that learning how to set the car up, how to make it go round a particular circuit in the most effective way, was a fundamental part of my profession. I had begun to realise how important it was, but Mercedes put a big emphasis on it and what they were telling me was spot-on: I didn't realise how much easier I could make my life simply by focusing on details.

As well as helping me with the fine-tuning of the car, Bernd also taught me how to use it to better effect on my way round a track. Again it was a lesson that initially went against the Webber grain. Bernd was asking me to use the kerbs: jumping the different types of kerbs and chicanes a circuit might present me with and using them to keep the car on the trajectory I needed.

I thought that looked bad: it was scrappy, it was hard on the cars and at times it could even give the impression that the driver was desperate, otherwise why would he resort to handling the car that way? Bernd cut through all that from the word go. He listened to me, then said simply: 'But your job is to get this thing round the track as quickly as possible.' And he was right.

You work hard to keep mistakes to a minimum, and making none at all is the aim, but Bernd was the past master at executing all the techniques that help you go faster. He left no stone unturned and that's why he was phenomenal in touring cars and in sports cars. He was one of the fastest guys I ever drove with or raced against. Looking back, he probably went up that steep learning-curve in the early part of his career; he arrived at Formula 1 before he had completed the curve and learned a lot of those techniques too late. Thanks largely to him, I was fortunate enough to learn them in time.

It would have been helpful to pick up that knowledge sooner, but I absorbed a lot from Bernd in that first year with him. In that crucial period of my career he was a real brother to me, my first real friend outside the UK. We both liked playing squash, we went running together, we obviously drove together in the same car and we would win many races.

We had a very good relationship – but that didn't mean he was a pushover. Schneider was one of the most ferocious competitors I've ever seen. It would be nothing for him to destroy a squash racquet when things weren't going his way on court. He was on a very short wick and he hated being beaten. So I learned a lot from him about many aspects of driving and controlling both the car and myself. He wasn't a politician – maybe that's why he didn't do as well as he should have in Formula 1 – but as a driving talent, he was phenomenal.

Speaking of car control and self-control, Bernd acted like a brother on one particular occasion I will never forget. It was all part of a very significant learning process going on in 1998. When we returned to the UK Ann and I rented a terraced house in Aylesbury. I used to drive from Aylesbury across to Mercedes headquarters in Stuttgart regularly; AMG were very good with their drivers, they gave us a car each, which again for me was just a phenomenal thing, going from the B-reg Fiesta to a Merc! That's how they wanted us to turn up at the events, it was all part of the professionalism. On one particular day, though, I got myself into a scrape that looked anything but professional.

It happened on the French–German border at Saarbrücken. I was going to a Mercedes truck function, where Bernd was meeting me from Cologne. I used to do this trip in the early hours of the morning to get it over as quickly as possible, timing myself from door to door (I made it in seven hours on one occasion), and I used to hook in pretty hard. On this occasion I became confused at the tollbooth at Saarbrücken and when I blasted out of there I got myself into the wrong lane. I was furious at myself for losing a whole 40 seconds, so I did a U-turn at the service station and headed back down onto the main motorway. The fact is I was going way too fast. Uncharted waters again, this particular motorway entry: down the bottom it really tightened up and it was a lot greasier than I expected. It was wet, and it got a lot wetter, and I couldn't use the merging lane, I had to go straight out into the lanes with other vehicles. I was thinking, 'Please don't let there be any traffic', but as it turned out there was a huge truck in the allegedly slow lane. He was doing 120 or so, I was going too fast, I couldn't brake and get in behind him, I couldn't accelerate to get in front of him, I was just going straight into the side of his truck.

Sure enough, I hit him and the impact turned me pretty much onto the front of the truck. Now it was pushing me down the motorway, and when I came off the truck I was totally paranoid about being T-boned because they drive so fast over there. That didn't happen, but instead I had a head-on with the central reservation, put the three-pointed star up where the windscreen wiper sits and absolutely destroyed the car. I wasn't hurt at all: I was cool when I got out and then about 30 seconds later the shock hit. It got worse when I realised the truck driver was out of his cab and intent on killing me. That much was clear, even though he didn't speak any English and my Polish is not that great. Thankfully a lady turned up who spoke multiple languages and managed to calm things down a little and eventually the police arrived as well.

Not knowing what else to do, I rang Bernd.

'Bernd, mate, I've had an absolute monster shunt, driving way too fast, I'm not going to make the function. What do you think I should do?'

He cut right through: 'Ring Norbert straightaway. Go straight to the top and tell him you've f#*ked up, driving like an idiot.'

I rang Norbert, expecting the worst, and said, 'Norbert, I've had a crash, I was driving too quick and the car's a write-off.'

He asked, 'How are you, are you okay?'

Once I had reassured him I was unhurt he started making things happen. Mercedes organised for the police to take me to a dealership where I picked up another car. The people bringing my wrecked car were told very clearly not to drive it past the dealership showroom where a new C-Class Mercedes was being launched. I did some work for the dealer in return, signed some photos and did an hour's worth of promotional activity for them, which struck me as quite a funny turn of events.

Another stroke of luck was that the accident happened not far from where Bernd's parents lived. I wasn't really up for driving by that time so the police took me to the Schneiders' house and I stayed there overnight.

My tail was between my legs, but the experience taught me another important lesson. It was a big wake-up call about pulling my head in – it's a good thing I was on my own because the passengers would have been in a much worse state than I was. The driver's was the only straight door on the car. Bernd's advice was brilliant: you've got to go straight to the top because that way the story is unfiltered. I think Bernd knew that because he'd had plenty of experience of those situations! For me, though, it was a nice little reminder from upstairs to rein it all in a bit.

*

If Bernd Schneider was the teacher when it came to sorting the car out, the man who took control of my personal fitness side was Tony Matthis. Tony was the ski coach of the Austrian World Cup team; Mercedes had been using him to get their driver squad into shape for some years. The place where I found out how far I had to travel in fitness terms was Zürs, in the Austrian Alps. I went there briefly with Bernd just before Christmas 1997; he told me to be sure and enjoy the trip because I sure as hell wouldn't find the next one much fun!

That second trip was for a training camp that took place early in 1998. It started well enough: we were given a day's grace to get out and do a bit of skiing, then we had a meeting with Tony in the evening to outline what was to come. I knew there was hard work in store, because I had recently done a big test in the car for Bridgestone at Jarama in Madrid. Bridgestone had taken me under their wing as a test driver on their sports-car program. They liked the fact that I spoke English, albeit with an accent! The Jarama schedule included testing about a dozen of the company's tyre compounds, which meant putting in 15 laps on each set of tyres. I then had to select the best front and rear tyres and carry out a full one-hour run. That was the first time I had ever driven for an hour non-stop, and it came after I had already done well over 150 laps. I lost 4 kilos in the process and I was buggered at the end of the day.

I had already begun to realise I needed to improve my fitness in the F3 race at Macau in late '97. It's one of the most demanding street circuits a driver will ever face and the experience really opened my eyes: even though I finished fourth, it was the first time that I had felt so uncomfortable in a race car. I'd been going for my little jogs round Aylesbury and thought I was pretty fit. I was dreaming – and Zürs certainly woke me up.

In F1 there was a changing of the guard in the mid-nineties with Michael Schumacher. It was Schumacher who opened everyone's eyes to the difference fitness – real fitness – could make. Michael had already been where I found myself now – in the Mercedes sports-car program – and he had become a bit of a beacon for me. I went on that training camp at Zürs with the Mercedes squad, including Bernd and Ricardo Zonta, the Brazilian who had just won the F3000 title – and I got pasted.

We had multiple sessions on each of the six days after a pretty solid pre-breakfast hike: some stretching, some skiing in the middle of the day, a run or some other activity in the afternoon. We used to do this walk on a nearby hill, where we'd put a pair of racquet shoes on and walk to the top. The first day I got there before everyone else, but they never saw me for the rest of the week because I was destroyed. I was so keen to do well on the first day, but I could never repeat that effort.

I couldn't fix the problem in a week, I just had to hug my teddy and get on with it. But I decided there and then I would never be humiliated in the same way again. When I got back I had changed: fitness was now front and centre on my agenda, and would remain so throughout my career. When I came back again these pricks were going to be in big trouble.

*

It's funny how a couple of words can change the course of a career. Early in 1998, a year after I introduced myself to Norbert Haug, the man in charge of the Mercedes-Benz racing program, I found myself back at the Australian Grand Prix. But this time I was at the wheel of a mighty 'Silver Arrow', the name originally given to Mercedes cars in Grand Prix racing before the Second World War. Even though I was 'only' doing demonstration runs, it was a wonderful opportunity to showcase sports-car racing to an Australian public with very limited knowledge of the category. For me, it was a taste of things to come in the season that lay ahead. The car I was showing off in Melbourne was the CLK-GTR in which Bernd had taken the inaugural FIA GT title for

Mercedes in 1997. I announced in Australia that Mercedes were putting me alongside Bernd in all 10 rounds of the 1998 GT series, whose long races – 500 kilometres, for the most part – demanded that drivers share the burden. In mid-year we would be taking the Mercedes name back to Le Mans, the world-famous endurance race in France, where it's fair to say the Mercedes marque had a chequered history.

In 1955 a Mercedes was at the centre of the most shocking accident in motor-racing history, when Pierre Levegh's 300 SLR flew into the crowd opposite the main grandstand, leaving more than 80 spectators dead. That tragedy triggered Mercedes-Benz's withdrawal from motor sport. Not until 1988 did the three-pointed star return to the circuit in the department of La Sarthe; they won the 1989 event, missed 1990 and were expected to dominate the 1991 race when a young Michael Schumacher was part of the line-up. Instead they were caught out by a minor component failure on two of their cars and left with their tails between their legs.

So the full-scale return of the Silver Arrows to Le Mans would obviously be the centrepiece of our working year. I've always been attracted to endurance racing and its twin challenge to man and machine. If you have any feeling for motor racing then Le Mans – Jaguar in the fifties, Ford vs Ferrari in the sixties, Porsche dominance in the seventies and so on – is ingrained in your psyche to start with. I was really looking forward to going there for the first time. First, though, we had to get the championship itself underway.

The 10-round series began at Oschersleben, in what was once East Germany. Our three-car force consisted of Schneider/Webber in one car and an interesting pairing of young and old in the second: three-time Le Mans winner (for Porsche) Klaus Ludwig and Brazilian Ricardo Zonta. Another privately entered Mercedes was to be shared by Jean-Marc Gounon and Marcel Tiemann. All year long comparisons would be drawn, inevitably, between Ricardo and myself – two young chargers in the same Mercedes family with a Formula 1 seat as a very realistic prospect if we did well. Score round one to the other old/new pairing: with our day compromised by damage to a wheel rim, third was the best Bernd and I could do as Klaus and Ricardo drew first blood.

Between Germany and the UK, where Silverstone was to stage round two, came a spine-tingling moment for me: my first experience of Le Mans. There is a pre-qualifying event there a month or so ahead of the race weekend itself, with two six-hour sessions in which the drivers are required to reach certain qualifying times in order to book their place in the race. We only needed to qualify one car as Bernd's achievement in winning the previous year's GT title automatically brought qualification for Le Mans with it. But we were bringing out the CLK-LM, designed specifically for the 24-hour marathon, so all six of the nominated Le Mans drivers, myself included, went down there for our first look at the car and, in my case, the track – all 13.8 kilometres of it. Despite all I had read and heard, it was a stunning experience. As soon as you get out there you understand the mystique that surrounds Le Mans, because it asks every question a racing driver needs to answer: fast corners, low-speed corners – and 330 kilometres flat out on the famous Mulsanne Straight! Bernd did the donkey-work and set third-fastest time overall; I managed six laps, but the length of the circuit meant that I was in the cockpit for 40 minutes while I did them.

Silverstone is another of our sport's most hallowed grounds, and soon after the buzz of seeing Le Mans came another high: the biggest win of my career to that point when Bernd and I turned the tables on the Ludwig/Zonta car at the British track in the second round of the championship. AMG's Hans-Werner Aufrecht asked me to take the lead role in our car for the weekend, so that was a feather in the Webber cap. Schneider/Webber in the championship lead, albeit by a single point!

Before racing at Silverstone even started I had another 'moment' that left a Mercedes with significant damage and its driver in need of assistance. One of the great advantages of racing at Silverstone is that I could commute each day from home. About halfway to Silverstone there is a village called Whitchurch. It has one of those funny little English mini-roundabouts, and that was my undoing.

Ann and I were in an E-Class Mercedes and as we approached the roundabout we came up behind a bloke who looked as if he was going to take the first exit and go left. In fact he was only veering left to swing round hard and do a 180-degree turn back round the mini-roundabout. He came back on me and turned into the left rear quarter of my car. If I'd been going faster he would have missed me, but the long and the short of it was that my E-Class now had a severely damaged rear bumper and light hanging off the back. I had no option but to press on to Silverstone with the car in that state. As luck would have it, as I turned off the road into the circuit entry, who should be in the car ahead but Norbert Haug. I went straight to Alan Docking to see if there was any kind of minor miracle he could work – I knew I was in a bit of strife as the left rear of the car was basically smashed in. I took it to the car park, reversed it into a corner, and from the front it looked beautiful!

*

On-track the news kept getting better: less than three weeks later Bernd planted the #35 car he would be sharing with Klaus and me on pole for Le Mans. Qualifying for the race proper is staged over four sessions on the Wednesday and Thursday of race week.

I put in another 12 laps of the Le Mans track during qualifying, focusing on setting the car up for the race. Bernd did a phenomenal job: we went there not believing we could find the one-lap pace to grab pole, but Wednesday gave us a glimmer of hope and he pushed like hell to get there on Thursday. The only man in the field to break the 3-minute 36-second record, Bernd was a full second quicker than the leading Toyota, which in turn was only just faster than our #36 car driven by Christophe Bouchut. It was just reward for the team's hard work, which included major test sessions over at Homestead in Florida, at the Paul Ricard circuit up on the plateau to the east of Marseille just before our Silverstone victory, and a final shakedown at Hockenheim in southern Germany. I had played my own role in that testing, too: every single Bridgestone tyre we had used in our GT racing and every tyre we planned to use at Le Mans had been tested by me and me alone.

I was thrilled to be at Le Mans, especially in a year that was a bit of a landmark even for that famous place. Nissan had been plotting their Le Mans campaign for some time, Toyota would be there, so would Porsche – and so would we, for the first time in almost a decade. Everyone was expecting record speeds in such a competitive environment. During those Paul Ricard tests I had a word with a former Le Mans winner, Martin Brundle, and he said, 'You've picked the right year to do it, mate, because it's just so competitive this time.'

There was a different animal to get used to. The CLK-LM was a Le Mans-specific car: in contrast to the GTR's 12 cylinders it had a V8 engine and was 100 kilos lighter. At Le Mans we were also allowed to use so-called driver aids such as traction control and an anti-lock braking system. It was even closer to a single-seater, in my view, than the car we had been sharing in the GT series proper. Bernd was used to those tools, thanks to his experience in the International Touring Car championship, and he was working hard to bring me up to speed not only with those systems but also with tyre management and fuel consumption. Formula Ford and F3 don't teach a young driver much in that regard because all you do there is go flat out! We had also figured out another crucial part of the weekend, namely who would be A-B-C in our car; that is, which of us would be allowed to sleep when – an important consideration when you have a 24-hour marathon at high speed ahead of you. I was B, the man in the middle, which meant I would be catching some shut-eye roughly between two and five in the morning of Sunday, and that suited me just fine.

I felt some trepidation about racing at night, not least of all because of the speed differential between the various classes of cars that race at Le Mans. It's a sobering thought that when you come to the end of a straight in your car you will still be pedal to the metal up around 300-plus when you reach the braking-board 200 metres from a first-gear chicane – by which time the GT2 guys have been on the brakes for about 150 metres already, so there is a difference of about 150 kilometres per hour between you.

Still, I was trying not to set too much store by this first appearance at Le Mans. For a start, I understood that however much testing and preparation you had done, in the pressure-cooker of that race a 50-cent washer could bring you undone. More than that, though, whether we won by 10 laps or blew up on the first one, I felt it didn't carry that much weight where my future was concerned. Just as well: I never got to turn a wheel in anger! Our lead man Bernd started the race but had to call it quits after just 75 minutes of the 24 hours when a steering-pump problem led to engine failure. Neither Klaus nor I got into the car. Becoming a Le Mans driver would have to wait another year.

Meanwhile there was a GT championship to be won. Bernd and I set about doing that in the best way possible: we won the third round at Hockenheim in Germany on the last weekend of June 1998. It was the maiden victory for the CLK-LM, albeit one race later than we had all hoped, and Bernd's signature was all over it: pole position, a double stint in the cockpit at the start, a 40-second lead when he handed over to me and an eventual 72-second margin of victory over the Ludwig/Zonta Mercedes.

The next race couldn't have been more of a contrast. We went to Dijon, in north-eastern France, and once again we were comfortably in control until traffic forced me offline and I picked up a piece of debris between the rear wishbone and the inside of my wheel rim. The friction split the rim and the tyre deflated, which pitched me into a spin and I had to crawl back to pit lane for repairs. With no points for us and with Klaus winning the race in the other Mercedes, our title hopes had taken a knock.

But you have to roll with the punches and come out fighting again, which is exactly what we did in round five at the Hungaroring just outside Budapest only a week later. Bernd and I led from start to finish from the car's fourth successive pole; we were a point behind our teammates as the GT championship prepared to head east.

A few days in Oz catching up with family and friends (my sister Leanne was about to give birth to her first child) did me the world of good. Immediately after that Bernd and I caught up with Klaus and Ricardo and regained the lead in the GT series. Not only that, but for me it was the most remarkable victory I had tasted so far. It came at one of my favourite circuits, Suzuka in Japan, and it was doubly satisfying because it was a 1000-kilometre test of endurance in high temperatures and even higher humidity – one of the worst combinations a driver can face. Sure enough, I started dehydrating, but I got over it quickly enough to take over the car for the final hour and bring it home again.

When we racked up victory number five in the next race back in the UK things were looking rosy for the #1 Mercedes. We were seven points in the clear with three rounds to go, and another 1–2 result meant Mercedes had retained the manufacturers' title. Round eight in the third week of September took me back to the scene of the crime: the A1-Ring in Austria where just over a year earlier I went through that first spine-tingling test for Mercedes. This time I had a shorter day's work ahead of me – a three-hour race – but there was plenty at stake again. Despite Bernd's best efforts in his final stint we were beaten by over half a minute. Our lead was down to three points; maybe it was just as well we had a month's break in the schedule before heading across the pond for the final two rounds in the USA.

Unfortunately I kept my least impressive performance of the year for the first of those two American races, at Homestead in Florida on 18 October. Once again there was lingering evidence of my inexperience: while we had all the technical back-up we could hope for, race-day specifics like wellness and hydration were left to the drivers' own devices and I wasn't getting my physical preparation quite right. I was also caught out by Klaus Ludwig's craftiness as I chased him late in the race – he forced me into a mistake and I went off. Now we were four points adrift, with one race left on the other side of the country at Laguna Seca. When we got to the business end of the race Zonta had 18 seconds on me. I tried very hard to catch him, but I went off on a large patch of oil someone had kindly deposited – and Ricardo had the same problem next time round. I fired in a string of fastest laps but just ran out of time and had to back off and keep an eye on the fuel gauge.

So the end result was second place in the FIA GT Championship by a margin of eight points. My disappointment was tempered by happiness for Klaus, since that was his last year in racing, but I also felt it had been a little unfair on Bernd. His partner came from Formula Ford and F3, whereas Ricardo arrived as the new F3000 champion to partner Klaus and was already getting test drives in Formula 1. I could go toe-to-toe with them most times but sometimes I struggled, partly because it was Bernd's car, basically, and he had it set up as he wanted it, and partly through sheer lack of experience.

I didn't realise until a few years later how lucky I had been to see how Mercedes went about their racing: the discipline in every area was exemplary. In terms of car preparation it was a super team. On the back of that success Zonta headed off to F1 with the BAR (British American Racing) team; meanwhile I was gearing up for a second season of sports-car racing.

*

The Mercedes arrangement had changed things dramatically on the professional front, and it almost changed my personal life at the same time. If I really wanted to go somewhere as a racing driver, 1998 also taught me that you have to be emotionally sound as well as physically together. There was a period in the middle of that year when I was an emotional mess.

My parents came over to the UK in the English summer of 1997. While they were thrilled about how things were developing for me in racing, they'd been less thrilled by the romantic relationship that was developing between Annie and me. I had suspected that Dad had sensed our growing feelings as he had been spending quite a bit of time with us in the UK but he hadn't raised any warning flags with me. I think it's fair to say that both he and I buried our heads in the sand as we didn't want to upset Mum by telling her the truth about my relationship with Ann. It was only when Mum came over in 1997 that it had to be confronted.

I felt totally torn between the new life I was carving out for myself in the UK and wanting to keep my parents happy and, more importantly, respect their feelings. Annie could sense the pressure I was under and didn't want to add to it: she was understanding to a point but she was disappointed that she was being made to feel uncomfortable in her own home, all because the Webbers hadn't communicated with each other very well. The irony was that by wanting to protect Mum in the first place and not telling her, Dad and I had ultimately made things worse. Disey is quite a traditional mum and she was terribly distraught and upset, mainly because of the age difference between me and Annie, and she was concerned that this would mean I wouldn't have a family of my own.

But even Annie and I didn't know ourselves where our relationship would play out at that stage. We had no expectations, we had been surprised ourselves how strongly our feelings had developed, but there were people telling us it wasn't right, it couldn't work. Admittedly, the pressure got to me and we agreed to put the personal side of our relationship on hold although we continued to share a house together. When I went back to Australia for a break, I started a relationship with a girl I'd known from high school. Mum and Dad were very supportive of this blossoming new romance and in this version of the movie Webber marries the hometown girl, they start a family and everyone lives happily ever after.

Annie knew that I had only scratched the surface of my racing career but she wasn't prepared to hang around and watch young love undermine all we'd worked so hard for. No doubt the 1998 Australian Grand Prix only reinforced the way Annie felt, because my new girlfriend and I made a

point of announcing our presence in a less than inconspic-
uous fashion, even to the extent of waltzing into the Yellow
Pages suite and laying down some new ground rules, such
as the number of autographs I'd sign and meet-and-greets
I was willing to do! Of course, this did not go down well
with Bob Copp and his colleagues, who were concerned
that their vision for me, and their investment, was about to
be derailed.

Annie was bitterly disappointed at my behaviour. Her
plan to take me to the highest level of motor sport was
starting to go horribly wrong, so she left Australia earlier
than planned and headed back to Europe. My family
arranged for Alan Docking to collect my belongings from
the house we had been sharing and the one and only car
Annie and I had at that stage. That left Luke and her stuck
in Aylesbury without any form of transport; she later told
me that she rented a car whenever she needed to travel for
work. Campese Management told her that they had been
instructed by the Webber family to terminate her role as my
manager and that Campese Management would be taking
over all aspects of my career, including the negotiation of
my driving contracts.

Meanwhile, I was off to Germany again, which was
bloody tough as it was now going to be my base in Europe.
I was in Stuttgart on my own staying in a hotel, although
sometimes I'd stay at Bernd's place, where I learned another
little quirk of European life: the continental breakfast!
He and I would come back from a 10-kilometre run, I'd
be absolutely ravenous – and he would have a little bit of
cheese and ham. I ended up virtually scavenging for food,
I was so hungry.

One thing I did enjoy was some of the development work Mercedes asked me to do on the road-going versions of the cars we were racing: it got me onto the autobahn, well north of 320 kilometres per hour, on more than one occasion. There would be an engineer sitting beside me punching the numbers in and saying, 'Schneller, Schneller!' – 'Faster! Faster!' – when I was already going fast enough for the wipers to peel off the windscreen and bend back along the side of the car like boomerangs. It was by far the quickest I had ever been in a road car.

By late April, as my first race with Mercedes was fast approaching, I was an emotional wreck. I had the pressure of wanting to do well in my new role; I had my family encouraging me to take a different path in my personal life; and there were plans in place for my girlfriend to come to Europe to attend my first few races.

I knew that what was going on in my private life was going to affect my driving, and I knew the new regime – a new girlfriend, a new management company – wasn't going to work. My family and I were dreaming if we thought I could survive and succeed in Germany on my own. I knew the guys at the Mercedes team but I couldn't exactly sit down and talk to them about my personal life – the last thing they wanted was a bit of *Dallas* in the middle of their sports car season.

While I knew Annie provided the support and guidance I needed in my racing career, I was missing her in so many other ways too. We were such a dynamic force in every sense; we could make things happen when we were together. We were teammates, soul mates, call it what you want. Maybe I had been blind to it but we had been on a

life journey together and it was going places. I realised I'd
screwed things up with her and there was only one way to
fix them again: call her. So I did – several times, in fact,
but she was quietly getting on with her life in motor racing
and at first the calls went unanswered because she was
away racing.

When she eventually answered, the only thing I could
say was, 'I want to come home.'

So after six months Annie and I resumed our relationship, both personally and professionally. I moved back in
with her and Luke in Aylesbury and settled down to the
serious job of being a professional racing driver, but now in
a stable home environment that I was comfortable with.

My dad never really had a problem with my relationship
with Annie. Mum knows now that there have been more
positives than negatives to it. She and Annie were slow to
bond but I can honestly say that their relationship has never
been stronger than it is now. They're never going to have
the stereotypical mother-in-law/daughter-in-law relationship, which I'm happy about as I've seen plenty of major
fallouts and disruptions caused by feuding mothers and
daughters-in-law! Nowadays they have a good friendship
and there's a lot of mutual respect between them.

As to Mum's concern about our age difference, that has
never been a factor for us. When we began to be more open
about being together, perhaps the top end of the age gap
shocked a few people. In those days people were less accept-
ing of a big age difference between partners, especially when
it's our way round. It's not such a big deal nowadays and it
makes us laugh when so-called celebrities reveal they're
dating an older woman or younger man! One of the most

amusing things is when we're checking in to hotels and we get asked if we require separate rooms, or if Dad's with us, they try checking him and Annie in together! Even now it still causes the odd raised eyebrow!

As to Ann's family's reaction, we had stayed with her mother when we first moved to the UK in early 1996 and Bettine was always very supportive of my career. She was wise enough to see the relationship developing between us but never felt it was her place to say anything either way. But when it had become blatantly obvious, she embraced it. Sadly Bettine died in March 2015 at 92, but she was sharp as a tack until the end.

In career terms, perhaps the most crucial lesson I learned in 1998 was about discipline. It's so easy for young athletes to be dazzled by the trappings of success, whether you measure those in material possessions or in the so-called glamorous lifestyle that people associate with sporting achievement.

I had gone from being almost down and out to being a paid professional driver. Seeing a few zeros at the end of your bank statement certainly makes a difference, and I can tell you it makes a big difference flying business or first class when you spend so much of your life in aeroplanes getting from one racing venture to another.

It was easy to think I'd made it. The question is: made what? There were still mountains left to climb and we weren't exactly rolling in money and there were some not inconsiderable debts to be repaid. With all the emotional distractions it would have been very easy for me to mess things up at Mercedes and be left with absolutely nothing again.

We were in a dilemma. On the one hand I could go into cruise mode and accept the good things coming my way: I was 21, I was being paid, and had nice little perks like an AMG car at my disposal in the UK and also whenever I was back in Australia.

On the other hand, we were trying to keep an eye on the real prize: getting to Formula 1. And that was a massive gulf to bridge. It used to annoy Mercedes quite intensely that I *was* still so focused on F1. It didn't matter to them that I had been brought up on images of single-seater cars flashing past me in Adelaide, and on videotapes of all the great F1 drivers of the day in action. They would much rather have had me concentrating on sports-car racing, a category for which I was massively undercooked at that time. I had only been in Europe for 18 months, after all. But I wasn't ready to let go of the F1 dream just yet, even if the route to that eventual goal might have changed in the last few months.

Ann and I thought we might dovetail my GT commitments with a season of F3000 in 1999 if we could find the funds, and we were probably better off being in Australia trying to drive the fund-raising. So we relocated in December 1998, partly because the Mercedes program for the following year was going to be quite short, with the focus firmly on the return to Le Mans and a limited number of American Le Mans series races. Realistically, it was a non-starter as Mercedes wouldn't have entertained it for one minute but we were still determined to keep my single-seater goal alive.

When we returned to Australia, we didn't go back to Queanbeyan but to Melbourne, where we rented an apartment on Queens Road, right opposite the Albert Park track. If I ever needed any motivation about keeping my F1 hopes alive, seeing the track being constructed over January and February and watching the place come alive in March was it.

5

Nightmare at Le Mans: 1999

IN THE EARLY PART OF 1999 I FLEW IN AND OUT OF AUSTRALIA on a regular basis as Mercedes were busy testing in Europe and America. We returned to the UK after the Australian Grand Prix – I remember it being all a bit last-minute and having to recruit one of Annie's friends to help find us rented accommodation back in Aylesbury. Luke returned to the same school and friends he thought he had said goodbye to three months earlier and we settled down in a rented house on a little estate called Watermead; the picture of domestic bliss was completed by a nice AMG Mercedes in the driveway.

And another Mercedes would be waiting for me in France.

I came into 1999 with big plans to go one better than the previous year and win a World Championship with Mercedes, but that hope was quickly dashed. At the end of February the FIA announced that the International

Prototype Cup, the category the AMG Mercedes team was scheduled to take part in, had been cancelled. 'Lack of interest from other manufacturers' was the reason given, just as we were getting into our testing stride back in California.

The dumping of the prototype series was cause for concern. It meant 1999 would offer very limited driving opportunities for me. At Mercedes we were left with only one target to aim for, although it was a pretty inviting one: Le Mans. In April AMG Mercedes announced that I would be the lead driver in one of three new CLR machines. Without the distraction of regular racing, there was a clear focus again, a clear goal: it was all about taking three Silver Arrows back to Le Mans – and winning.

The build-up to the 1999 Le Mans 24-hour race was the best time in my racing life up till that point. It was really rewarding and a lot of fun because Bernd and I did the bulk of the preparatory work. We crossed the Atlantic regularly to do a lot of testing in America because the weather was better over there. There's no track you can really compare with Le Mans, but thanks to the great American team-owner Roger Penske and his link with Mercedes, we went to Fontana in California to simulate conditions in La Sarthe as best we could. It was a track where you could do a bit on the banking, but on the infield section you could test the engines at full noise, the gearbox, the tyre constructions, everything. A lot of people didn't know where we were testing as we were getting ready for this one crucial race. And in between times we had so much fun taking in Champ Car races, playing golf, all sorts of stuff – it was a bit like the boys on tour!

We were working with a real purpose, though: getting those cars bullet-proof. Bernd and I did a lot of training together, and we were totally focused. The sessions would be five or six days long, and we were attempting to complete 30-hour simulations, 25 per cent longer than Le Mans race duration. In our first test at Fontana we had three cars running; two of them failed, but the car I was in actually finished the test – 1000 laps of the Fontana road course. You could say the car won: it wore out the drivers! Gerhard Ungar, AMG's chief designer, was well aware of the healthy rivalry among the drivers, and he kept hammering it into us that we were all going to be in the race; it wasn't a competition to see who was doing the quickest lap times, it was all about testing the car. But after three or four hours' running it was like qualifying out there. We were giving it everything, because after all he did say it was about testing the car and if you want to really test it then you have to do your best to simulate a race scenario.

I wasn't going to drive with Bernd in 1999. Mercedes had pretty much given me my own car for Le Mans, which was a thankyou for the year before, so I was with Jean-Marc Gounon and Marcel Tiemann. They had both been in the privately run Persson Mercedes outfit the previous year. In the other cars would be Pedro Lamy, Franck Lagorce and Bernd, then Christophe Bouchut, Nick Heidfeld and Peter Dumbreck in the third entry. The 24-hour classic was due to take place on 12–13 June, with the traditional pre-qualifying on 2 May. Our #4 car had been pre-registered for the race as a reward for AMG's title win in the '98 FIA GT series, but I was still keen to get back to La Sarthe, build on the handful of laps I got before the previous year's race and see what this new car could do – we were expecting top speeds in excess of 350 kilometres per hour.

What we were *not* expecting was the mechanical failure that struck our car, with me on board, in that May pre-qualifying session. I was just going into the second chicane on the Mulsanne Straight when the front right suspension collapsed. That was a very unusual failure on the front lower wishbone: it simply pulled out of the tub as soon as I started braking. It was the first time this had ever happened. It sent me spearing across the gravel trap, then I spun and hit the barrier. It was a big moment, but I got it all together and I was able to get out of the car all right. The preparations, as you might expect, were so thorough that we actually had mobile phones in the cars, so the onlookers were taken aback to see the driver putting in an emergency call to the team back in the pits! Team sensitivity also came into play: one of the mechanics grabbed a camera from a nearby photographer and destroyed it on the spot. But the mishap meant our car was pretty much out for the rest of the day's running because it was in a difficult place for the recovery team to get at.

What had just happened came as a complete surprise. We had been doing those 30-hour simulations and we'd had to turn the car off because every other part of the team, the drivers and mechanics in particular, was destroyed. As a result we were pretty confident that the cars were going to be reliable for the race. Now, all of a sudden, there was this question mark.

After pre-qualifying, there was major panic because we could see we just weren't quick enough. We were off the pace compared with the Toyotas, though there was some talk that they might be running light, show-boating to spook the opposition, and even the Panoz looked pretty quick. There was a hint of desperation creeping in and by that stage there was no time to fix the problem. When the race itself is only four or five weeks away there's not a great deal you can do to re-invent the wheel in performance terms.

Any Le Mans victory is sweet, but this year's looked like being a really prestigious race to win, with official entries from Toyota, Porsche, BMW, Nissan and quick drivers like Martin Brundle, Thierry Boutsen and JJ Lehto, or Le Mans specialists like Tom Kristensen. It was a very, very hotly contested year in terms of the intensity and pace of the race.

We took ourselves off to Hockenheim and did some testing on the old circuit, the layout without the chicanes, which meant we were able to run at incredibly high pace, taking a bit of down-force off the car to help our top speed. At Le Mans you need the balance between cornering and top speed on the straights, you need to get through the Porsche curves coming back towards the main straight there – we needed to be competitive on every part of the circuit. Within the team our thinking was, 'Okay, let's put a bit more performance onto the straights with the aerodynamics and make the car a bit more slippery, and go there in better shape for the race.' The critical area is the undertray at the front of the car. We had these little 'flicks', aerodynamic add-ons which we could put on at each side of the nose to give us more down-force should it rain, and we thought that with Bridgestone tyres, and with the track rubbering in and becoming grippier over the race weekend, we still had a chance to win. Armed with what we had learned at Hockenheim, we went back to Le Mans for the famous race itself.

It would turn into the worst race weekend of my entire career.

*

Practice was going along all right until Thursday night, 10 June. I was pretty happy with what we'd done in my car so far, even if we were struggling a bit for outright pace when Marcel was at the wheel. I had only done three timed laps in the car myself and I was out there doing some final reliability checks, getting my eye in. That's when I came up behind Frank Biela in his open-topped Audi on the section between Mulsanne Corner and Indianapolis at the southern end of the circuit, where you brake for the hairpin and then accelerate up to sixth on the way to the first kink. Biela was cooperating nicely, I was going with the flow – I loved driving in the twilight and it's nice to punch out the lap times round there. I was pretty close to him just after the apex when the front of my car started to feel light. Nothing unusual there: these are big cars, they punch a big hole in the air and when you get close up behind someone else the car loses a bit of down-force here and there. I wasn't unduly concerned at first. But I quickly realised, 'I can't bring this back . . . this thing's going to go up.'

It happened so fast that it was just like an aeroplane taking off. In fact that's exactly what was happening: at this point I was probably doing close to 300 kilometres per hour and the car was just taking off. I should point out that at Fontana Bernd and I had been slip-streaming at 330 kilometres per hour and never had a problem, though of course it's fine on a billiard-table track like that. At Le Mans it's bumpy and very narrow on the run down to Indianapolis. I jumped on the brakes, but it was too late. I couldn't see Frank's car any more, I was going straight up. I could see the sky and then the ground and then the sky again, I could almost see the headlights clipping the trees – it was dusk, not really dark – and I was a passenger in this 1000-kilo racing car 10 metres in the air doing 300 kilometres per hour. Much of the Le Mans circuit snakes through a forest; I knew how thin the windscreens were on those cars, they're not designed to be taking trees on, and I thought, 'That's probably the only thing that will see me off, I'll probably cop it if I go into the trees.' I also knew there was a kink in the circuit so if the thing kept tracking straight I *would* go into the trees. I was thinking clearly, but I was also massively frightened. By this time I'm in mid-flight, a long way up, and everything's silent – that was the spookiest part, there was just no noise.

And it's all in slow motion as this thing that weighs a tonne feels as light as a leaf in the wind. Ground, sky, ground: I knew I'd done a flip, but I lost my bearings. Frightened, yes, and yet paradoxically I was calm and completely relaxed.

It's true what they say: at a moment like that your life does flash before you. The images, the chapters that machine-gunned themselves across my mind as they did when I was in the air were phenomenal. My sister Leanne had had her first baby the year before. I thought of them, and then, 'I'm too young,' then, 'Bloody hell, it's Thursday night at Le Mans, maybe this is it.' The whole thing seemed to take five or six minutes but it was probably only three or four seconds.

When I hit the ground I knew I was still within the track fencing – and I was very relieved to know I was still here. In fact I had come down on the right rear of the car; it was on its roof for a short period, apparently, but I don't really remember a huge amount about that. The air-box was ripped off and there was quite a bit of structural damage to the roof, but somehow it finished on all fours. I had just done several back-flips – some eye-witnesses said the car had gone over three times in mid-air – and landed.

I stopped as close to a marshals' post as I could get. Obviously I didn't have any real control, but I did have some brakes left and I managed to pull over to the left-hand side of the track. The marshal was actually gesturing to me to come a little bit closer: he clearly had no idea what I had just been through, he had just looked up to see this damaged car arriving at his post. I was relieved, yes, but now I was also shocked.

'What the f#*k have I just been through?' was the question racing through my brain. It was an unbelievable moment – the emotion you go through, trusting that car like your bloody mother 90 seconds beforehand, then you think you're going to cop it, then the car does look after you in the end. Get your head around that!

What happens after that is bizarre. The racer in you automatically starts thinking, 'Shit, we've lost track time, we don't have another car, what are we going to do?'

There was some concern about my neck, so I went to the medical centre for a check-up. (They later charged me for the bloody X-rays!) Actually the ambulance couldn't have deposited me in a more public position if it had tried; just about the only people I couldn't see were the only ones I really wanted to talk to. I wanted to tell Ann and my dad, who had come over for the race with Spencer Martin, that I was okay – fine, but pretty rattled, because by this time it was all starting to sink in. Dad was struggling. He will tell you now that Le Mans '99 was the lowest point in all his travels around the world to watch me race. 'When Mark's Mercedes took off, it happened out the back of the track, which is very long, and it was difficult to find out what had happened to him. The worst thing of all was that nobody, *nobody* in the Mercedes camp could look me in the eye for an hour and a half. They were the longest, most agonising 90 minutes of my whole life. And when they finally called me down to the medical centre I didn't really know what I was going to find. When I got in there and Mark was OK, he was able to drive again, the relief was enormous. Nobody wanted to know me that day and it was the loneliest time I ever had to endure.'

In the medical centre they gave me a sugar cube loaded up with lots of alcohol. The nurse also came at me with some pretty mean-looking scissors to cut my suit off – another slight problem as I was wearing only a vest underneath, no other underwear at all. Thankfully I had no major injuries, but I was pretty stiff in the upper body, through my neck, back and shoulders because I'd suffered whiplash. I knew how lucky I had been.

I went straight back to the hotel, which meant I didn't see any of the engineers until the following day and it was then that I realised that the team did not accept my version of what had happened. Their response? 'No, that couldn't happen, the car couldn't possibly flip end over end.'

We looked at the data and they knew the car had taken off, but there was no evidence in the form of footage or even still photographs to confirm what had happened. There was just a bent car and what I said – although Biela confirmed he had seen the bottom of my car as I went up. I took part in a question and answer session with the press, maybe two cars did get a little close, but no one from the team saw anything – no photos, no TV – the seriousness of what had happened just had not registered, even with me to a lesser degree. A new car was built, I went through some intensive treatment with the team physio and got ready to tackle Le Mans again.

Warm-up on Saturday morning is the last chance to check the car before the 24-hour ordeal. I was ready to go. The plan was that I would get out there, do a short run, and then let the other guys do their stuff. So I jumped in the new girl, and I was going out there to show her who's boss. In my eyes I was still on target to win this bloody race. Everything in my car was brand-new, so it would be a question of nursing everything – pads, discs and so on – in readiness for the race itself.

I followed Bernd out of the pits, and in the queue was Brundle in the Toyota. In fact there were a few big guns cruising around, a couple of Mercs, a couple of Toyotas, and we were filtering our way through a few of the GT2 cars as I settled in, my first time back out on the track since the shunt on Thursday. We were getting up to speed on the long Mulsanne Straight for the first time, short-shifting in fifth and sixth as we warmed everything up. On the approach to the hump, I was cruising at around 290 kilometres per hour as Olivier Beretta in the Oreca was going over the crest. Even in the warm-up you're not taking it easy, you're going pretty quick, because you've got to get everything up to temperature so the guys in the pit crew can check it after the installation lap, especially when you're in a virtually new car. I'd driven over 100 laps if you take pre-qualifying and practice together, and that part of the track had never been an issue. This time was different.

We'd had a little vent put in the side window for cooling, and with my right hand I went across to close it because it was a bit cold in the cockpit. When I put my hand back, I started taking off again. This time I got to the top of the crest probably doing 280 kilometres per hour . . . and the car didn't come down the other side. Once again the front of the CLR got light and it took off.

I just could not believe what was happening. It simply had not crossed my mind that it could happen again. I hadn't let it: I was still the Mark Webber from before the crash, whether that was naïveté or stupidity on my part, I don't know. But within half a lap of the first accident I was in exactly the same position again – and this time the mentality was different. These were no longer uncharted waters. I'd been here before.

Two thoughts went through my head. The first was for the team: what the f#*k were those guys doing, giving me a car like this? And then: 'There's no way I can be that jammy again; I don't want any pain, I want it to be over quick.' These were no ordinary crashes I was going through, they were massive.

Here we go again: sky-ground-sky, but a bit quicker because I was even higher this time, and this one seemed a bit more violent, it wasn't as smooth. There were more trees on my left but once again, the car didn't go into the scenery, it landed back on the track. I think the car touched the barrier a few times and so it was spinning, and this time it stayed on its roof, it didn't right itself. Now, when you're doing over 200 kilometres an hour on the roof it's bloody noisy and violent, that's the first thing. Then you start to worry where the car's going to end up: how long is the escape road, what are you going to hit next? I started to panic a bit because in those cars there was always the risk of fire. I was paranoid about getting trapped in there, and at the same time I was so fired up with the team because I knew I was doing nothing wrong, I *knew* it wasn't me. I was being ripped off here.

Halfway through the slide I thought, 'When's this going to stop? I want to go home now, I've had enough of this. I've already made my decision, this is it.'

I took my seatbelts off because I wanted to be ready to get out. Surprise, surprise, that dropped me out of my seat so all of a sudden I was trying to hold myself up in the car. I had thought I was about to stop but the car was still travelling at around 140 kilometres per hour on its roof. I was very lucky I didn't hit anything hard because, looking back, getting out of my belts was probably the most stupid thing I ever did. Had I gone into a tyre barrier I would have been very seriously hurt. Every now and again I could hear my helmet touching the ground, sliding along upside down, thinking, 'I don't particularly want it to wear through because my head's next!'

When the car finally came to rest, a touch of panic set in. There was some smoke around and fluid coming into the cockpit, but it was lubricant as a result of all the hits the car had taken. Next I started feeling very frustrated with the other drivers: why was no one stopping to help me?

I didn't realise it at the time, but the whole scene was totally under control. The marshals were there pretty quickly, it only seemed like an eternity. I was trying to lift this bloody car off me but there was no chance. In the end they were there within six or seven seconds and just scooped me up. I got out and sat on the banking outside the track. My hands were bleeding, and I was shaken up, but by the time I stepped over the Armco, I had made my decision: I wasn't going to do this bloody 24-hour race, I was never getting in that car again, I was never racing a sports car again.

I just could not commit myself to it.

I rang Jürgen, the team manager, and he said: 'Mark, what are you doing to our cars?' He was fuming with me, that was his gut reaction not wanting to believe there was a fault with the car, and for me, that was another big kick in the balls. It was a very, very long trip back to the pits – I never wanted to see that car again, but ironically the car that took me back followed the truck with the wreckage on it.

The next 24 hours, as it turned out, were massive in terms of where my career might go. My first thoughts were for my teammates in the other two Mercedes entries, but the team had called them in and put the cars in the garage. We had those little aerodynamic flicks I mentioned on the front of the cars, which would kill our top speed but would be good for grip, so they put some of those on and the other guys finished the warm-up. It was clear to me that there was a strong chance the same thing would happen in the race. How can you do a 24-hour car race, especially with the performance differential through the Le Mans field, and not come up against a bit of lapped traffic here and there? I tried my best to convince them all we were playing with fire, and I could see there were a few boys in the team who were really worried. They knew I wasn't making this up – something here wasn't right. The front floor tray was fitted incorrectly on the car that I was driving but they were clutching at straws: there was no clear evidence that this had caused the flip.

When I got back there was a big curtain between me and the people running the team. I was totally blown away by what had just happened, and now I was also starting to feel isolated. I spoke to Norbert and Gerhard and the other Mercedes guys, and this time things were a bit different, because now there was footage, there were photos and they could see that it had really happened the way I said it had, and how disappointed I was. The guys who were siding with me most were Franck Lagorce and Jean-Marc Gounon, and Pedro Lamy was clearly quite worried too. At that stage I was so paranoid that I thought *anyone* could go up, not just the Mercedes cars. What sort of Russian roulette were the drivers playing out there?

I was petrified for Bernd, my best mate, and I begged him to rethink his decision to race. 'Bernd, mate, you can't race this car, there's no way. After all we've been through together, this is too dangerous, it's just too close to the edge.'

But he had been with the team for years and by now he was convinced he would be OK, they'd put those flicks on the car which they thought would fix the problem and everything would be fine.

Fine? We're in total f#*king chaos, we've got the biggest hole in the bottom of our boat, it's a disaster. Mercedes had turned their backs on Le Mans in the wake of the 1955 tragedy; this new situation was not calculated to reassure people about modern Mercedes cars being quick but safe. Safe? We had cars taking off!

We batted the issue around for a while and I was so upset that I made the decision to leave before the race even started. I'd had my guts ripped out again – I felt alone and that the team had not stuck with me. Norbert's response was, 'Do one thing for me, do the drivers' parade, see the fans, say hello,' and I agreed.

On the one hand, it was phenomenally brave for them to go through with racing – on the other, it was quite insulting. I felt a sense that it was 'only' Webber it had happened to both times, but if it had been Bernd they wouldn't have raced. After the parade I went back to our motor-home to pack up. I was shattered; I took it very personally.

Ann said, 'Things happen for a reason, we'll move on from here,' and in fact I was already starting to draw a number of positives out of what I'd just been through.

I knew I was still a quick driver, I knew what I was doing, and most of all I knew I was right. By now the race was underway, but we had no television in the motor-home and no way of knowing what was going on.

Then the telephone rang.

Dumbreck's Mercedes had flipped and he had gone into the trees.

I lost it then. I burst into tears, and then I ran flat out to the pits, about a kilometre and a half away. I was ropeable. When was this nightmare going to end?

I was thinking, 'If he's gone, I'm going to kill these bastards, I'm going to kill them. I know exactly what he's gone through, and it's everything I feared: he's in the trees, he's gone in there . . . He's going to be injured for sure.'

I went straight to Joschi, the engineer, and asked him, 'Is it true?'

You could see it was, by the panic that had set in at the garage. Everyone, all the people in the team, looked horrified. Now it wasn't only me it had happened to. Maybe it *was* their car and their 'fix' was not working. Immediately they pulled the other car out. Franck was in Bernd's car at the time and he told me he had already made his decision to come in because he had actually seen Peter take off.

At that point I didn't care about Mercedes, I was only interested in Peter. Amazingly, he was all right, although it took 20 minutes for that information to filter through. Bernd, Pedro, Franck and I sat in one of the drivers' rooms for 40 minutes and didn't say a word to each other. Grown men blown to pieces: we couldn't speak, we didn't know where to start. I went to see Gerhard, the technical brain behind the car, who had convinced the team to give me a chance in the first place. We'd been through a lot together, he was a passionate guy and so committed to his work, but this time Mercedes had got it wrong. He was sitting across the table from me, and his eyes were full. He was a super bloke, but he was sitting there all by himself as it all fell apart around him – no communication, no organisation. I slept in that drivers' room that night and when I woke up next day this bloody race was still going on . . .

We started the long drive home in the motor-home we had used as our Le Mans base and every time it swayed I got nervous, that's how bad a state I was in. Bob Copp navigated us back to Paris. He told us later that people in the team had been pointing the finger at me, believing that the driver was at fault, not the Mercedes car. Bob thought

I was suffering some kind of delayed reaction to what I had been through as he found me dull and distressed on that journey. He was convinced the Mercedes people had not spent nearly enough time talking to me or Peter Dumbreck. My dad agreed: 'Mercedes didn't in my opinion handle the situation terribly well at all. It was pretty clear to me that they weren't interested enough in Mark's welfare.'

I was so badly shaken that it took me a week to get comfortable even in road cars. I remember Thierry Boutsen saying through a friend of a friend that Webber would never be the same again after what had happened, but again I quickly resolved to prove him and any other doubters wrong.

There was the sheer disappointment, as a racing driver, of never getting to turn a wheel in anger at one of the most legendary tracks in the world. I knew it was going to be tough, and I was ready for that, but in the end the 1999 experience was tougher than anything I could have imagined. There was no official contact from the race organisers; nor was there any debrief within the team, no crisis management plan to work from, no PR strategy in place. I was just a driver in the scheme of things, and I felt very much on my own.

But what is it they say? 'What doesn't kill you only makes you stronger' – so I must have come away from Le Mans twice as strong because the race had tried to kill me twice! By July 1999 I could not have been any further away from the Formula 1 dream if I had tried. My career was supposed to take off with Mercedes. I had come back down to earth with two of the almightiest bumps you ever saw.

6

A Pawn in the Game:
1999–2001

THE IMMEDIATE AFTERMATH OF LE MANS WAS HARD. I WAS still in a bit of a daze for the first few days. Worse still, I felt there was a lack of concern from my team. A whole week went past and we didn't get a single phone call from Mercedes. They had a lot on, but one of their main soldiers was in pieces and I would have been glad of a little more interest.

On the other hand I can fairly say that Le Mans was, paradoxically, the best thing that ever happened to me. Brutal, shocking, frightening, horrible – it could have been the end of me. Instead I was able to look at it differently and turn it into superb medicine for motivation, the best I could have had.

At first, though, it looked as though my journey had gone horribly wrong. I had told Mercedes-Benz that I couldn't drive those cars again properly, or at least not as I used to, so I'd be no use to them. There was talk, briefly, of trying to keep the relationship between me and them alive: Norbert Haug offered to help me in single-seater racing in the USA, but I just didn't want to go that way – I hadn't moved to Europe as a stepping-stone to the United States.

There was talk later in the year of my going into IndyCar racing with the Forsythe team but 1999 was also the year in which the popular Canadian IndyCar driver Greg Moore was killed in a Forsythe-Mercedes at Fontana, in California, at the end of October. I had met Greg when Gerhard, Bernd and I made a boys' trip to watch some American racing and he was an amazing guy. His time ran out so early, and it was another blow that gave me pause for thought: 'I've got to really focus and get the single-seaters in Europe going again.'

But there was still the small matter of my contractual arrangement with Mercedes-Benz. When nothing was forth-coming from them, Ann and I took the initiative and went over to Germany to meet Jürgen Mattheis, the team manager. He knew where we were coming from, and he agreed that sometimes marriage ends in divorce, but then he said, 'Now we have to go and see Norbert.' Between our meeting and our arrival at Norbert's office the whole tone had changed. How dare we want to try to distance ourselves from this? We didn't know what we were talking about! Ann was a nice little girl from Australia but she knew nothing, and I thought, 'Right, I get the picture here!' They were extremely patronising, and while I can't remember exactly how the meeting ended, I know it didn't end well.

We weren't prepared to be patient. Annie certainly wasn't: the next time we went back over there she actually walked out of the office. They had bigger fish to fry than their Australian bloke, I knew that, but what were we going to do about it?

I was doing nothing – and that's not a good place for a racing driver to be in. We were anxious to start rebuilding my single-seater career, but any time I drove another car – in F3000 testing, for example – we would receive a letter from AMG's lawyers saying we were in breach of contract. When we protested that we had clearly terminated the contract, they asked for a payment to release me – starting off at US$1,000,000.

The figure had something to do with their belief that they had actually made a long-term investment in me as a driver, but there was only one possible response to that, so we laughed and said, 'What – I was nearly killed twice and you want a million dollars?'

The bottom line was that I felt they had lost faith in me when they didn't listen to me and I had certainly lost faith in them. We were prepared to go to court to sort it all out if we had to, but we didn't believe that Mercedes really wanted that. Nor did we; our priority was just to go racing, but it dragged on and we stayed strong until the figure came down to what Mercedes-Benz had originally put into my F3 career.

I'd like to set the record straight though, and say as clearly as I can that the Mercedes 'university' was an awesome experience for me, and I've always enjoyed a good relation-ship with Norbert Haug. He and I got past the Le Mans episode and moved on.

But by late 1999 my three-pointed-star romance was well and truly over. The severe case of the Benz was all finalised around November because I needed to be clear of anything to do with Mercedes before I could get on with my racing life.

*

Ann and I were determined to keep the Formula 1 dream alive. We promptly jumped from the frying pan straight into the fire. I walked away from being a professional racing driver and took the risk of putting my reputation on the line once more by starting more or less from scratch to reignite my single-seater career. And that's where Irishman Eddie Jordan, or EJ for short, comes into the picture.

Ann knew Eddie from way back. EJ had a reputation for fostering young talent – he gave Ayrton Senna his first F3 test – and he had been keeping an eye on my progress. After Le Mans 1999 we asked if we could have the benefit of a bit of friendly advice. Eddie made himself readily available at a time when he had plenty on his plate; Damon Hill's position in the Jordan F1 team was looking precarious in the build-up to the British Grand Prix. Whether Eddie knew it at the time or not, he was my lifeline and I was clinging to it! He told me I was welcome to use the gym at Jordan F1, which is where I bumped into the Jordan team principal Trevor Foster. Hearing from Trevor that my ex-Mercedes teammate Ricardo Zonta was 'the next big thing' simply added fuel to my motivation.

You can tell the desperation creeping in when I confess to having turned stalker again. On the Thursday of British Grand Prix week in July 1999 I decided to follow EJ when he left the Jordan factory. Ann and Dad were with me; the plan was to way-lay him somewhere, but Eddie's driver was probably wise to the fact that some nutter was on their tail on the M40 motorway and he managed to shake us off when they dived into a service station and disappeared. I've never been sure in my own mind what I was going to say or do if I actually came face-to-face with EJ, especially as he had already been more than generous with his time over the previous few months.

I wasn't the only serial pest. Ann was making herself just as much of a nuisance with endless calls to Ron Walker in Australia, trying to drum up financial support. Later, and to his eternal credit, Ron confessed it was because we were so damned persistent that he always took our calls. That's what was so awesome about individuals like Ron and EJ: we had a small band of people who *would* take our calls and leave the door open for us. We must have driven them crazy.

Things happen for a reason, as we always say. And the reason that one of the most important things in my life happened was Eddie Jordan. Not long after Le Mans I was with EJ in his office up at Silverstone. Two weekends after my Le Mans experience Heinz-Harald Frentzen had taken Jordan's second Grand Prix win in France. Jordan were looking pretty sharp, so I was hoping to pick up some shakedown work – the initial, very limited try-out of a new car, or some F1 testing for them. I thought I could do the job. Eddie did keep my hopes up for a while on that score, but it eventually came to nothing. Still, imagine a kid from Queanbeyan chewing the fat with EJ!

On that particular day at Silverstone he said, 'You've got to meet one of my sponsors from Australia. He's an absolute nutter: he's over the road testing in F3000 so go and introduce yourself.'

Off I went to the Silverstone track, just across the road

from the Jordan factory. I walked up to this man, Paul Stoddart, and said, 'G'day mate, I'm Mark Webber and I want to drive for you.'

His answer was, 'Okay then, we'll do a test.'

Paul Stoddart looms large in the next three or four years of my career. 'Stoddy', as everyone in the business knows him, is a boy from the Melbourne suburb of Coburg who made good. What thrust him onto a bigger stage was his purchase of ex-Royal Australian Air Force planes from the VIP fleet in Canberra in 1989, and all the ancillaries that went with them. That was a major stepping-stone to his own overseas expansion through his charter company, European Aviation, and the beginning of a lucrative period in his life that would lead to Formula 1.

Paul had been a club racer back at home and retained a keen interest in cars; when money came his way he was only too happy to channel some of it into his first love. He did so in part by accumulating an amazing number of historic F1 cars and occasionally racing them himself; more significantly, by 1996 he had also become a sponsor of the Tyrrell F1 team, but his hopes of acquiring it lock, stock and barrel were dashed when someone with even more money came on the scene – British American Tobacco. By 1999 he had switched his sponsorship support to Jordan, which is why Eddie was keen for me to meet Stoddy, and perhaps capitalise on our Australian connection. There was a time when it looked as if there might be a Formula 3000 hook-up between them, but that never materialised. Paul would end up instead in a partnership of sorts with Tom Walkinshaw, another prominent name in UK motor-racing circles. Tom, an uncompromising Scot, was by then head man at Arrows in F1; he had Australian connections through Holden and was another motor-racing man with an eye for a deal. Big fish swim in small circles . . .

The result of my first encounter with Stoddy was a test in one of his F3000 cars. The first time I got back in a racing car after being nearly killed at the greatest sports car event in the world was in September 1999 at . . . Pembrey, a tiny circuit just to the west of Llanelli in South Wales. Still, who was I to complain? McLaren had taken Prost and Senna there for private testing on the tight little 2.348-kilometre track with its variety of corners, so if it was good enough for two multiple world champions, it was good enough for me. But the contrast between the Circuit de la Sarthe, legendary home of the 24 Hours of Le Mans, and this little Welsh track was not lost on me. The only positive way to look at it was as the first step on a long road back.

I was expected to do well simply because I had been with Mercedes as one of their lead drivers. But because my 1999 season had been entirely centred on Le Mans and the sports car series had been cancelled, I hadn't been in a racing car for three months. That's an eternity in any racing driver's life, and consequently I wasn't really as car-fit as I would have liked. Even so, the test went well and Stoddy said, 'Definitely, come back again.'

My next test for Paul was at Donington Park in the Midlands on 13 October, on the same day as another young Australian called Paul Dumbrell, but our two agendas could not have been more different: one Aussie was paying Stoddy shedloads for the privilege of testing his car and the other – me – was trying to persuade him to invest enough money in me to let me do the F3000 championship the following year.

It was a far more serious hit-out than Pembrey; I got in over 40 laps in the European Formula F3000 car and it felt good to be in a single-seater at a reasonably quick track again.

Next, in the second week of November, came the official test session at Jerez ahead of the 2000 F3000 season, which would embrace 10 rounds starting at Imola in Italy. Stoddy gave me another chance to show what I could do. Being out on the Jerez track in south-western Spain for that official test with a bunch of other drivers was a good feeling. It had been a lonely few months. Each team was allocated two new sets of tyres, one of which you had to bolt on at the start of the day, and I wore the first set out just getting back up to speed. But I was fourth-fastest in the final session and over a second quicker than Marc Hynes had been in the same car – always the crucial comparison – so it ended well enough.

Two weeks later the various teams moved north-east to Barcelona and I was quickest on the opening day of the test there. I wasn't playing catch-up any more and had the chance to show some genuine speed for the first time.

Late in 1999 I was in Monaco hosting some guests of Yellow Pages and I took the opportunity to announce that I had finalised a deal with Paul Stoddart and his European Formula F3000 team. What we had negotiated was a package deal. One component was the full F3000 championship in 2000, which meant 10 races in support of the European Grands Prix; another was some testing for the Arrows F1 team, because Stoddy and Tom Walkinshaw had agreed to join forces, meaning the F3000 outfit would essentially be the 'junior' Arrows team; and the third component would be occasional guest drives for sponsors and other VIPs in Stoddy's two-seater car. The package was worth £1.1 million; to simplify matters Paul converted it to a loan which I would pay back as and when.

This was far removed from my Mercedes deal, and I was no longer a paid driver, but we had nothing else. We certainly had no money to pay for a drive. I would be racing in Formula 3000, but racing with a team that had only qualified for the previous year's series by the skin of its teeth.

Still, I was back in single-seater racing, even if it was far from an ideal scenario. Beggars can't be choosers; I had to make this gamble pay off. Looking things in the face, I was just a reject. I was out of sports cars and hadn't been in a race for 14 months. The little voice in my ear was back: 'Mark, what the hell are you doing?'

*

Every driver remembers when he first got his chance in a Grand Prix car. My first F1 opportunity came in December 1999 when I went to Barcelona to conduct a two-day test for Tom Walkinshaw's Arrows F1 team, which Stoddy had organised and dangled in front of me as a bit of a sweetener for the F3000 deal, hoping that it might just twist a corporate arm back home in Australia to get behind me. Imagine, an Aussie in an F1 car!

Tom wasn't blind to the publicity an Aussie connection would bring, because he was already a well-known player in racing Down Under. He set up Tom Walkinshaw Racing back in the mid-seventies both as a business in its own right and as a vehicle for his own driving talent, which was good enough to make him European touring car champion in 1984. In 1985 he was in the thick of things at the Bathurst 1000, Australia's own 'Great Race', when John Goss and Armin

Hahne co-drove a TWR Jaguar to victory and Tom shared the drive with Win Percy in the sister car that finished third.

Tom, who died in December 2010, was never a stranger to controversy, either on-track or away from the circuits, but as a team owner he did a hell of a job. It was Walkinshaw-run Jaguars that won Le Mans twice in the late eighties, with top drivers like Martin Brundle and with an emerging technical genius by the name of Ross Brawn. Later Tom became Engineering Director in the Benetton F1 team in 1991 as it began the rise that would see both the team and Michael Schumacher win back-to-back world titles in 1994–95. Two years after that Tom had his own F1 team, Arrows, and persuaded the reigning World Champion, Damon Hill, to leave Williams and drive for him.

At my Barcelona baptism I couldn't believe the lightness of the vehicle, how nimble it was and how precise. Then, after five or six laps, you start thinking like a racing driver again, you realise it's got some understeer or some other characteristic you've encountered before. Then it's a matter of putting your trust in the car and getting over that balls-out-down-the-front-straight feeling and getting on with the job. You can't really prepare yourself for that experience and, reaching the end of the straight, standing on the brakes and feeling the old eyeballs hanging off the nose as you pull 4.6G, is not something you forget in a hurry.

It was really rewarding finally to drive a 'proper' racing car again. In fact it was 10 times everything I had done up to that point in my career. My compatriot Chris Dyer, later to play a key role at Ferrari, was the engineer for the day. The car in question wasn't brilliant – Arrows had managed just a single point in the 1999 World Championship, after all – but it wasn't a heap of rubbish either. I was sitting in the garage as the guys warmed the car up, thinking, 'This is pretty special!'

Jean Alesi smoked out of the garage right next to mine in the Prost car and the whole place came alive. My own plan of attack was pretty basic: do the simple things right, don't be too cocky about doing what was really a pretty basic job, don't go about it as if my life depended on it. It was more a reward than a real stepping-stone to my F1 dream, but we had been working night and day to make something happen again and so it *was* a big day in a lot of ways.

I'm no businessman, just a driver, and it's common knowledge that drivers are not supposed to be the sharpest tools in the box. But there are some decent street-fighters in an F1 paddock. There was no way I was going to do anything that day to try to really impress them because there wasn't the opportunity, but I knocked a fair bit off the learning curve and there were lots of little rewards for me in the car. But looking back I wasn't so much a cog in a machine as a pawn in the game that was going on between the team owners: the Eddie Jordans, the Tom Walkinshaws, the Paul Stoddarts – the people who really pull the strings.

*

Formula 3000's a strange category. In testing at Jerez again in late January we were doing okay, although we weren't chasing out-and-out lap times, then in Valencia at the start of March there were 19 drivers within a second of each other. You just never knew where you were. By the time we went to Silverstone for the final test on 23 March I had announced a personal sponsorship deal with Aussie icon

Foster's, which in those days enjoyed a major presence at F1 circuits around the world.

The Eurobet Arrows F3000 team was launched at Leafield on 4 April 2000, the cars sporting the same orange and black livery as the Arrows F1 outfit. Lola chassis as standard, Ford Zytek V8 engine pushing out 470 horse-power, and a 10-race season ahead with an Australian driver desperate to get back out there and show what he could do in a racing car.

I had a great start at Imola when I qualified third and took my first F3000 podium, a great relief since it was my first single-seater race for two-and-a-half years and my first race of any kind since October 1998! Things got even better in round two at my adopted 'home' track, Silverstone, where I qualified on the front row in the wet and went on to win the race, just as I had done for Mercedes in the FIA GT series two years earlier with Bernd. But a three-race string of 'DNF' results in Barcelona, at the Nürburgring in Germany and in Monte Carlo put a serious dent in my early championship hopes. Those results proved two points: if you qualified poorly it was hard to stay out of trouble among the midfield hotheads, and if you went to Monaco in less than peak condition you were cooked.

In qualifying for that Monaco race, trying to put in the big lap, I put the car in the barriers; in the race I was lying fourth when dehydration caught me out and I lost it at the left-hander after the chicane. My physical condition had let me down, and as a consequence my concentration had wavered – and that's a recipe for disaster in Monaco, which is so physically and mentally demanding. But I made a vow to myself that Monaco would never catch me out again.

Little did I know how big a place it was going to occupy in my career.

If Monaco was tough, so was the next round at Magny-Cours in France on the first weekend of June, for different reasons. In the strange world of motor racing you can finish well down the field but know in your own heart that you have performed as well as you possibly could. That's what happened in France. I suffered a right rear puncture when I ran over some debris early in the race, re-joined dead last after a tyre change and fought back to finish sixteenth. Ann still swears it was one of the best performances of my career.

Hockenheim in Germany brought my final visit to the podium for that 2000 season, which I finished in third place behind Bruno Junqueira and Nicolas Minassian. At the start of the season I would have been happy with an overall finish in the top six, so there was real satisfaction in breaking into the top three.

*

Racing in F3000 was important, but my main objective through 2000 had really been to focus on F1, keeping myself in the frame however I could, and that included doing some further testing. Not for the first time, things turned pear-shaped. I was scheduled to have a major test in the first week of July at Silverstone with Arrows, in the latest car on the full Grand Prix circuit with a proper allocation of tyres to work with. It would have been my first serious Formula 1 test, a day to get into it and feel the car properly. We'd organised for some of the people who were helping me that year to come along and watch.

But about 10 days out from the test Tom Walkinshaw

threw a spanner in the works with a contract which he wanted me to sign for the following year – before I got in his car. Stoddy went ballistic. In the middle of that year, the July test was a big opportunity to try out the pukkah race car against some of the other drivers there; it was going to be a pretty big day for me, to say the least, and Paul was fighting my corner.

The proposed contract would have bound me to Tom. Finding myself in a very weak position, it would have been incredibly easy to buckle – you've got your name on the side of the car, they've done everything to put you in that situation and you're absolutely busting to do it – but I said 'No'. Things got pretty juicy between Tom and Stoddy for a while, and that was the end of that test.

Just a few hours later we strolled down to the Benetton garage and renewed contact with Gordon Message, whom I had met several years earlier in Adelaide. Gordon was now Sporting Director at Benetton and said he would work on Flavio Briatore, the Italian who was then in charge of the team. Meantime Ron Walker had come over for a meeting with Bernie Ecclestone, the man who effectively ran Formula 1, during which Ron said how keen he was from an Australian promoter's point of view to get my backside in a Grand Prix car.

Bernie said, 'He's under contract to Tom, isn't he?' but of course I had refused to sign at gunpoint. When Ron said 'No', Bernie rang Flavio there and then and told him to 'give the kid a go'. Then Gordon phoned us back and it happened!

'It' was a three-day evaluation test from 11–13 September 2000 with Benetton, whose drivers Alex Wurz (funny how Alex kept popping up at my first tests) and Giancarlo Fisichella had just helped the team finish fourth in the World Championship. Admittedly they were light years behind Ferrari and McLaren, but still, this time I would have a genuine chance to show what I could do in a quick F1 car.

The test took place at Estoril in Portugal. Before going down there I had a chat with Ricardo Zonta, my old teammate and sparring partner from our Mercedes sports car days, who had since raced in F1 for BAR and Jordan and knew the track.

Ricardo said to me: 'It's bumpy, I hate it, enjoy!'

I studied the circuit like hell on videos because I'd never been there before. I was training really hard to convince myself that I was ready, trying not to leave too many stones unturned. My agenda: keep mistakes to an absolute minimum, fit in as best I could with the team, drive as quickly as I could, draw on all my experience, channel and focus it all into those three days. I just loved the balance of the car. I was lucky because Wurz is a tall bloke so I had a lot of room in the cockpit. I felt comfortable, and that was a massive confidence boost. I drove on the first day of the test and wasn't a million miles off Ralf Schumacher's session-leading time in the Williams, but next morning Fisichella got in 'my' car and blew my time away.

'Bloody hell,' I thought.

The team said, 'Don't worry, the track was rubbish yesterday,' but I was *very* worried.

When I went out again, within five or 10 laps I realised it *was* just the track conditions that had made the difference and this time my times were very close to Giancarlo, who had laid down a benchmark of 1:21.710.

On Tuesday afternoon I was down in 1:22 territory, then

on Wednesday I was given the same tyres and fuel load as
'Fisi'. The team told me they would be happy if I got within
six-tenths of a second of their F1 regular; in the end I was
two thousandths shy of Giancarlo.

Who's to say how fired up the Italian was, and how seriously he treated the whole exercise? He came in to do a
benchmark time but he'd seen enough of that car, he'd
been driving around in it all year only to be told he had to
go down to Estoril and do this extra chore. But Benetton's
Technical Director Pat Symonds was there with Gordon,
and they gave me a totally fair crack. It was a dream week
for me, and it was all done very professionally. By that
time Computershare, an Australian-owned share-registry
company, was already on board with us in F3000 and its
help was important in making that Estoril test possible. The
Morris family, who founded Computershare, very quickly
became a part of Team Webber; they have attended many
Grands Prix around the world and Ann and I remain friends
with them to this day.

In the midst of finalising the contract for Estoril, Annie
and I were also making what now seems the unfathom-
able decision to buy our own house. Looking back at it
now, it was utter madness: I had nothing guaranteed for
the following year, so how the hell were we going to pay
for a house? I think our logic was that we had been paying
other people's mortgages for way too long: wouldn't it be
better if we were putting our money towards something
we could call our own? Annie found a detached house that
needed a bit of TLC in a village called Mursley, close to
the outskirts of Milton Keynes, which became home, and
the hub for Team Webber, for the next four years. It meant

Luke had a bedroom of his own for the first time, a place where he could put pictures of his own sporting heroes up on the wall, and it was somewhere the three of us could call home.

We forged lasting friendships with neighbours Val and Jackie Christensen and other villagers like Tim and Debbie Parker. While Ann and I had kept our relationship private in our professional lives we were openly living together and ensconced in a village community. There were never any questions asked and we were readily accepted for who we were. It was as close to a normal lifestyle as we had enjoyed up until then, and more and more people were beginning to share in our journey. It was a happy and exciting part of our lives as our dream started to come true.

*

The conversation was brief and to the point. 'Look, Webber, I fucking talking now. You want the deal or no?'

'Oh, yeah . . .'

The short reply came from the Queanbeyan end of a telephone line connecting me to Europe and the phenomenon called 'Flav': Flavio Briatore, one of the most colourful, controversial and successful men to have functioned in the F1 paddocks of the world in the last quarter of a century. The deal in question was my contract to be Benetton's F1 test and reserve driver in 2001.

It was a mismatch in boxing terms: a 24-year-old bantamweight trying to break into the big time against a 50-year-old Italian entrepreneur already established as one of the heavyweights of the game. He's certainly got a presence, especially for a youngster trying hard not to let himself be overawed by anyone, and you have to concentrate very hard to understand him, especially on the telephone. He talks very fast and when it comes round to the numbers he talks even faster, so dates, terms and conditions are always very quick – but never ask him to repeat them because he'll kill you!

For a man who started professional life as an insurance agent, Flavio Briatore has come a very long way. His connection with F1 came about with his meeting with Luciano Benetton, head of the clothing empire which was then still in its infancy. It was Flavio who went to the USA and got Benetton's business up and running there in the mid-eighties. By then Benetton had acquired the Toleman F1 team, and in Mexico in 1986 Gerhard Berger secured the first Grand Prix victory for the most colourful team on the grid. The first F1 race Flavio attended was the Australian Grand Prix in Adelaide in 1988; in 1989 he was named Commercial Director of the Benetton F1 team. An early significant move of Flavio's was to bring Tom Walkinshaw into the team's management structure.

Flavio's greatest gift when he came into F1 was the ability to spot emerging talent. He realised immediately the potential that Michael Schumacher had and signed him for Benetton after just one race with Jordan. It was also Flavio who pushed through the strategic alliance between Benetton and Renault that led to enormous success with world titles in 1995. He set up his own management company in 1993, bought and sold F1 teams like Ligier (which became Prost GP) and Minardi, lived the billionaire lifestyle after which his modern business is named and later became involved in one of the biggest scandals in recent Grand Prix history in Singapore in 2008.

Above Some of my earliest memories are of riding motorbikes on the family farm – even though it was frustrating to be so small and it would often result in burns to my legs from the exhaust or engine! Here I am in 1979, age three.

Above Me with Dusty, one of my grandfather's sheepdogs.

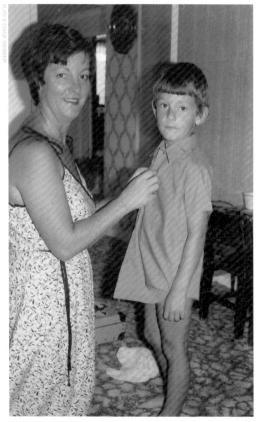

Left Striking a pose in 1982 as my mother, Diane, gets me ready for my first day at school.

Left My hero, granddad Clive, was probably the biggest influence on my life. He founded the family business, Bridge Motors, in 1955 with two petrol bowsers on the main street of Queanbeyan and I'll always be grateful for values he gave my dad which in turn got passed on to me. This photo was taken in 1987.

Above Small bash for my old man celebrating his birthday in 1990. My cousins Adam and Johnny are blowing out candles while Leanne and I are eyeing off a piece of cake!

Right My final days of karting in Australia in 1993. The category taught me pivotal lessons for the adventure ahead.

Left My first big single-seater win in Europe – the prestigious Formula Ford Festival at Brands Hatch, England, in 1996.

Right Taming the beast that was the Mercedes CLK-GTR at Laguna Seca, California in 1998.

Below Learning from the Master. I was so fortunate to work with Bernd Schneider in 1998 when he was still hungry and keen to pass on all of his experience. Bernd changed the way I went about my profession forever.

Above A light-hearted moment at Oran Park in 1995 with Bob Copp of Yellow Pages, the guy who made the brave decision to sponsor me during those crucial early years.

Above Proof I've always had cool haircuts! This is my first ever visit to Brands Hatch, age 19 in 1995. Ann's son, Luke, was only four at the time – he's 6 feet 2 inches now.

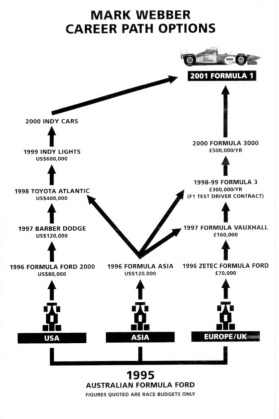

MARK WEBBER
CAREER PATH OPTIONS

2001 FORMULA 1

2000 INDY CARS

2000 FORMULA 3000
£500,000/YR

1999 INDY LIGHTS
US$600,000

1998-99 FORMULA 3
£300,000/YR
(F1 TEST DRIVER CONTRACT)

1998 TOYOTA ATLANTIC
US$400,000

1997 BARBER DODGE
US$120,000

1997 FORMULA VAUXHALL
£160,000

1996 FORMULA FORD 2000
US$80,000

1996 FORMULA ASIA
US$120,000

1996 ZETEC FORMULA FORD
£70,000

USA

ASIA

EUROPE/UK

1995
AUSTRALIAN FORMULA FORD
FIGURES QUOTED ARE RACE BUDGETS ONLY

Opposite Terrifying moments at Le Mans in 1999. I was praying the car would stay within the barriers and not go into the trees lining the circuit. It took me four or five months to recover mentally. Going 300 kph plus on the roof is not ideal...

Above Me and Flavio Briatore in 2005. It was sensational to have him box my corner for 15 years straight.

Above Another pivotal day in my career – testing for the Benetton F1 team at Estoril in 2000.

Left My very first podium finish in Monaco in 2001 with Super Nova. The Formula 3000 cars were physically demanding and would often open up the driver's hands, especially on the gear shifts. You can see the tape over our hands to minimise blisters.

Above Leading the Formula 3000 race at the 2001 French Grand Prix that I eventually won.

Right Sitting on fellow Aussie and five-time world champion Mick Doohan's 500cc bike at Donington in 2001. Mick and I are still tight buddies 15 years later.

Above My first Formula 1 Grand Prix at Melbourne in 2002. To say it was a big day at Albert Park would be an understatement. Minardi owner Paul Stoddart is sharing the podium with me.

Above With rugby superstar and fellow Queanbeyan lad David Campese in 2003. Thank God 'Campo' bought into our vision and supported me when the thread of my career was about to snap. In this shot Campo and I are at his old rugby store in The Rocks, in Sydney.

Above Chatting to Michael Schumacher after a GPDA meeting in 2003. Michael certainly liked to orchestrate things on and off the track. Here he is teaching me about the business of the sport.

Above The Jaguar R4 in 2003 was a real beast. This was the window in F1 where the drivers had to be at the peak of their fitness.

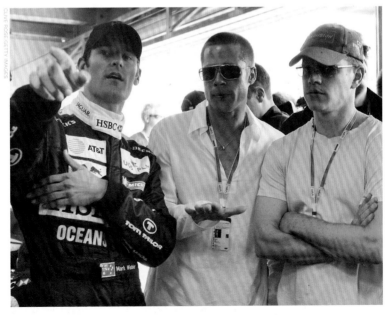

Above Hanging out with Hollywood stars Brad Pitt and Matt Damon in Monaco 2004.

Above I loved watching Steve Waugh
play Test cricket. He was a gutsy
bugger and inspired me to lift my
own bar.

Right My first Formula 1 podium in
Monaco 2005. Strangely enough,
it wasn't a particularly special day for
me. I felt I was capable of a much
better result.

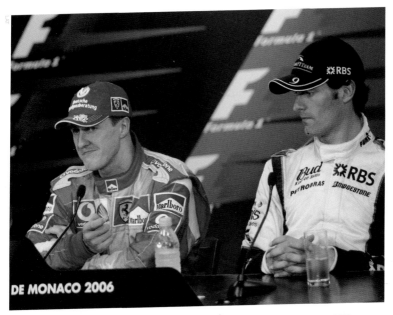

Above One of the most awkward press conferences of my career came in Monaco 2006. Michael Schumacher is in the hot seat this time for the infamous Rascasse incident.

Above Triple F1 champion Sir Jack Brabham heavily influenced my father's love of motor sport. It was an honour to have the support of such a brave and pioneering Australian throughout my racing career.

Opposite Family and friends sometimes joined me at Red Bull events. This is in Turkey, 2007. Luke is about to s*** himself!

Right A man of great presence, Dietrich Mateschitz always had something to teach me. Dietrich didn't come to many races and it was even rarer to have him on the grid as pictured here in 2008.

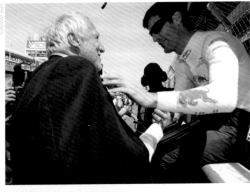

Left Riding with the lie, Monaco 2008. Lance Armstrong and I had many open discussions together. One of my best buddies, Morris Denton, is riding behind us.

Below Arguably two of the most popular characters in the F1 paddock, Tokyo 2008 – Jenson Button's father, John, and my old man, Alan. Both are legends in my eyes.

Above Running Tasmania's rugged coastline in the fourth Mark Webber Challenge in 2008. Thirty minutes later I was off my feet and en route to hospital with a broken leg.

Above I was very lucky to survive my collision with a four-wheel-drive with the injuries I did.

My first personal contact with Flav was when I did that Estoril test, after which I went to see him with our lawyer, Simon Taylor. To start with we were negotiating a test driver contract with some options in the future, obviously totally in their favour. Simon was asking some other questions and I was thinking, 'Don't ask anything that's going to piss him off, for Christ's sake!'

There were some points that did need to be addressed, but we left very happy because I was going to be paid to be a test and reserve driver. I remember Simon saying, 'I think they've got a soft spot for you and they really do want you.' The other thing both Simon and I remember is that Flavio did two very disconcerting things while we were sitting with him: one was to massage his belly most of the time, the other was to take constant calls from Naomi Campbell.

I was back in Australia while we were trying to close the contract and Simon said, 'Look, just ring him up and ask him about those two points and see how you go.'

I rang Flavio's PA and she said he would ring me back. He always does.

When he came back on the line and I said, 'Oh Flavio, just two points . . .', he uttered those immortal words: 'Look Webber, I fucking talking now! You want the deal or no?'

Mum's asking me, 'How d'you go, mate?' and while I'm figuring out how to explain Flavio to Disey, Dad's chipping in: 'What do you think's going to happen, mate, do you think you're going to lose it?'

None of us slept a wink that night, thinking, 'Oh bloody hell, what have we done now?' So we got back to Simon and said, 'Quick, get it all done!' The deal was signed the following morning.

I couldn't believe I had landed a full-on test and reserve driver deal, although the only part of it I wasn't particularly keen on was that Flavio wanted me to do another season in F3000. I thought mixing the two together was going to be quite difficult, but he said I had to keep racing, because I had to stay sharp. I wanted to focus on the testing, but he was right. I needed the racing edge.

So I was in a good place early in 2001. It got better in May when I signed with Flavio again, this time to be my manager. It was a huge call on my career. I never imagined anything like that happening, but he was prepared to back me. I had done enough on the track to show that there might be something in it for him because he is a businessman, but what also helped me was that he had a couple of other drivers like Antônio Pizzonia and Giorgio Pantano, who had very good records in the junior categories. They were testing for Benetton at the time; an absolute piece of luck for me was that the team (and, I suspect, Flavio in particular) called for some driver fitness tests. I was committed to fitness by that stage and totally confident I had reached the right levels. Flavio was big on that side of driver preparation after his time with Michael at Benetton, so they really did put their drivers through the mill at the Human Performance Centre at Benetton HQ, a phenomenal facility which was ahead of its time.

When I went down there and met an Englishman called Bernie Shrosbree they certainly put me through the wringer, and my fitness went to a new level again. Bernie's an ex-SBS marine. He's also a good judge of character: it's not about what scores you pull on the rowing machine or the bike, Bernie is much more interested in what's between the ears and the fire within. Bernie's dealt with the biggest egos in the world.

'Purely looking for the character of the individual and, most importantly, the commitment on the physical and mental side,' is how he explains his approach.

Already at that stage Flavio was aware of a simple fact about me that might work against me in F1: my physical size, especially my height, and the weight that came with it.

'Webber,' Flavio had said to Bernie, 'maybe a bit big, a bit old?'

I think it was the drive Flavio saw in me, so to speak, and Bernie's assessment that got me the contract. Looking at things from my side, by mid-2001 I had become a regular in the Benetton F1 cockpit as I dovetailed F3000 and my F1 testing role, but the focus was firmly on what lay ahead – and that meant a seat in a Grand Prix car as a fully fledged race driver.

To move to the next level as a driver I needed someone who really knew the ins and outs of how F1 works. Paul Stoddart had invested £1.1 million in my career through a combination of F3000, the two-seater work and the planned F1 testing – the most expensive component and the one that never actually happened. Paul had converted the total value of that package into a loan. The medium-term arrangement was originally that Paul would take a 20 per cent commission when I started to earn money from my racing; either that or we would pay it back in two lump sums as and when we found ourselves in a position to do so. But it really wasn't Stoddy's job to go out and get me to the next level.

I didn't really have anyone looking out for me, nosing around on my behalf with my interests at heart. Stoddy was being more than fair, but he also had more than enough on his plate – he wasn't going to make the time to go and pump my tyres up among the other F1 movers and shakers. So at Annie's suggestion I went to see Flavio about signing up with him. She was prepared to acknowledge that the time had come for her to step back. My reputation was on the up-and-up, and while she was well known in her own right she didn't have the clout to keep opening doors for me. Nor did she particularly want to move in the F1 paddock.

I said to Stoddy, 'I need to go to the next level: you could potentially take a cut of me in the future, but what if I can get you that money back and I can put that commission someone else's way?'

Stoddy's immediate response was, 'The best way would be for Flav to buy out your contract with me: let's see if we can get him to do that.'

We went to Flavio with that idea at Monaco in May 2001 and he agreed. I put pen to paper on a 10-year deal with his management company. He was combining two roles as team manager and driver manager, but all my business dealings from then on were with his right-hand man Bruno Michel. Paul and Flavio came to an arrangement of their own. Stoddy was genuinely happy for me; he knew I had someone who was on the inside and knew the system very well. I was swimming with the sharks now. I'm little, but I'm in there!

*

Given that Flavio was keen for me to keep racing, I had signed to contest the 2001 FIA International F3000 Championship with the reigning champions and perennial front-runners Super Nova, headed up by the highly respected David Sears, and I was looking forward to going there. If you asked him now, Flavio would freely admit that we made a rod for our own backs by combining the F3000 race series with a heavy schedule of F1 testing for Benetton and their new engine supplier, Renault. But once I had convinced myself that I had to do F3000, Super Nova represented my best chance of doing well in the category.

David Sears had guided a string of very talented drivers to success: Ricardo Zonta and Juan Pablo Montoya were just two of the names on his list of previous drivers, while Nicolas Minassian had finished 2000 as F3000 runner-up for the team.

It all began well enough. At the major F3000 test session at Silverstone in early March I ended the first day fastest and over the two days I was second quickest. In the end, though, the season turned into an absolute nightmare. I've never crashed so many cars as I did that year, just through a total lack of respect for the F3000 machine. I never bent one bit of carbon on the Renault-powered F1 car but I destroyed the F3000 quite regularly. I had been busy all winter with F1 testing, with an additional stint in Estoril when Fisichella discovered a hairline crack in a bone in his right leg and couldn't drive.

With hindsight, the season-opening Interlagos F3000 race was the shape of things to come. Qualifying on the fifth row wasn't a big help, but I fought back well to come through for second place and a handy six points – until the stewards handed me a 25-second penalty for overtaking David Saelens before we crossed the timing line after a safety car period. That was a real kick in the guts for me and for the Super Nova team.

There was only one way to bounce back and we did it by taking pole and the race win at Imola next time out – the famous occasion when I drove with a broken rib sustained under severe G-forces in F1 testing. It was a big break-through at that early stage of the season, but F3000 bit back when I crashed in Barcelona qualifying and could do no better than seventh in the race. Austria was worse: I was out on the opening lap when a big shunt ahead of me – I had qualified sixth – left me with nowhere to go and two other cars up my chuff. Once again there was only one way to come back from those disasters, and Monaco was the best possible place to do it.

After the previous year's fiasco, when dehydration had cost me a strong result, Monaco had haunted me. In 2001 I was determined to show the place who was boss. I had changed my hydration strategy, my fitness levels were very high, and I said, 'Righto, I'm in charge this year, I'm going to rip this race to pieces.'

Pole position was the first step, though I tried too hard to go even faster and put the car in the barriers; after that I had to pay the guys back for their hard work by winning and I did it despite two safety car periods. Pole, fastest lap, race win: it was one of those days when you wonder, 'Where's everyone else?' That was a taste of things to come as well, but for the time being I was delighted to be Super Nova's first Monaco winner. It was also my first race as a member of Flavio's management stable and he was understandably chuffed.

Front row and second place at the Nürburgring kept the momentum going and when I won again at Magny-Cours I was the first driver to stand on the top step of the podium three times that season. Things were looking pretty promising until a fourth in Britain and three straight DNFs put paid to any chances I had of the title in my second year.

When we won, we won easily, but when it didn't happen we were fighting for second, third, fourth, fifth, so that was positive. Overall, though, the workload between F1 testing and F3000 racing proved too much. My shunt at Spa in the penultimate race was massive, and summed things up rather well. Once again frustration kicked in because both qualifying sessions were wet, I was on provisional pole for the whole session, but it dried out in the last five minutes so I came in and put slicks on, went back out and we ended up fourth and fuming. I was determined to crack the famous ultra-fast corner called Eau Rouge and just blast past the other guys up the hill that follows. We lowered the car's settings on the grid to try to dial out some of the oversteer, but that made it a touch heavy. Through Eau Rouge, whether the car was now so low that it bottomed out or not I can't say for sure, but it got out of control and I was gone. I ended my day in hospital, where I spent a few hours under observation before being given the all-clear.

September had started badly. The month would end with another trip to hospital, but this time it was all for the right reasons. The previous year had seen Lance Armstrong publish his book *It's Not About the Bike*, and it bowled me over. Armstrong had already won the Tour de France three times. It was an event, and he was a rider, that commanded my respect and admiration, particularly as I had started road cycling myself by then. Here was a man who had come through testicular cancer that spread through his brain, lungs and abdomen. As the book's title suggested, it was about one man who had to fight for his very life before he was able to pick up his professional cycling career again. His story was very inspirational to me, especially after what I'd seen my grandfather Clive endure.

September 2001 finished with the F1 race at Indianapolis, which was on my schedule as test and reserve driver for Benetton. Armstrong was treated in Indianapolis at the Indiana University Medical Center, so off my own bat I went to the hospital to see if I could meet some of the people who worked with him. I wanted to see if the book, this amazing story, was real. Just how special was this man?

In the book he refers to the nurse he was closest to and says, 'This is what an angel looks like.' I found her: she was called Latrice Haney and she was certainly real. She also confirmed how hard Armstrong had fought against the disease. Ann and I stayed in touch with Latrice for years afterwards and she gave me a fascinating insight into what a great athlete had been through, and the people who had helped him come out the other side. I can't help wondering what people like Latrice think of Lance Armstrong now.

*

I would really have liked to win the 2001 F3000 championship because that was my last chance to win a title in the junior categories. If I'd stayed on for a second year in British Formula Ford maybe I could have done it; if I'd stayed on for a second year in Formula 3, maybe I could have done it there. But even if I had stayed on for a third year in F3000 I probably wouldn't have done it, it's just that sort of category. In the end I finished runner-up to Justin Wilson.

Flavio put a lot of pressure on me to win that title as well, but in the end he saw what I was doing in the Benetton. There were some days when I would be very close to regular drivers Fisichella and Jenson Button despite my limited opportunities in the car, but it was a tough year because I was the first guy to drive with Renault's 111-degree engine as they prepared to return to the Grand Prix scene. At the December 2000 Silverstone test the thing was popping and banging for two days as we struggled with no power and no down-force, so throughout the following year we had to work pretty hard on it. What impressed me, looking back, is how motivated the team stayed and how hard they kept pushing. Fisi drove an amazing race in Spa on 2 September, 2001 and ended up on the podium.

My 2001 season had been split between a fairly basic car with the clutch on the floor and a gear-stick to play with, and a state-of-the-art Grand Prix car with traction control, paddles on the steering-wheel and all sorts of other toys. The F3000 car was 10 to 12 seconds a lap slower and a totally different beast. But the category itself, with its sheer unpredictability, helped me learn to deal with adversity. It was good training for F1 in the sense that it was an unbelievably competitive era in F3000. The first few laps were always very aggressive, and any kind of battle helps to harden you. I didn't want to be delivering pizzas in Queanbeyan if I got the year all wrong and maybe I tried too hard.

Just a couple of days after the final race in Monza I was back in the Benetton for three days at Silverstone. This time, I got my first long runs in that year's car, the B201 – and my time was a bee's dick slower than Button's. Every time you drove the car that year there were new things on it: we really were test pilots. We can't give this to the race driver, he might hurt himself – you have a go and see what happens!

But that didn't matter because my single-seater career was back on track. We were back in the hunt to try to get a race seat in Formula 1. At the end of 2001 Jenson kept his seat, Benetton now being wholly owned by Renault and renamed accordingly, and was joined by Italian Jarno Trulli, but Flavio told me: 'In '05 I want you and Alonso as my main drivers.' This is at the end of 2001 and I haven't even done a Grand Prix yet!

Fernando Alonso had just finished his debut season in F1, racing with Stoddy's Minardi team. He may not have scored any World Championship points but he had certainly caught the eye with his trademark combative style and the maturity of his approach. In the years to come I would form a close bond with the Spanish driver and some of my fondest memories of my F1 career are of epic encounters with Fernando on some of the greatest racetracks in the world.

But Fernando's name cropped up again during an episode that encapsulates the ups and downs of that year. What was I saying about the single-seater career being back on track? Late 2001 brought one of the great highs of my life to that time. On 21 October, with well-known F1 journalist Tom Clarkson, I launched into a bike ride from John O'Groats to Land's End, an epic 1627 kilometres to raise money for the never-ending fight against cancer, which had touched my family when Clive succumbed to the disease. Tom and I trained hard at the Renault Sport Human Performance Centre and we often did laps of the European Grand Prix circuits on race weekends on two wheels to get the stamina levels to where they needed to be for our 14-day marathon. It was a rewarding time – except when I heard, midway through the ride, that Alonso was leaving Minardi to take up a new role as Renault's F1 test and reserve driver. What did that mean for me?

I finished a hectic year in the cockpit with a final three-day F1 test in Barcelona at the end of the first week in October and wondered where that testing role and my F3000 campaign had all left me. All I knew for certain was that 2001 was the steepest roller-coaster I had ever been on.

7

Base Camp at Everest

RECENT YEARS HAVE SEEN A MARKED INCREASE IN THE number of drivers having to bring sponsorship money or some form of financial backing with them to F1 teams, even those that are not perennial back-markers. At the start of 2002 Paul Stoddart, who had acquired his own team by buying Minardi a year earlier, signed a driver with a lot of personal backing – but it wasn't me. Stoddy offered a race seat to Malaysian Alex Yoong, but at least the funds Alex brought with him gave Paul some wiggle room where his second driver was concerned. I still had no deal with him at that stage and our never-ending hunt for support went on.

Flavio always complained that the bloody Australians did nothing for me, but that wasn't true. We had Ron Walker making the Webber case from Australian Grand Prix head-quarters, we had Telstra on board, and everyone in Team

Webber was pushing like hell to bring money into the fighting fund. Flavio was distinctly unimpressed by what little we did have. 'Aussie pesos,' he growled. 'They're doing well! Don't they understand? This is nonsense – they must try harder!' That's the whole point, of course: when you come from a big island at the bottom of the world it's hard for the people down there to realise how the world of F1 works, and how hard *you* have to work to create your own place in it. Getting people to understand the need for funding – substantial funding – was always an uphill battle, but it made us all the more grateful to the people in Australia who did rally round.

In desperation I even rang Bernie Ecclestone and reminded him that I had qualified for a super-licence (the piece of paper a driver needs to race in F1) for the past two years running, thanks to my results in F3000. So I said to him we might as well just have Formula Ford and Formula 1: what were all these other categories for? Normally Bernie will lend a sympathetic ear if he thinks a young driver trying to break into F1 has a case; he's not always the intimidating character that the media portray, as I found out later when I got to know him a little better. But at this crucial stage of my career all he said was, 'Sometimes life isn't fair.'

It wasn't until the proverbial minute before midnight that I finally did a deal with Paul Stoddart that would get me – at last – to where I wanted to be: in Formula 1, as a race driver. We finalised it at Terminal 4 at Heathrow with Bruno Michel, Flavio Briatore's right-hand man, and Stoddy. By then all the other F1 drives were gone, things were looking bleak again and at one stage we didn't even know what was happening with the Minardi team itself.

I had been determined not to get carried away before I had concrete proof that the Minardi deal, which was being rumoured in the racing media, really was happening at last. I'd had my hopes built up so many times only to be dashed each time, so while I was grateful to Paul for the opportunity I don't think I believed I really was a Grand Prix driver until I actually arrived in Melbourne. And since Paul owned not only a Formula 1 team but also his own airline, European Aviation, we arrived in Melbourne in some style!

We flew in Stoddy's 747, calling in at Kuala Lumpur to say hello to my new teammate's personal sponsors, then on to Avalon airport outside Melbourne. To fly down there with the cars underneath us in the cargo hold for my first Grand Prix weekend was absolutely surreal. It wasn't exactly how I would have done it, but I knew where Paul was coming from: an Aussie driver making his F1 debut at the Australian Grand Prix with a team owned by an Australian, and in his home town to boot! He wanted to milk it for all it was worth.

Ron Walker and Steve Bracks, then Premier of Victoria, met us at Avalon and there was a three-hour media marathon before I could make my way onto a Canberra flight for a touch of normality, a barbecue at my sister's farm near Queanbeyan with family and friends. Leanne and her own family are a long way removed from the racing scene and it was a short, sweet antidote to the mayhem.

Next day Webber the likeable larrikin, as one of my teachers had called me, was back at Karabar High talking to the senior students and, in one of life's little ironies, preaching the need for safe behaviour behind the wheel. In a pattern that became familiar ahead of each year's Australian Grand Prix, the next few days were a blur as I went from one engagement to the next. Not exactly the ideal preparation for a rookie F1 driver's first Grand Prix but they were all commitments I felt I had to honour for the people who had done so much to help get me to that Melbourne race in the first place. But I won't deny the sense of relief I felt when I finally got into the inner sanctum of the F1 paddock.

There was just one problem: the Minardi team and its car were totally underdone for my World Championship debut. Before heading Down Under, a brief test at Valencia in Spain was all I had managed in the car that was to be mine for my first F1 race. When I visited the Minardi factory in Faenza I could not believe the size of the place: it was like a good F3000 team, it just blew me away that a Formula 1 team could operate from such a small base. Straightaway my admiration for Fernando Alonso, who had raced for Minardi in 2001, went up, because it underlined that big doesn't always mean better and you can make an impact even with limited resources.

I felt a huge amount of pressure: it was going to be very, very bad if the car broke down in the first five or six laps, because people's expectations were impossibly high after all the media hype and we had to spend so much time damping those unrealistic expectations down. It was, of course, really special to drive my first Grand Prix in my home country. Not many drivers get that opportunity. But in terms of putting on a good show, I wondered if later in the championship would have been more suitable.

Still, I was staying as positive as I could. I was there, that was the main thing, and to my mind in those early stages it was all about trying to ruffle some feathers, being somewhere I shouldn't be, or at least where so many people had told me I never would be. 'How the f#*k are *you* going to make it to Formula 1, coming from Queanbeyan?' Here was the answer to the oft-repeated question: M. Webber (Australia) on the grid in Melbourne in Minardi Asiatech PS02 #23. Even if I was nervous about the outcome of my first race there was a considerable degree of satisfaction in simply being there in the first place after so many years of trying.

In Melbourne race distance is 58 laps. It wasn't going to be the longest time I'd spent in a car, but I was on the track, a street circuit, with the guys perceived as the best in the world, and the plain fact was that I was going to be one of the slowest on that circuit because of the car I was driving, and there wasn't a lot I could do about that. I was going to do my absolute best with what I had, but I knew the car was very unreliable.

The story of the race weekend itself is pretty straight-forward – but almost unbelievable. For a start we out-qualified the Jaguars, which a Minardi was not supposed to do. As for the race, things played into our hands quite beautifully. Ralf Schumacher's Williams took Rubens Barrichello's Ferrari out off the start-line and the ensuing carnage meant there would be fewer cars in the hunt for a good result. When the crash happened I thought the red flag was going to be put out for sure.

We're out there – eighth or ninth or whatever – and it didn't matter what I did, with the equipment I had there was no way I was going to be overtaking anyone. There was only one car behind me and that was my teammate! From lap 3 we were already behind the safety car, and the differential and traction control were starting to play up. All weekend we were also having a nightmare in the pits: whenever we grabbed first gear and tried to pull away, the anti-stall would kick in because there was a bug in the software relating to the pit-lane speed limiter. Whenever you came into the pits you would hit the pit limiter once to go to the mandatory pit-lane speed on the way to your garage. But when you were ready to leave, boom, it kept putting on the anti-stall and you were going nowhere. What the team wanted Alex and me to do in the race was hit the cruise control, do the regulation 80 kilometres per hour as we came in, then just before braking into the pit box, hit the button again so the cruise control went off.

But what happens when you do that? The fuel flap goes down.

When I pulled up the pit crew just went ballistic, screwdrivers flying everywhere, until team manager John Walton came on the radio and calmly said, 'Mark, hit the pit button.'

I did as John-Boy asked: the flap went up, the guys were able to insert the hose on the refuelling rig where it was supposed to go, and I was able to take fuel on board and rejoin the fray.

At that stage in the race I wasn't thinking about my position too much. There was a more pressing question in my mind: how was I going to get to the finish? This car and I had never done anything like this sort of distance together before and it was sending me all sorts of distress signals to say it was definitely going to let me down, the only question was when. For the last 25 laps or so – almost half the race distance – I was short-shifting, moving up through the gears quickly to avoid stressing any of the components unnecessarily and doing everything I could to nurse the car home.

Then I saw Mika Salo coming in the Toyota. He was much quicker and I thought, 'Once he starts getting within 10 seconds I'll start to stretch my car a bit more.'

I surprised myself by staying so cool: I knew there wasn't long to go, we were in the points, which was pretty massive in itself, and I could see the crowd coming closer to me with every lap that went by.

When Salo cruised up on the back of me I was pretty much driving flat out; that was all the car could give me. I was drawing on all my experience to keep him behind me. On the grid Stoddy had said to me, 'Just bring it home, mate.' But when I was in position to score two World Championship points for fifth on debut in a team that needed those points so desperately and Salo was catching me, Stoddy came on the radio and said, 'Under no circumstances let him past.'

The rules had changed all of a sudden! But I knew the difference between two points and one point. The potential revenue was as high as $25 million, I believe. It was important to Stoddy and the team so I just kept my cool.

My Christmas came in March when we went down the front straight for the first time with Salo behind me but not getting all that close. I thought, 'We're in with a bloody chance here to hold him off!' It was going to be pretty serious if we did that.

Another lap went by and he was all over me round the back of the circuit. There were a few places where I would stay out of the throttle to let him close up and give him more disturbed air behind my car. The pressure was building: we were getting deeper and deeper into the race and I knew he was going to get more and more aggressive, which meant I was going to have to be more and more aggressive in blocking him, and the crowd were getting more and more animated. Then suddenly he spun! On oil that had been there the whole race.

Alex, my engineer, came on the radio yelling, 'Salo's off, Salo's off!'

I came out of Turn 3, where there's a little kink, and I checked in the left mirror which is normally where you look for the bloke coming up behind you at that point on the track – and I couldn't see Salo's Toyota.

I thought, 'There's no way he can be beside me, where the hell's he gone? This is strange, really strange . . .'

It only got stranger. I was on the last lap . . . but then I realised it wasn't: the crowd's reaction had confused me. I'd seen on my pit board *2 to go* and then my mind started to play games. Were there still two to go? The leaders had lapped me: when was the chequered flag going to come out?

The crowd was going mental, and it all just happened – the most unbelievable moment of my life. Fifth place and two points on my debut: the World Championship was in its 53rd season, hundreds of drivers had contested hundreds of Grands Prix and I was only the 50th to score points in his first F1 race.

As soon as I crossed the line to clinch that fifth place the tears came. I couldn't believe it had actually happened. The crowd, the PA, Stoddy . . . the whole thing was a blur. You could see it in everyone's eyes: it wasn't just a sporting event, it had turned into something a bit special for the locals. But I used up a lot of luck on the first one!

After the 'real' podium ceremony featuring Michael Schumacher, Juan Pablo Montoya and Kimi Räikkönen, Ron Walker and his media man Geoff Harris came down to the Minardi garage and said they were going to get me up there for the Aussie crowd. It was a highly irregular breach of protocol that might have cost us those two precious points if the authorities hadn't shown a human touch on the day.

I wasn't so keen on being shoved up there, mainly because my back was killing me: I didn't really fit that well in the car and I just wanted to get hold of my physio, fellow Aussie Rod 'Rocket' McLean, because it needed unwinding. I was uncomfortable with it in another way, because a podium, especially in F1, is such a difficult thing to achieve. I felt the only men entitled to be up there were the ones who had finished in the top three, not some local bloke who was fifth. But it happened on the spur of the moment. Then Sabine Kehm, Schuey's press officer, came down to our garage to say Michael had requested the pleasure of our company in the Ferrari garage. He and I had some photos taken because, shrewd operator that he was, he'd won the race and he didn't want the new local hero to keep him off the next day's front page!

Emotionally I was fine: well, in the car I was, but when I got out and saw Dad I struggled to keep myself in check. Poor Mum was in the grandstand opposite the Minardi garage with half of Queanbeyan who had travelled down for the race. Understandably she wanted to share in the celebrations and when the crowd was allowed onto the track one of my mates basically hauled her up and over the safety fence so she could join us. I must have been in shock because

after I had a shower, a massage and a bit of a private celebration, the rest of the night was an absolute blur.

I remember Annie being very insistent that before any
more celebrating could be done she needed to get her press
release out. All I can say is thank God for email: no more of
those endless faxes, just a press of the Send button was all
it took for the news to go round the world within minutes.
Minardi threw an impromptu party that we called in at
before going on to enjoy the rest of the night in private.
I recall meeting up with friends from Queanbeyan in the
Crown Casino but we didn't know where to go! We tried
getting into a night-club but were refused entry. It was only
as we were walking away that someone at the club realised
who I was and came chasing after us to invite us in. We told
them where to poke it!

Days later I spoke to several people and said it was a
shame they hadn't been in Melbourne for the race – and
they had been! What we had done only really sank in when
I got back to Europe and experienced the response from Italy.
It helped me appreciate the enormous following Formula 1
enjoys around the world, and how happy the fans were to see
battlers like the little Minardi team enjoy some reward.

The great Murray Walker, 'the voice of Formula 1', rang
me in tears. That was one of my only regrets, that Murray's
familiar, steely voice, so well known to me from my early
days of watching F1 on television, wasn't calling my first
race as he had retired by then. We really did know that
those were probably going to be our first and last points of
the year, and did we make the most of it! I don't mean just
with the partying that went on, but also in respecting what
had happened that day, how good the team had really been.

To cap it all off, Annie had met a bloke called Danny Wallis at the Foster's pre-race party and he said he would give me $5000 if I finished the race. We rang him on the Monday after Grand Prix weekend, and he did!

*

While Aussie fans painted Albert Park green and gold as if 'their' man had won the race, the Formula 1 world I had stepped into was another colour entirely: red. I became a Grand Prix driver while Ferrari were in the middle of an astonishing run of success that saw them win the Constructors' Championship six times in a row from 1999. Michael Schumacher had been keen to get in on the photographs in Melbourne because he had become used to lording it over the F1 scene. A broken leg at Silverstone in '99 had prevented him winning the drivers' title that year, but his first World Championship as a Ferrari driver came in 2000 – the Scuderia's first drivers' crown since Jody Scheckter way back in 1979 – and he retained it the following year. In fact his winning margin of 58 points over McLaren's David Coulthard in 2001 was the biggest in the 52 years of World Championship history to that date. In 2002 he would go even higher: there were 17 races that year – and Michael Schumacher was on the podium at every one of them! He won 11 races, beating a record set by Nigel Mansell with Williams in 1992, which Michael himself had equalled three times previously. His winning margin in 2002 was 67 points.

When I say Schumacher won 11 races, that's not quite the whole picture. In 2002 a subject that would come back to play a major part in my own F1 career many years later raised its ugly head: team orders. In Austria, which was only the sixth round of the 2002 season, Michael's Ferrari teammate Rubens Barrichello thrashed him in qualifying to take pole, then led the race handsomely before bowing to team orders right at the very end and allowing Schuey to cross the line ahead of him. It turned pretty ugly after that, with Michael taking the winner's trophy and promptly handing it to Rubens, who ended up very sheepishly on the top step of the podium with the first- and second-place trophies in his arms. Ferrari's argument was that they needed to guarantee their lead driver maximum points in his title campaign – with 11 races still to go!

There was another red-faced moment in Indianapolis when the Ferrari drivers, who had waltzed away with the race from the start, shuffled places right on the line. Some said Michael was trying to repay Rubens for Austria, as the Brazilian was eventually declared the winner of the American race. Team orders were banned at the end of the season.

My own first F1 season, with all the uncertainty over finances, was tough away from the track and it was a lot more bruising on it. I hardly fitted in the Minardi Asiatech and I was black and blue after every bloody race. But that first result in Australia was a huge financial relief for Stoddy and while there were alarms like Spain, where we had to pull out because of concerns over our cars' rear wings, we did enjoy some other reasonable afternoons.

One of them was my first time back in Monaco since that memorable day in 2001. I was going very well, up in the top eight, then late in the race a front tyre stripped a tread and we finished eleventh. Monaco was memorable for another reason: the curious incident of the camp-bed in the night. If anyone thought life was all beer and skittles now that I was in F1, they should have seen where Stoddy had us staying in Monaco. Rumour had it that the 'hotel' was a former brothel, and all I can say is that they must have had inventive clients. The rooms weren't big enough to swing a cat in. And Team Webber was occupying only one of them, which meant Dad was on a camp-bed inches away from his son and, as usual, snoring his head off. He used to feel very bad about it, but that was small consolation if you were the one having to get up and race the next day. I issued the usual warning – he always used to wake up with pillows and shoes strewn around him where someone had thrown them at him the previous night but they made no difference. So in desperation I got up and snapped the camp-bed shut with Dad still in the middle of it. He woke up then and stopped snoring . . .

*

After only a few rounds of the championship the racing press was full of stories about Stoddy not being able to make it through to the end of the season. Bernie Ecclestone himself was quoted as saying, 'This is quite a high-powered game so they perhaps shouldn't have been here.'

To be fair, Stoddy kept me in the loop, helping me understand how much pressure they were under. 'Mate,' he said to me in Austria, 'we are absolutely on the edge here . . .' It was hand-to-mouth stuff for him, that season: Minardi was almost like a family-run operation, with all the Italians from the original Minardi days when Giancarlo Minardi himself brought the team into F1 back in 1985. Paul loved all those guys and kept them on, and I really enjoyed working with all the Italians, but he knew I was pretty important to him as well. I wasn't going to make or break his team but my presence certainly helped. And he wanted to do the right thing by me. 'I want to make sure that we give you the best opportunity,' he said to me, 'you've got to move on from here.'

Moves were already afoot. Flavio and Bruno were worried that Minardi wouldn't last the whole season. In career terms it would have been catastrophic for me to have another six or eight months out, particularly at this level. Flavio started talking to Niki Lauda, the triple World Champion who had been put in charge of the new Jaguar F1 project. Flavio was particularly keen for me to do a test in the middle of the year; Jaguar's drivers were Eddie Irvine and Pedro de la Rosa and the Spaniard was under fire.

The test drive with Jaguar took place right at the end of June in Barcelona. I was beating Irvine and de la Rosa in the Minardi regularly, so Niki was pretty keen to have a look at me as well. I couldn't believe what I saw in the Jaguar camp. I'd be there an hour early, making sure I got absolutely ready, being as professional as I could be – and Irvine would be getting a massage! Not quite ready yet, go out to his garage 10–15 minutes late, do the installation lap . . . I was blown away. This was one of the first big teams in Formula 1 I'd seen at work and I thought, 'Bloody hell, these drivers are getting away with murder!' I guess I still had a lot of the Mercedes discipline in my head because I'd been given such a good schooling there. I had it drummed into me that no driver is bigger than his team and vice versa. These guys have worked their arses off all night to get the car ready and you come out 10 minutes late? It's not on.

Once I got over the initial culture shock the test went well. The Jaguar had phenomenal horsepower compared with my Minardi. It wasn't the best car in the world by any means but it had a lot of power and felt quite different. In around 50 laps I was within a couple of thousandths of de la Rosa's times. It was pretty clear that Jaguar were going to replace both their drivers; I didn't care which, as long as I got one of the seats.

Once I was reasonably sure that Jaguar wanted me, we got on with the rest of our Minardi season, which was made easier when Stoddy won his claim for payment of television monies, easing some of the pressure on him and the rest of us. We had a great weekend at Magny-Cours in France, leap-frogging both Toyotas and coming home in the top eight. Stoddy said afterwards he felt my drive that day was better than the points-scoring debut in Melbourne.

We capped the year off with another top-10 result in Japan and I finished 16th in the World Championship, which earned me F1's equivalent of an Oscar: the 'Bernie' for Rookie of the Year 2002.

Two little episodes may help to paint a picture of how life was beginning to change. At the end of that rookie year I was invited to go to Slovakia, of all places, to do a magazine interview, attend a couple of functions and, as I understood it, help to raise the profile of F1 in that part of the world, possibly because they were toying with the idea of staging a Grand Prix of their own. Maybe the magazine in question had approached all the other F1 drivers and had been turned down!

The journey took us out beyond Bratislava itself, and it became apparent very quickly once we landed that this was going to be no ordinary trip. First of all, my 'interpreter' was a stunner; she could have been some kind of movie star.

'I'm with you for three days,' she purred, 'anything you need, just ask . . .'

Fortunately, Ann had come with me!

Late in 2002 I also allowed myself a moment of self-indulgent fun: I bought a BMW M5. I think there must have been a bonus clause of some kind in my Minardi deal and I used some of the money to acquire the Bimmer.

Dad was pretty ticked off with me, and he was right: what did I need a BMW M5 for? We had a seemingly endless series of Renaults on hand, but clearly I thought I deserved something a bit more special.

The BMW nearly got me into trouble one evening when I was on my way home from a function. I was honking along when a police car passed me coming the other way. I looked in the mirror, saw the brake lights glow and the flashing lights come on. In a split-second I made the decision to continue: the chase was on! I was in the right car, I knew the roads extremely well, although the question did flash through my mind: 'Mark, why are you doing this?'

I only had five miles till I was safely home, the adrenaline was off the charts, so I went for it. I didn't have to pass another car, which was good – and bad, because it meant my pursuers could still see me. There were lots of left-right, left-right flicks as I got closer to home, and they worked in my favour. I parked the car in the garage and waited 15 minutes with it ticking away as it cooled down – would the noise give me away? – and Annie upstairs wondering why the hell I hadn't come into the house.

There was no knock at the door. I lived to fight another day. It was a silly thing to do, but maybe I thought I'd already scaled the heights. As it turned out, I was only at base camp at Everest.

*

By November 2002 I was a confirmed Jaguar driver. Niki Lauda was very complimentary about the mid-year evaluation test I had done with his team. I was surprised, to say the least, when we began getting down to serious business within just a few weeks of that test. I was mowing the lawn at Mursley, trying to take my mind off what might or might not be happening, when the call came through from Bruno Michel confirming the move. All that was needed was my signature on the contract, so I jumped in the car, still in my shorts and with grass clippings on my trainers, and drove to the Little Chef restaurant on the A5 roundabout close to the Jaguar factory to meet Bruno and Jaguar's lawyer. It all felt a little weird: it was the first time I'd experienced the way things worked in the F1 paddock.

When Flavio had announced that we were talking to Jaguar I said, 'How will Stoddy feel about this, Flavio?' but I quickly worked out this was how things were going to be. I'd been in Stoddy's F1 team for five months and I knew my career wasn't going to be at Minardi forever; you simply have to move on.

The F1 landscape was changing slightly for my second season. Michael Schumacher would win 'only' six races, but it was his sixth title, something even the peerless Juan Manuel Fangio, the dominant force of the fifties, had not been able to achieve. The points system had changed, maybe in response to Michael's dominance, with drivers being rewarded down to eighth place in each race rather than sixth as before. We had eight winners that year, which was twice as many as in 2001. One of them was Fernando Alonso. He became, at that time, the youngest winner in World Championship history when he took his maiden victory for Renault at that year's Hungarian Grand Prix. We also had one-lap qualifying as the authorities began what often seemed like an endless process of tinkering around the edges of the sport. Just as a footnote, the F1 entry list did not include Arrows, the team I had contemplated joining a couple of years earlier. Tom Walkinshaw ran out of cash and inspiration midway through 2002 and was never seen on an F1 grid again.

I thought the switch to Jaguar was the perfect step up after my debut year. Jaguar was one of the most famous names in British motor-racing history, with multiple victories in the Le Mans 24-hour race back in the fifties and a superb sports car tradition. Now, though, Jaguar had become the identity under which Ford went racing in their own right when they bought the Stewart Grand Prix team at the end of 1999.

Jackie and Paul Stewart, his elder son, had done a pretty reasonable job of starting a new team from scratch and becoming Grand Prix winners in only their third year in the World Championship. Then Jackie had done a shrewd piece of business in handing the reins over to the Ford Motor Company with whom he had enjoyed such a long association. But four points in 2000, followed by nine in 2001, were not the stuff of which title-winning teams are made, and a company the size of Ford has little room for patience. By the end of November 2002 Niki Lauda, who had been instrumental in signing me for Jaguar, was no longer there himself!

Ford decided a shake-up was needed; the new man in charge, Richard Parry-Jones, insisted that performance on the track was the only measure by which progress would be judged. There were now two P's in the Jaguar pod in the shape of David Pitchforth and Tony Purnell, running the race team itself.

'Pitchy' was great: a Yorkshireman, solid as a rock, and everybody loved him, but he was never going to do the schmoozing and cruising; he was never one for the politics of the F1 world. Tony was the boffin of the two, while Dave was far more down-to-earth, but the noises they were both making were encouraging. Tony had been quoted as saying that he was laying the foundations for something outstanding in years to come and that he was looking five, even 10 years ahead. To me it seemed they could construct something worthwhile if, I thought, they didn't end up having their hands tied behind their backs by the parent company. All right, we were a lean machine, one of the leanest on the grid, but we could take it one step at a time, build some momentum and, who knows, by 2005 we might find ourselves in a position to start winning races.

A new team of people had been thrown together and we had 'Jungle Boy' in the other car. That was Antônio Pizzonia, the Brazilian, four years my junior (I was 26), who had cruised through the apprentice formulae and picked up the British F3 title on the way to becoming a Jaguar driver. In pre-season testing the R4 proved very unreliable: we were doing a lot of engine development work with Cosworth, and we were working hard on the aerodynamics.

At the first test session in the first week of January 2003 I managed the grand total of 17 laps in the car. Michael's

Ferrari set the pace in the 1 minute 15 bracket. We were down in the 1:18s so clearly there was a bit of work to be done. But I believed there were still a lot of good people in the team and that we could make real progress together.

Unfortunately that wasn't much in evidence in Melbourne. I made rather a meal of the new one-lap qualifying format, and the first race of the second phase of my F1 career ended prematurely with a broken suspension component at the rear of the car. In Malaysia we were running in the points in eighth place but a catalogue of mishaps conspired against me: there was a persistent fuel-feed problem, I had a drama with my clutch at my pit stop that cost me half a minute, and to cap it all off the fire extinguisher went off in my face! I posted another DNF.

In April 2003, at Interlagos in Brazil, three remarkable things happened. The first was that we put the R4 on the second row of the grid. You have to remember that the F1 'tyre war' between Bridgestone and Michelin was in full swing at that time. The R4 went through its Michelins very quickly: I used to bring them up to the proper racing temperature as soon as I could, but the car was still very hard on them.

Qualifying was an area I thought was going to be a real challenge in 2003 because the system had changed to virtual one-lap banzai runs, whereas I used to like building up to it, having a few runs and getting everything ready. So at one of our winter tests I asked my engineer Pete Harrison to drop in a short run randomly throughout the day. We would go out fresh and pull out a big lap.

'Boom – just keep surprising me', I told him.

In the long run it turned out to be a bloody big strength and Brazil was one of the first signs it was paying off.

On Friday we took advantage of changeable conditions to take provisional pole ahead of local hero Rubens Barrichello in his Ferrari; he got his own back on Saturday in dry running when we were carrying a tad more down-force than either the Ferrari or David Coulthard's McLaren, but we still set third-fastest time, just five one-hundredths off the final pole position lap. Rubens was on provisional pole when I started my lap at the end; the crowd were apparently going quieter and quieter the further I got round.

Come the race it was wet again; we had too much water in the foot-well and Tim Malyon, my rack-runner (the bloke in charge of the car's electrics), was highly nervous. So was everyone, really – a Jaguar on the second row? The stress levels were off the charts.

We had a problem on the grid with the throttle: it wasn't calibrating properly. For the first few laps the team were ringing up, saying, 'Press this button, press that button,' asking me to clear and reset functions in the car.

This was also the race where I had my first little ding-dong with Michael, wheel-to-wheel for several laps. We had to run the car heavier than it needed to be because we couldn't suck the last 15 kilos or so of fuel out of the tank. So, what with one thing and another – and remember I'm not used to being among these big boys at this stage of my F1 career – I was trying hard to tell myself to stay cool. It was a race of heavy rain and multiple safety cars. In fact we started behind the safety car and it stayed out for the first eight of the scheduled 71 laps. The conditions caught out some of the biggest names in the field. Michael himself was lucky not to come off far worse than he did when the Ferrari skated off on the river of water running across the track just past Turn 2 and he narrowly missed a rescue truck.

The second remarkable event of that Brazilian weekend came on lap 53. I was running seventh after my second stop, working my way back through the field on intermediate tyres, when disaster struck. I had been trying to keep the tyres cool whenever I could, and that included coming uphill to the last corner at Interlagos. It had worked for the previous two laps, but the tyres had turned into virtual slicks and that was what caught me out. I went into the barriers, bounced off and back across, and that hurt! I remember my legs were going everywhere and how hard my knees were banging together. The impacts knocked all four corners off the car and I was left in a canoe, to all intents and purposes, sitting in the monocoque that had kept me relatively safe through my biggest F1 accident yet.

It wasn't over, though: Fernando's Renault came barrelling round and hit some of the debris. It sounded like a bomb going off, so as well as worrying about myself I was now concerned for him. The race was stopped. When I got out of the wreckage the first person I saw was one of the long-serving F1 snappers, Steven Tee, and his eyes were out on stalks. Steven's seen plenty in his F1 time so I knew I had just been through something pretty spectacular.

I wasn't taken for a medical. My physio, Nick Harris, asked me if I was all right so I dropped on the floor and did 60 press-ups to persuade him that I was. One of the most annoying aspects of the whole episode was that the race result was eventually declared at a point on lap 54 when I was lying ninth. Since points were now being allocated from P1 to P8 and I had been running as high as seventh, what would have been my first points for Jaguar and my first in over 14 months were snatched away from me. Talk about adding insult to injury.

And the third remarkable event of that eventful weekend? Just three races into our relationship Jaguar asked me to sign on again, but this time for five years! A year before, I had been on a three-race deal with Stoddy; now I was being offered five seasons!

By the time Imola and Barcelona had come and gone, my signature was on a new contract for the following year, with multiple-year options. We had suffered another non-finish in Italy when a driveshaft failed, but Spain brought our first points together – no nasty surprises this time – when I finished seventh. I really felt that race, after a test session at Mugello, not far from Imola, had fixed our reliability problems. I also felt I couldn't do all the hard work I was already involved in for the next season's car and then go somewhere else. In any case, the first Jaguar I drove was far from a shocker and it was a lot better than my debut year. We had already produced a stellar effort from pit lane in Austria, where I set the third-fastest race lap behind the two Ferraris; that was the performance that first attracted the attention of Frank Williams, but more on that later.

Silverstone brought one of the most bizarre and most alarming moments of my entire F1 career. Things were going well for us at that stage; we came off successive sixth places in one week at the Nürburgring and Magny-Cours and I was inside the top 10 in the championship, but the Silverstone race was overshadowed when I came round at Becketts – and saw a spectator in the middle of the track.

It turned out he was some kind of protester, dressed in a

lurid green and orange get-up, and he was running towards the F1 cars as fast as he could. It was the most incredible thing I had ever come across on a racetrack. Whatever he was protesting about, it didn't matter to me: he was putting other people – me among them – in an appalling position. I was pretty shaken up by the thought that I might have been racing my heart out as usual, and ended up killing someone. There would have been kids in the crowd and it made me even angrier to think that he was prepared to risk them witnessing a horrendous accident. As a footnote, the same man, whose name was apparently Cornelius Horan, made headlines at the 2004 Olympics in Athens when he attacked a Brazilian runner in the marathon.

Around the same time Silverstone was the location of another, more welcome event. Team Webber gained a new member when Kerry Fenwick came on board. She had ambushed Ann while we were watching Kerry's then boyfriend, Australian racing driver Will Power, compete in F3. She told Ann we needed her to come and work for us! Ann hadn't even thought about the need for a PA but Kerry wouldn't take no for an answer and she hounded Ann until she invited her to come and do a half-day for her, working in the spare bedroom at home which had been converted into an office. It was obvious from the start that she was a chip off the same block as Ann and very determined to drive Will's career. She figured out that aligning Will with Team Webber might open up some opportunities and contacts for him and to a degree she was right. We later invested in Will's World Series by Renault season and although F1 proved a bridge too far for him, he went on to carve out a very successful career in America, winning the IndyCar title in 2014. Kerry has remained with us and is responsible for maintaining order in our office and household.

Normal service, or something like it, was resumed two races later when I produced what I felt was the best drive of my fledgling F1 career. We qualified third again in Hungary, then a strong first stint laid the foundations for another sixth-place finish. Though I lost out to Montoya in the stops and was overtaken by Ralf Schumacher fairly late in the piece I thoroughly enjoyed myself, not least of all because it was the first time we could look at the results, point out that we owed nothing to other people's misfortunes and believe that we had achieved the position purely on merit. Seventh at Monza next time out would be my last points of a season in which I scored 17 altogether and finished 10th in the Drivers' World Championship.

*

At Germany's famous Nürburgring in 2003 Ann and I were able to make a significant announcement, one which had nothing to do with my driving career. We were setting up the inaugural Mark Webber Challenge, a new adventure race in Tasmania, set among some of the most ruggedly beautiful scenery Australia has to offer. The first 10-day Challenge would take place in November after the completion of the Formula 1 season.

The inspiration behind it was a familiar one for most top-flight sportsmen and sportswomen: the desire to give something back. The idea was to force people out of their comfort zone, which just happens to be the title Steve Waugh picked for his autobiography, one of the finest sports books I have ever read. Steve was coming with us to

Tasmania as were James Tomkins, a member of Australia's 'Oarsome Foursome' of Olympic rowers, tennis Grand Slam tournament winner Pat Rafter and the athlete who thrilled the whole country with her magnificent 400-metre sprint victory in the 2000 Sydney Olympics, Cathy Freeman.

Designed to showcase Tasmania as a world-class adventure destination, the inaugural Challenge took in a thousand kilometres and a range of sporting activities that included cross-country running, mountain-biking and kayaking. In addition to its fund-raising aims, the Challenge answered another need. It would really help with the all-round conditioning a modern F1 driver requires to do his day job. You want as many strings in your bow as you can have to prepare you for racing the car on the limit lap after lap and for the bloody big bang that's also going to come one day – as I had seen in Brazil.

Grand Prix drivers have to condition themselves to make sure they don't get run down during a hectic schedule of worldwide travel and racing. They are generally fit people, they can take the strains and the pressures of the different countries we race in, and specialist trainers had always encouraged me not to have what they call too tight a pyramid. You want your physical fitness to be built on a good, broad foundation, and that's what I had been working towards for years: going for a long paddle, going for a long run, sprint sessions, lifting weights, swimming, covering as many bases as I could. The Mark Webber Challenge encapsulated all of that, and it had two other key elements for me: the chance to work within a team, and the competitive urge to see how I might go against some pretty serious athletes.

Being on the Challenge – seven so far – puts me in a completely different world from the one I normally operate in. In F1 you live in a fishbowl, where price means more than value, relationships are built on false foundations and the moral compass is sometimes distorted. The Challenge was the perfect antidote to what Ann often calls 'that Formula 1 life', a professional environment that became more and more disenchanting as the years went by. To me it is a happy coincidence that we announced the creation of the Mark Webber Challenge at the place where, six years later, I would rise to the challenge of being a Grand Prix winner.

Although I wanted to test my own limits, the Mark Webber Challenge was not conceived as a competition, more as a personal test for anyone who wanted to join me in one of the most beautiful but also most daunting places on our planet. Since its inception, I believe it has become one of the most respected multi-sports challenges an athlete can face.

The first Mark Webber Challenge was incredibly physical: big, big days, and 10 of them – one of the hardest things I've done in my life, by a long way. One of the most pleasing things for me after the first Challenge was the reaction from Bernie Shrosbree, the rugged ex-marine who played such a part early on in my own quest for genuine fitness. It was Bernie who introduced me to the whole idea of multi-sports training; he came on my team for the first Challenge, when there were some demons in me asking, 'Well Mark, can you get through this thing yourself?'

After those 10 days Bernie said to an interviewer, 'Mark is walking 10 feet taller than he was 10 days ago.

The Challenge was mentally more difficult than he anticipated; he had some incredible bad moments – a bad fall, a knee problem, but whatever condition he was in, he wanted to stick with it.' Bernie added that James Tomkins had noticed a change in me as well. Apparently his comment to Bernie was, 'He's flipped over to pure leadership.'

It was a relief to me that I had come through it, but the last thing anyone should think is that the event that carries my name is all about me. It's about encouraging people to step outside their comfort zone and discover what they are capable of. Every participant has his or her story about why they are there in the first place – it gives me goose bumps when I first hear those stories. I'm reminded of Wayne Bennett's memoir, *The Man in the Mirror*, one of the finest sports books you will ever read. The book and its author have been twin sources of inspiration to me for years. The poem Bennett borrowed his title from sums up everything I believe: if you can look yourself in the eye, you have passed the sternest test of all. I believe many of the men and women who have come with us on the Challenge have passed that test – even if they didn't think they would.

*

After the extreme high of the inaugural Mark Webber Challenge in Tasmania in November 2003, the start of the 2004 racing year brought me back to earth with a bump. It would be an understatement to say that we expected more from R5, my second car at Jaguar, than it was willing to give us in 2004, a fact I quickly grasped at the first test session in January in Valencia where we were a full two seconds off the front-running pace. In F1 terms that's a huge margin, and while things seemed to have improved by the second test in late February, the season simply underlined our shortcomings.

We always had a good engine but we never seemed able to capitalise on any virtues the car possessed. The year can be summed up pretty easily: four points-scoring races in Bahrain, the Nürburgring, Silverstone and Hockenheim, but instead of the hoped-for podiums the best of those four results was sixth in Germany.

Among the few highlights was my first F1 front-row start in Malaysia, next to Michael's Ferrari. Being next to Michael's Ferrari in 2004 wasn't easy for anyone; his final World Championship-winning season was a stunner, with a new record of 13 race victories – 12 of them in the first 13 rounds. So it was a big lap!

I hadn't always felt comfortable in Malaysia because there are no reference points, no markers to help a driver on that wide and varied Sepang layout, and it was good to crack that circuit. But all that hard work went out the window when we endured a start-line fiasco with the clutch. It had oil all over it, so when the lights went out the Jaguar was going nowhere.

That led to one of my most aggressive first laps, because of course I did go *somewhere* – back down the field to seventeenth. By the end of the first lap I had clawed my way back up to eighth. I overtook Ralf Schumacher, which he didn't like, so he came charging up from behind, gave me his front-wing endplate in the left rear and left me with a puncture.

I had to limp all the way back to the pits, damaging the floor and the diffuser in the process, so when I came back out again the car just wasn't working. I spun under braking for the final hairpin and retired. Monaco brought two days from hell with fires, hydraulic failures, electronic glitches; it wasn't until the British Grand Prix at Silverstone in mid-July that I took my first World Championship point at Silverstone. I dedicated my eighth place to 'John-Boy' Walton, the team manager at Minardi who had died after a sudden heart attack the previous week.

Most of 2004's good things came away from racing: an enjoyable visit from George Clooney, Matt Damon and Brad Pitt as they publicised the movie *Ocean's Twelve* in Monaco; a trip to the Great Wall and the Forbidden City when F1 added China to its annual travel plans; and the opportunity to go bike riding with one of my then sporting heroes, Lance Armstrong, at the end of the season.

Best of all, late in 2004 Ann and I bought a beautiful property in the small town of Aston Clinton in Buckinghamshire. It put us close to the heartland of British motor racing, with Silverstone close at hand; it's not so far from Heathrow and other airports, which is always a major consideration when you lead the life of an F1 driver; and it is a listed building, meaning it has certain heritage features that make it part of English history. Annie in particular has poured a lot of time and effort into the house; the dogs and I have become familiar with every blade of grass on every track around the place. It must have been a good decision: I've been there longer than I was with any of my racing teams and we have no intention of leaving!

8

'This Can't be Happening . . .'

During my two years at Jaguar Racing its marketing guru, Nav Sidhu, came up with the idea for the team to generate some publicity by getting on the bandwagon with a couple of blockbuster movies which were just about to be released in the UK. The first one was *Terminator 3: Rise of the Machines* in 2003. The premiere took place on the Monday evening after the British Grand Prix, where I had raced with a promo for the film on the side of my Jag.

I had the dubious honour of driving the R4 up the red carpet in Leicester Square in the heart of London, wearing my tuxedo, with the whole cast, Arnold Schwarzenegger included, in attendance! Mum, Dad and a friend from Australia were over at the time and they joined Ann and me for the screening. We were separated when we got inside the cinema, but we had already agreed that it probably wasn't our kind of movie and that they should keep an eye out for us leaving about 20 minutes into the film and follow us a few minutes later.

I duly slipped out after 20 minutes. Annie followed me a few minutes later and we waited . . . and waited. I couldn't work out why Mum and Dad hadn't appeared, so I went back inside on the pretext that I had forgotten something. Our seats had been next to Jenson Button, who still had a close contractual relationship with Williams at that time, and he gave me a very odd look when I came back, started rummaging around and then disappeared back outside again. Still no sign of Mum and Dad! This went on for a while; Annie went back in and did the same as I had just done, so by this stage JB must really have been wondering what the hell was going on! Annie then went and fetched an usher with a flashlight and the two of them went looking.

This time Mum and Dad must have spotted her. We certainly couldn't have made it more obvious if we'd tried. Still no sign. By now I was fuming as I wanted to get home but we had all come in the same car. So Annie and I headed off round the corner for a bite to eat.

The story is important because it was the unlikely start of my relationship with one of the greatest names in F1. When my phone rang a few minutes later, it was not my parents, but Sir Frank Williams. He said that much as he would like me to join his team for the 2004 season, his existing drivers were still under contract.

But he would be happy to have me in 2005.

*

Sport's a lot like life. In the end, it's the people in it who matter – not the numbers, not the statistics, not the petty politics but the people like Sir Frank Williams, founder of Williams Grand Prix Engineering, who live through their sport and are driven by the desire to excel, whatever the circumstances they find themselves in.

In March 1986 Frank found himself in circumstances he could never have imagined. A racer through and through, Frank by his own admission was driving his rented Ford Sierra too fast for the road to Nice airport after an F1 testing session at the Paul Ricard circuit in the south of France. When the almost inevitable accident happened, Frank suffered severe spinal injuries that left him a quad-riplegic, paralysed from the shoulders down. But almost 30 years later Frank is still at the helm of the World Championship-winning F1 team that carries his name.

Over the years Williams had attracted drivers of the stature of Nelson Piquet, Nigel Mansell and my boyhood hero, Alain Prost. In 1994 he had finally got his man when Ayrton Senna left McLaren to join Williams. Within weeks the great Brazilian driver was dead, killed in one of Frank's cars at Imola in northern Italy. It was a blow almost as devastating as the one Frank suffered on that road in France eight years earlier. If you looked closely at a Williams F1 car in 2014 you would see the familiar double-S logo and the words 'Ayrton Senna Sempre' – 'Ayrton Senna Always' – to mark the 20th anniversary of his death.

Sport's a lot like life in another important way. Some-times the heart rules the head, because sport is emotion or it is nothing at all, and sometimes our passions run away with us. When a man like Frank Williams called me and asked if I would like to drive for him, how could I say 'No'?

Flavio wanted me to go to Renault after my spell at Jaguar. His master plan had been to have a Webber–Alonso pairing by 2005 and we were on the brink of it. But I looked at Williams – the man and the team – and I saw pretty well everything that I liked in Formula 1. My compatriot Alan Jones had helped Williams win their first titles at the start of the 1980s. Drivers as different as the stylish Piquet and the bulldog Mansell had won countless races in their cars. The name and the man behind it had been enough to lure Senna away from the team that took him to his three world titles. More importantly, the Williams team had emerged from its recent doldrums to win the last race of the 2004 season in Brazil.

Their current drivers Juan Pablo Montoya and Ralf Schu-macher were both moving on at the end of 2004; Williams wouldn't name my teammate until months later but obviously they were pretty keen to get the deal with me done and dusted and I took that as a feather in the Webber cap. In fact my new teammate was to be a German by the name of Nick Heidfeld. 'Quick Nick' had won the 1999 F3000 title; since then he had been to the short-lived Prost team for his F1 debut in 2000, moved on to Sauber for three seasons and spent 2004 at Jordan.

For me, the decision was easy. I followed my heart. The interest in me from Williams had begun as early as my sixth race with Jaguar. At the A1-Ring in Austria in May 2003 I set the third-fastest lap of the race, bettered only by the two Ferrari drivers, Michael Schumacher and Rubens Barrichello, and even then I was only five hundredths of a second behind the Brazilian.

Williams started sniffing around, and just over a year later the approaches became serious. Ann and I thought this was, at last, the opportunity to launch ourselves. I remember driving the race-winning Williams from Brazil 2004 at the end of that year and thinking, 'This is going to be awesome.' The Webber backside was going to be in a car previously graced by names like Jones, Reutemann, Piquet, Mansell, Prost, Senna, Hill, Villeneuve . . .

The deal first offered in 2003 was confirmed on 28 July 2004, and I called it 'the most significant milestone in my career to date'. As a result I endured the lowest time in my entire F1 career.

*

FW27 was the first car to come from a new group of Williams people headed up by my compatriot Sam Michael. Sam had just been named Technical Director in succession to Patrick Head, the design genius behind Williams's early title-winning cars, who had been made Director of Engineering. Williams were making sweeping changes; they had also appointed a new aerodynamicist in Loïc Bigois, who came with serious credentials, and the chief designer of the new car was Gavin Fisher. But they seemed to have been caught out by late regulation changes to F1 aerodynamics for 2005.

When I drove the FW27 at Jerez early in January I somehow posted the quickest time, but without telling anyone I privately thought, 'Bloody hell, we're gone . . .' As early as that first test I rang Ann and told her we'd made the wrong decision. Ironically there is a moment in *Terminator* 3 when one of the top brass trying to counter the latest invasion says disbelievingly, 'This can't be happening.' I knew how he felt.

All of us in the F1 paddock broke one long-standing record in 2005: with 19 races between 6 March and 16 October it was the longest season in the sport's history to that date. Bahrain and China had come on to the calendar in 2004; in 2005 they were joined by another new venue, Turkey, which would be the scene of some drama in my own career a few years later. The tweaks continued: we weren't allowed tyre changes mid-race, which may have been a contributory factor as Ferrari's six-year stranglehold over F1 came to an end. They were a Bridgestone team, and the change seemed to suit Michelin better. McLaren were super-strong, as you would expect from a driver line-up of Räikkönen and Montoya, but there was a young Spaniard by the name of Alonso who threw a spanner in their works.

A second test with my new team in Barcelona later in January was followed by a pre-Australian Grand Prix publicity stunt that involved me driving a Williams F1 car over the Sydney Harbour Bridge – quite an eerie experience with no other traffic allowed up there with me.

That year's was the 10th Australian Grand Prix to be staged in Melbourne, and for me it was a pretty exhausting week of media engagements and behind-the-scenes stuff that left me once again relieved and happy to get into the paddock and shut the gates behind me.

The race itself was low-key, to say the least. I qualified third in the new split format, but that didn't translate into a top-three finish because I got bottled up behind David Coulthard's Red Bull Cosworth and came home fifth. Oh yes, and Giancarlo Fisichella, Fernando's teammate, came out and won the first race of 2005 in a Renault. Talk about rubbing salt in the wound!

After Melbourne we went to Malaysia, which should have brought my first podium. But I touched wheels with Fisi between Turns 15 and 16: as I was passing him, he got on the dirty stuff on the inside of the next corner, his rear tyres were shot, he braked too late, needed to use me to get his car round the corner and ended up on top of mine. I had a taste of what was coming when Patrick Head, who was still very much a driving force at Williams, got stuck into me about that – 'stupid place to pass' and other comments along those lines. Two sixth places in Bahrain and Spain were some consolation, even though I believed we were doing far too much of our learning about FW27 in the races themselves rather than having the car sorted out by the time the red lights went out.

Thank goodness for some light relief: Barcelona brought one of those occasional rewarding experiences I have enjoyed so much through my career in the form of a pro-am tennis tournament staged by Barcelona-born tennis star Arantxa Sánchez Vicario and her brother Emilio, no slouch on court himself.

With the help of my compatriot Chris Styring, who also organised tennis hit-outs in Melbourne to help the Mark Webber Challenge Foundation, they always put it together superbly: there were several of the top Spanish stars there (and it was an eye-opener to realise just how huge tennis is in Spain, particularly on clay), but there were also French players and a handful of people from other sports, includ-ing me. It was my first snapshot of being on court with professional players and seeing how phenomenally good they were. The mutual respect among elite athletes from different disciplines is obvious, and those tennis players were just such great people to be with. If memory serves me correctly I actually won the tournament once, but I think the standards had been deliberately lowered to help the amateurs! Interestingly, one of the photographs we have from those days shows a young Andy Murray standing at courtside looking on. He obviously learned from what he was watching!

Then came Monaco. The Monte Carlo race did bring that long-awaited first podium, but it was a disaster. I had absolutely towelled Heidfeld all weekend, every session. In the race we were stuck behind Fernando; the team made a call to bring Nick in and make a pit stop, which I'd had in mind because I was worried about losing more track positions. The way it worked out, I was pissed off that they gave Nick the chance to stop, come back out, enjoy two laps in free air and jump Fernando that way. I lost a position to my teammate, finished third to his second, and my engineer was livid. Heidfeld's engineer had a lot better relationship with the man in charge of Williams's strategy than mine did, so it was a bit of internal fun and games, which is why I was disappointed. I knew I was better than my teammate all weekend and he finished up on a higher step to me, that's what made me look so unhappy.

The Nürburgring was another no-score even though I qualified on the second row again. I was taken out by Montoya's McLaren while I was trying to defend my position against Trulli and Alonso, but fifth place in Canada in mid-June – my first points in Montreal – poured a little oil on what were clearly troubled waters. And then Indy! That was the year of the absolute shambles over the tyres when only six cars actually raced. Ours weren't two of them.

Before we got there I was caught up in a little adventure that's worth recounting. I was asked to do another appearance, and for once I was really looking forward to it. This one involved a group of us – Alex Wurz, for one, and some NASCAR drivers as well – going to Colorado for a three-day cycling camp at which there would be some pretty serious scientific testing to go through. It was being put together by Morris Denton of AMD, then sponsoring Ferrari, and Chris Carmichael. Anyway, off we go to Montreal airport on Sunday evening post-race, check in, see our bags trundle away on the conveyor belt, and shortly after learn that we can't actually fly to Chicago to pick up our Colorado flight because the city's O'Hare airport has been closed in by bad weather. Too late for those bags – they're on their way. Frank's personal pilot heard about our plight and came up with the perfect solution. They were going to fly down to Indianapolis later in the week, the North American races being back-to-back: why didn't we borrow the plane, with Frank's blessing, to get to our interim destination?

Great plan, until we were informed that we couldn't take off in Canada and land in the US in a private aircraft without a full US visa, and we were travelling on the visa waiver system. No problem: the resourceful pilot suggested they take the plane over, land at Burlington, very close to the border, and meanwhile we cross over in a rental car and pick up the flight from there.

Then we discovered that the same visa issue would stop us: you couldn't do a one-way trip in a rental car either. Talk about trains, planes and automobiles! By this time it's early Monday morning; eventually, somehow, we got hold of a van that deposited us on the airfield to pick up the flight to

Colorado – and our bags were waiting for us there! Doubly amazing because we had gone to great lengths to explain, after the Montreal check-in fiasco, that they should be sent to Indianapolis. Bear in mind that this is security-conscious America post-9/11: where those bags had been and how they got to Colorado I will never know.

Once we all, bags and drivers, finally got to the famous Brickyard it was pretty clear early on that trouble was brewing. There were monster shunts: my former sports car teammate Ricardo Zonta, test driver for Toyota, was the first to find himself in trouble, on the infield section on Friday after his left rear tyre failed. Worse was to come. That afternoon Ricardo's Toyota teammate Ralf Schumacher went into the wall hard on the banked Turn 13 when, he said, he felt something give way on the left-hand side of his car as well. The medical men forbade him from taking any further part in the weekend.

So alarm bells were ringing early on about the casing on the Michelin tyres, and we were experiencing a lot of loading on that side of the cars on the Indianapolis banking. Ironically it was Jarno Trulli in the other Toyota who grabbed pole position on Saturday, but that turned out to be a furphy as they had put a thimbleful of fuel in the TF105 to rescue some good publicity, and possibly because they already knew their man would not be in the field the following day. I qualified ninth, with a disgruntled teammate back in 15th between the two Red Bulls.

Ours was not a happy camp for other reasons, namely the widening rift between Williams and our engine partner BMW, but there were more immediate problems to contend with. We had our normal team meeting that night, and it never crossed our minds that we wouldn't be racing next day. We just thought there would be some magical solution. Different tyre pressures, a change of camber on the wheels, and it would be all right on the night. The show would go on.

But in the background Michelin were in a state of near-panic. At Williams we drivers were kept a little bit in the dark. There was a further meeting that night down in the pits with all the Michelin teams' technical directors trying to work out what to do. The French company had brought in some different casings by then, a stiffer sidewall meant originally for the Barcelona race; in fact they threw everything at the problem overnight. On Saturday morning one of the Williams cars had a bulge on the sidewall of a tyre, which is the first indication that the tyre in question is about to fail. We limited ourselves to short runs, said we'd do qualifying, take it from there and have a look at our options for the race. Everyone got through the qualifying session and the tyres were fine.

But Michelin were adamant that the specification of tyre available to us was not guaranteed safe for racing speeds unless those speeds could somehow be reduced through the banked section of the famous oval. Don't forget Michelin were supplying two-thirds of the field, but they'd got their calculations wrong and we couldn't use these tyres on this track. So then it was down to the FIA and Michelin to work things out. There were a lot of voices from within the Bridgestone and Ferrari camps, saying the show must go on, which is understandable when you are at one of the temples of motor sport and people have come from all over America to see what's supposed to be the absolute pinnacle of motor racing taking place in their own backyard.

By now it was all about these fans and what we could do to give them something for their money and their support. In the end we couldn't find a way to do anything. Whenever some compromise was put forward the response was just 'No, no, no', there was no real flexibility. We were not going to take part in the United States Grand Prix. Early in the season, assessing the new Williams, I had said to myself, 'This can't be happening.' On the Indianapolis grid I came across Bernie Ecclestone and he was saying, 'This shouldn't be happening . . .'

But it was happening. It was bizarre, really, getting ready and knowing you weren't going to do the race – in front of 130,000 paying customers who had come expecting to see a Grand Prix. We did the formation lap, then all of the Michelin-shod runners peeled off, the Ferraris blissfully raced off into the distance and that was the Grand Prix of America that year! It was the one race Michael managed to win all season. By the way, it was also the last time a team known as Minardi ever scored points in Formula 1: Christian Albers and Patrick Friesacher were two of the other four drivers on Bridgestones! We were booed as we were leaving the track, and no wonder. I really felt for Michelin because they are a brilliant company, with top people. They just got it wrong.

The Indianapolis fiasco came about largely because of the disunity among the people at the highest levels of the sport. The same applied to us as a group of drivers. As the movie *Rush* showed so well, it's nothing new for drivers to have wildly varying opinions, especially when it comes to the biggest issue of all: safety. One of the most absorbing aspects of today's F1 racing, as it was back then, is the activities of the GPDA, the Grand Prix Drivers' Association, in which I was a pretty active participant for much of my F1 career. Interestingly, it was Michael Schumacher who first approached me to play an active role just a couple of years into my own F1 career.

The Indianapolis affair was one of the most challenging periods for the GPDA during my close involvement. As the situation developed we had Michael clearly taking a position with Max Mosley, the FIA President, who was insisting that the race go ahead; the rest of us in the GPDA were worried about safety, because if you had Michelin tyres clearly it was a problem. David Coulthard took a phone call from Max, a pretty stern one, saying 'Pull your head in,' which we weren't happy about as a group. Michael didn't really support us much, so David, Jarno, Ralf Schumacher and I got together and compiled a petition saying we weren't happy with the way the issue had been handled and we'd like to do something better in the future. Even the Bridgestone drivers signed. All except Michael.

Ralf said to me, 'Mark, you should go and talk to Michael about it.' I said, 'Bloody hell, why don't you go? You're his brother, surely you can make him listen?' Michael was much closer to the FIA than the rest of us. He attended a lot of their meetings on safety and technology and was much more up to speed with developments. Some of the younger drivers were probably intimidated by him, but I wasn't. Every now and again he would side with us but if a change wasn't what Michael wanted, then it didn't happen. When Michael left I think the atmosphere in the GPDA got a bit warmer. We were keen to feel that if anything ever did go wrong or we needed to take a stance or a position on an issue, we'd try to make a united front – not always easy when so many different cultures are represented on the grid. We all tick differently. But we tried to take a leaf out of Jackie Stewart's book, because for him driver unity was paramount: in his day guys were being killed on a pretty regular basis.

Other points of contention were Max Mosley's plan to have us pay enormous fees for the mandatory super-licences (we would never have won that battle if we hadn't been unanimous), twilight racing in Melbourne, cockpit safety, a discussion prompted by the death of Henry Surtees, the son of John Surtees, the only man to have been World Champion on two and four wheels, or new venues like Singapore and its night race.

But the GPDA has its lighter side, too. I remember one meeting where Felipe Massa piped up and said, 'Hey guys, I've been thinking . . .' and all of us just fell about laughing. 'Felipe, surely not? Don't tell us – put it in the minutes! Write it down . . . Felipe's been thinking!'

Once we had stopped rolling on the floor we remembered to ask him exactly what he had been thinking.

Back comes the little Brazilian: 'Aw, shoot, I've forgotten what I was going to say!'

*

Hard as it may seem to believe, our 2005 season went downhill from that June low point in the USA. At Magny-Cours the aero 'improvements' we put on the car were actually more of a hindrance than a help. More significantly for me, my cockpit overheated when a rubber grommet inserted to block an unused aperture dropped out and the heat from an electronics box outside my cockpit built up to unbearable levels. I've still got the scars on my right hip to this day.

Meanwhile Nick pitted repeatedly in the other car in the second part of the race as his fears about the car's suspension grew. I opted out of a test session in Jerez to allow my French burns to heal a little more, had a first-lap accident in Germany that damaged a track rod in the suspension . . . and then the brown stuff *really* hit the fan.

To some extent it was a relief to get to the last race in Hungary at the very end of July before the European summer break. I should have remembered that this would be my 13th race in a Williams. My first dozen had yielded the princely total of 22 points and 10th place in the Drivers' Championship, 55 points and nine places shy of the man whose Renault teammate I might have been, Fernando Alonso. Nick and I came home sixth and seventh respectively in the Budapest race. I said at the time that seventh place and a couple of points was a nice way to go into the summer break, but that little note of optimism was quickly snuffed out on the first Monday of that otherwise welcome three weeks off.

Frank and Patrick summoned me to Williams HQ in Grove, Oxfordshire, that day to tell me they were 'massively disappointed' with my performance in their car. The results hadn't met their expectations of me. Patrick delivered most of the dressing-down, then asked if I had anything to add.

I felt like telling them where to poke their drive, but all I said was, 'Actually no, see you later.'

To cap things off Patrick and Frank finished by saying, 'We've got you for another year but if there's a way we don't have to have you that would be fine.'

'Okay,' I thought, that's a nice way to start the break.'

From then on I just worked for myself. I didn't go to the factory as much, my relationship with the team was pretty distant. The boys on my car were good, but it was the first time I had struggled with the management of a racing team, and this was the one where I had expected to feel most at home. I turned up at the next race and just got on with driving the car.

Socially I always got on well with Frank, Patrick and Sam Michael and their respective families. I went to the speedway in Swindon with Sam and Loïc Bigois, too, in fact speedway became a regular feature of our race weekends: we used to settle down in the motor-home to watch it, with a bunch of Williams personnel who were two-wheeled nutters, me supporting the Aussies like Jason Crump and Leigh Adams while they were cheering on the Poms. People from other teams would join in; to me it was a nostalgic snapshot of what life in the paddock must have been like before everyone got caught up in their own little F1 bubble.

I went to Grove expecting that sort of togetherness. Williams should have suited me down to the ground. From the outside they looked as if they were doers, racers, they wanted to get on with the job. You learn the truth quite quickly.

I don't need an arm around me, but I do need to be among people who enjoy their work, and the majority of the people at Williams clearly weren't in that category. In fact they looked as if it was the last place they wanted to be. To walk into that factory after being at Jaguar was like walking into a morgue. They'd hardly lift their chin away from their computer and I thought, 'This can't be right.'

And I've been proved right. It was never like that at Red Bull and we enjoyed tremendous success as a team.

I don't know why Frank and Patrick bothered to ask me if there was anything I wanted to add, because they would never listen to anything I said in the first place. They didn't need help, they were still living off their past successes. I haven't met many, in fact I haven't met *any* drivers who loved their time at Williams. I've never heard anyone, be it an engineer or whoever, describe Williams as a brilliant working environment.

Frank is an inspirational person: the guts and determination he's shown for so many years is phenomenal. He is clearly one of life's special individuals. To give you an insight into his competitive streak, he used to ask me how long it took me to get from home to the Grove factory and I found myself trying to set personal best times to see how I stacked up! But as a race team? Williams wasn't for me.

I could see that Sam Michael was massively overloaded, working 70–80 hours a week, and Loïc Bigois looked like a man who simply never saw daylight. I tried to tell Frank: key personnel need to be motivated and happy, they've got homes to go to, they've got partners and children, surely he could at least find a PA for Sam to take some of that load off his shoulders. It cut no ice with Frank.

At Jaguar I used to compile my own reports every two to three weeks, suggesting areas where I felt we could work together to improve the car – which is the object of the bloody exercise – and it went down well. Not at Grove: they wouldn't have any of that. It took me six or seven months to work out that I was banging my head against a concrete wall, so I just had to go out and drive the car, however bad it was.

What I hadn't understood before putting pen to paper was that the Williams–BMW partnership was a vessel heading for the rocks, and I was part of the shipwreck. First their engine-supplier, then key sponsor Budweiser: Williams were losing support right, left and centre. By season's end it was also announced that Hewlett-Packard would no longer be the team's naming rights sponsor.

For me the timing simply couldn't have been worse. I should have gone to Renault, which Dad was very keen for me to do. In 2005 Fernando won seven races and became, at that time, the youngest World Champion F1 had ever seen. If only . . .

But to go to Renault with Flavio's company managing both Fernando and me was going to feel strange. For business reasons it would have been risky to have both their drivers in the same team – there could only be one winner and the other would lose value. Renault hadn't done anything prior to that either. No one could have predicted what they achieved in 2005 and again in 2006.

In the early stages I was still trying to be as positive as I could. This was Williams. It would turn around. It wasn't until the middle of the year that I thought, 'You're dreaming, it's not going to happen.'

The first race after my visit to the headmaster's study took us to another new F1 venue, Turkey's spectacular if slightly remote Istanbul Park. I had two rear punctures, which was because of the diffuser hitting them, but apparently that was my fault too. Eventually I tried to pass Michael and he wasn't too keen on that idea so we crashed. I was fourth at Spa, which should have been a podium: I couldn't believe the team put me on new intermediate tyres at a time when we needed scrubbed ones on a drying track. In Brazil we saw Fernando win the World Championship for the first time. I was genuinely happy for him. As I wrote in my BBC column at the time, I liked his way of going about the job: turn up, get in the car, no fuss or drama, just get it done. I was miles away from being where Fernando was, but at the end of 2005, at Suzuka, a little carrot was dangled in front of me when I finished fourth again, battling with McLarens and Renaults, after what felt like the fastest race I had ever driven in F1: flat-chat from the first corner and 53 qualifying laps to follow!

There were times when Patrick acknowledged that the FW27 wasn't what it should have been. There was a big problem with the wind-tunnels, which I was told were in-accurately calibrated. It was as if they had two watches and they didn't know which one was telling the right time. But I was under contract and in the end no one else wanted to drive for Williams, so I stayed!

All the same, we were already looking for an escape route. After all, my stock had taken a big hit. The team that was supposed to turn me into Australia's next World Champion had taken me to the dizzy heights of 10th place overall. Right now I had to keep things sensible or else my career was finished. As the midsummer break had shown, I wasn't greatly valued within the Williams set-up, so I started thinking only about myself.

In 2005 Williams had scored 66 points. In 2006, when Fernando won seven races and claimed the title for the second year in a row, we managed just 11, of which I was responsible for seven. If you compiled a highlights reel of our on-track efforts it would be very short: there weren't any!

I wasn't the only one feeling the pinch. Midway through 2006 Keke Rosberg, my teammate Nico's dad and the 1982 World Champion, told me Nico had been relieved to get to the mid-season pause to enjoy a break from the Williams environment.

Ironically one of my main memories of that second Williams season revolves around Michael Schumacher, evoking memories of Indianapolis the previous season. But this time the focus was entirely on the man himself.

What if a famous F1 driver deliberately did something on-track on Saturday to spoil his main rival's chances in the following day's race? What if the rival in question was so incensed by this behaviour that he threatened to lie down in front of the famous driver's car on the starting-grid on Sunday?

In 2006 the battle for the World Championship raged between Renault and Ferrari all season long. Monaco was race seven; only one-third of the season had gone. Not quite time for desperate measures, you might think. By that stage, though, Renault's Fernando led Ferrari's Michael by 15 points (in those days it was still 10 points for a win) and Renault were 19 points to the good in the Constructors' standings. As qualifying in Monaco unfolded, Michael had provisional pole – but he knew Fernando still had one run up his sleeve. Coming round on what looked like being his own final run, Michael was quick in sector 1 but slower in sector 2.

And then it happened.

'It' was what looked like an amateurish mistake, except that an amateurish mistake is the last thing you would expect from a man who at that stage had already won all seven of his world titles and the small matter of 86 Grands Prix. Coming into Turn 18, which television viewers will know as La Rascasse after the restaurant that sits inside the hairpin there, Michael seemed to be approaching at something like his usual speed, but he braked so hard for the tight right-hander that the car locked up and he had to regain control. He duly did so, without letting the car touch any of those menacingly close Monaco barriers. No damage to the car, then. There was just one problem: his engine had stalled, leaving the #5 Ferrari inconveniently – or conveniently, depending on where you were sitting – parked in the middle of the track.

Fernando was already well into his own final crack at pole position. At the second sector split the Renault was three-tenths of a second up on Michael's own best time. Pole position was in Alonso's grasp. Except that there was a red obstacle in his way as he tried to get round on to the final sprint to the line.

Fernando wasn't the only one who still had a chance to go quicker: Kimi Räikkönen's McLaren and my own Williams were both still on target to improve. So we came round to find Michael's Ferrari parked up there . . . We didn't read a huge amount into it straightaway, but then the alarm bells started ringing. Michael had provisional pole after his first set of fresh tyres; on the second set of fresh tyres he made a mistake and he thought he was going to be vulnerable; other people were a real chance of taking pole away from him. So he was making sure no one could improve.

The stewards of the meeting thought long and hard about what they had seen and no doubt watched it all again many times over behind closed doors. After several hours the sensational news broke: Michael had been found to have 'deliberately stopped' in the middle of the track, preventing the #1 Renault from setting its final qualifying time. Fernando had said to me at dinner that night in Monaco, 'If he doesn't get a penalty I'm going to finish the formation lap and get out and lie in front of his car!'

Schumacher was relegated to the back of the grid. Alonso was on pole, and my Williams would start from the front row for only the second time since I joined the team and the third in my F1 career to that date.

To most insiders, the punishment failed to fit the crime. Many people were saying Michael should have been excluded from the meeting altogether. Not Jean Todt: the Ferrari team principal was a picture of indignation, saying the stewards had 'ruled out the possibility of driver error'.

Too bloody right! Michael Schumacher making a beginner's error like that? As Keke Rosberg, the 1983 Monaco winner for my Williams team, observed: 'Give me a break . . .'

There had been other notorious Schumacher incidents. In 1997, at the European Grand Prix in Jerez, his Ferrari collided with Jacques Villeneuve's Williams and Michael was subsequently stripped of all his points for that season; in Adelaide in 1994 Michael's Benetton took out Damon Hill's Williams, leaving Michael as World Champion, though no action was taken over that particular incident. On both occasions Michael was leading the title race by a single point. I wasn't racing in F1 in those days, but I was with him in Monaco, I was on track that day and I felt I had a right to my own opinion.

This was the occasion when he disappointed me most. Knowing how Michael ticked, I thought: 'I'm going to confront him at some stage about this, just on my own, I'm going to go and tell him what I think.'

So I did. I went to see his personal PR manager, Sabine Kehm, at the next race at Silverstone and asked if Michael had some time.

I'd had many discussions with him in the past about lots of things – I was a GPDA director because of him, after all – but this was different. I said, 'Michael, I just want to talk to you about Monaco. And please let me finish.' He was very good at interrupting!

I repeated, 'Let me finish what I have to say. You made a decision when you knew things in qualifying weren't going quite to plan. What you were thinking was, "How can I do something now to control the rest of the field?" I want to tell you that first of all I thought it was amazing that you had the presence of mind not to crash the car because you were thinking of your mechanics. You were caught in two minds: damage the car, or save your guys a lot of hassle. That's why it wasn't executed all that well in the end.'

Then I added: 'I was disappointed you did it, really disappointed. I'm not expecting you to tell me if it was for real or not, but I wanted to come and tell you on my own, not in front of everyone else at the GPDA – because for sure it's going to be brought up.'

And he said, 'Mark, sometimes you go down a road and you can't turn back.'

It was exactly what I wanted to hear from him. He told it to me straight and it showed me what he was prepared to do in order to win. I was happy he had the respect for me to tell me the truth. Michael was an absolute phenomenon, but the levels he would go to just to keep being successful . . .

That's the way he was wired, he was such a ferocious competitor, always on the edge. Would *you* be comfortable in your own skin, looking in the mirror, saying, 'This is what I did to achieve some of that success?'

At the next GPDA meeting when, sure enough, the Monaco incident did come up, I was very relaxed about it because I'd taken issue with Michael individually. But some of the other drivers were getting ticked off with me because they claimed I wasn't standing with them. I encouraged some of the other guys to follow my lead and talk to him directly, but obviously they never did.

Back on track, two sixth-place finishes in Bahrain and Imola were the peak of our performance at Williams in 2006. Why? We simply weren't good enough. With FW28 the switch from Michelin to Bridgestone was a big change because feeling how they perform is a big part of a driver's skill set. In fact we enjoyed almost zero continuity. We lost BMW engine power as they moved to join Sauber, and Williams used Cosworth's CA2006 V8 units instead; and in Rosberg I had another new teammate to think about.

The final race of that 2006 season summed it all up. It was in Brazil, as usual in those days, and it was an unmitigated disaster. Both Williams cars were out on the opening lap – because we had tangled with each other. Nico rammed into the back of me; I lost my rear wing, he lost his front. I limped round to the pits to retire; Nico carried on but crashed heavily in the second-last corner and brought out the safety car. My exasperation with Williams came out when someone asked on the radio if Rosberg was on his way back too, and I couldn't resist a misplaced crack at the blond, self-consciously good-looking guy in the other Williams cockpit. 'No, mate,' I answered, 'Britney's in the wall . . .'

My last race for Williams could hardly have gone worse, and my next comment – 'What a waste' – summed up not only that Grand Prix but the whole season. In fact, this could be said of the whole two years I had spent with Sir Frank's team. My second year at Williams was effectively a long goodbye.

In case it all sounds like doom and gloom at Williams, other aspects of life under Frank and Patrick did raise a chuckle, and Jackie Stewart was at the centre of a couple of them. Jackie was still a prominent member of the team through his connections with sponsors the Royal Bank of Scotland. When I first went to the UK one of Australia's most respected motor-racing people, journalist and former top driver David McKay, had mentioned me to Jackie and asked him to keep an eye out for me. He certainly has: Jackie and Lady Helen, and their sons Mark and Paul, have been kindness itself in the intervening years and have included Ann and me in their lives as if we were family. Those Williams years brought my first close professional dealings with Jackie, and an insight into just how meticulous this legend of motor racing could be.

There seemed to be endless demands on us drivers away from the track in those years, and on one occasion in Hong Kong we were due to attend a couple of public signing sessions. Jackie had decided he would like to sign all of his picture cards in the car en route – and that's where the problems began. His PA Niall Brennan had been out on the tiles the previous night and he was still at breakfast when JYS issued the instruction that those cards had to come with him in the car. Unfortunately for Niall, in his less-than-perfect state he took the pile with a few JYS cards on top – and all of mine underneath. You didn't want to be in the gun with Jackie after committing a *faux pas* like that and wasting his precious time.

Jackie loves being well dressed and could never understand my preference for jeans and sweatshirts. Different generations, I guess. In those years he would insist on trying to get me into more acceptable clothes, which meant multiple visits to Dougie Hayward, the Savile Row tailor who had supplied him with his suits for years. Dougie by this time was well into his eighties and found it hard even to move around the shop. His suits were a bit different, to say the least, but the meticulous side of JYS came through again: one cuff had to be a few centimetres shorter so that it would be easy to shoot the sleeve back and display the timepiece, supplied by Rolex of course, underneath.

One of the bonuses of my career at the top level of motor racing was the chances it brought to see and do some different things. Two other moments from the Williams years took me to opposite ends of the spectrum. One was a visit to Iceland for Hamley's, the big London toy store, and that was a cool trip, if you'll pardon the pun. I took Annie with me and we went to the capital, Reykjavik, but I also got the chance to go on a mountain-bike trip out into that unique landscape. So barren, and so remote – so much so that we were all encouraged to hop off the bikes, strip down to the absolute buff and hop into the warm water from the geysers! It was a terrific experience, just one of those little perks that came with the job.

The other end of the spectrum was a trip to Croatia in the recent aftermath of war in that part of the world. One of our marketing people, Matt Jones, had fought in Serbia; we went over there and our trip included a visit to a school. It was an eye-opener in a completely different way: graffiti, barbed wire, facilities as basic as you could possibly imagine. Talk about getting out of the F1 bubble.

Grove was a tough part of my career: I had to restart after that two-year stall. To be honest, it was worse than simply stalling. I had gone backwards, just when I had been travelling nicely. From Minardi to Jaguar to Williams, that was a normal, in fact a very positive progression for a Grand Prix driver. But it's amazing how fast a phenomenal corporation or team – the Lakers, an NRL team, a Williams Grand Prix Engineering – can implode when success is not happening any more. I was there for the first phase of that implosion at Williams.

Frank's one of the most sensational team bosses ever, and that partnership between Patrick and him was deadly for a long period, but when people of their stature fall off by five per cent it's equivalent to a lot more as it filters down: it translates into 30 per cent among the people in middle management and by the time you get to the factory floor you're toast. In fact it wasn't until 2014, with Mercedes power, that Williams really showed signs of becoming a force in F1 again. The dynasty continues with Frank's daughter Claire doing a splendid, unfussy job as Deputy Team Principal.

Ironically Williams did approach me again after those unhappy two years, but by then I was comfortably installed at Red Bull Racing, in a racing environment that suited me down to the ground.

Besides, I often say you do a lot of learning when you get your arse kicked. When you win a race by 30 seconds you don't learn much, not only about that day, but about how to handle yourself and deal with getting beaten. And if you've been beaten fair and square, if you've done everything you can, they're the days when you learn that you've got to come back and work harder. That's what happened to me at Williams. At the end of 2006 my stock was at its lowest since I arrived in F1. My record now read five seasons, 86 Grands Prix, one podium finish, 25 races in the points, of which three had come in 2006, and a career tally of 69 World Championship points. While I had taken some enjoyment from my time at Jaguar, my last two years with Williams had been a period in the F1 desert. Some expert witnesses were ready to come to my defence: the annual review of the F1 year in *Autosport* magazine said, 'Here was a classic gritty Williams driver. The tragedy was, this was no longer the classic Williams team.'

There was only one question in my mind: where to next?

9

Smile Back on
the Dial: 2007

IT'S STRANGE, BUT THE YEARS THAT DEFINED MY F1 CAREER
and gave me my greatest successes are the ones I've struggled to find the motivation to write about. I don't think it's
because I'm disappointed how it panned out for me personally because I've never forgotten where I came from, or
what I managed to achieve. When I left Australia to follow
my dream, I was determined to stay in Europe for as long
as possible. That could have easily been no more than six
months but as it turned out, I'm still racing 20 years later
and remain a paid professional, and we're becoming few and
far between these days.

The real problem stems from the fact I fell out of love
with Formula 1. I was disappointed to discover a darker side
of the sport which I was unaware of when I was racing for
lower-ranked teams. But when there are race wins and championships at stake and the big money that goes with them, you

enter a world where you simply become a pawn in someone else's game, where politics and hidden agendas are the order of the day. I remember Sir Frank Williams saying when I signed for his team that I was the most apolitical person he had ever met in F1. I knew what the word meant all right but I couldn't understand why he would use it; after all I was just a racing driver so what did politics matter . . .

Disillusionment with life on the inside, as it were, was increasingly matched by disappointment with how the sport was evolving. I'm old-fashioned; as a Grand Prix driver I loved to race and liked those races to be sprints from start to finish. In recent years, that component has been diluted almost to the point where the drivers are either vastly over-qualified for the job they have to do or the job has become so easy that anyone with half an idea could graduate to F1 with relative ease. Where once being granted an F1 super-licence was a privilege and something you aspired to – you could only get one if you had finished in the top three of an FIA-affiliated championship – in more recent years it seems you can apply for one on the back of a cornflakes box!

I also became frustrated with the sanitising of the sport and how attempts were made to quash any kind of indi-viduality, which is why larger-than-life characters are sadly missing from the sport these days. I found it insulting to be told what my response should be to certain questions, sometimes about subjects that carried us outside the safe (or blinkered) confines of the paddock – like going to race in Bahrain, where the escalating civil unrest had resulted in the 2011 race being cancelled. I was carefully drilled by Red Bull Racing's PR machine about what to say – or not to say – to the media so it didn't go down well with RBR's powers-that-be when I said to the press, 'So, Bahrain?' and tried to answer their questions as honestly as possible. I was a grown-up, a man in his mid-30s at that time, and funnily enough, I was capable of forming an opinion and was interested in what was happening in the wider world beyond F1.

This is such a sad feature of F1 nowadays; at one stage at the height of the Max Mosley sex scandal I was asked my opinion, and Red Bull Racing's Dr Helmut Marko actually said to Ann that we should try not to buck the system, just play the F1 game whenever we found ourselves in the paddock. Maybe it was his way of warning us about how to behave to get ahead, but he didn't like it when Ann politely asked if that meant checking our brains in at the turnstiles on the way in!

After the debacle at Grove I didn't want to argue with Flavio again. He had said Renault, I had said no, and Alonso had ended up with two world titles in a row! When Flav started nudging me towards Red Bull Racing, I could see the sense in that, and the potential they had in their ranks.

There was the initial attraction that Red Bull Racing had been built on the foundations of Jaguar, my old team, which meant a return to familiar territory at Milton Keynes. Ford had decided to offload its F1 racing arm in the European autumn of 2004; while Red Bull got it at a fairly good price, Dietrich Mateschitz, the Austrian billionaire behind the Red Bull brand, made a three-year commitment to keep it going. Three years is a long time in Formula 1, so he was clearly prepared to invest some of the money coming from worldwide sales of his famous energy drink, launched in his native country in 1987.

Dietrich is a modest and private man who shies away

from the spotlight. I only ever saw him at one or two Grands Prix or tests each year as he wasn't involved in the day-to-day running of the team, leaving it to the people he had put in charge. But over time I got to know him better away from the racetrack and would visit him regularly at his office situated within Red Bull's Hangar 7 at Salzburg airport in Austria. He has a great passion for aviation, and Hangar 7, an edgy building with a futuristic look about it, is home to his amazing Flying Bulls collection of historic planes and helicopters, and numerous Red Bull-sponsored racing cars.

Within a year of the Jaguar purchase Dietrich Mateschitz and former Austrian F1 driver Gerhard Berger had also acquired another of my former teams: Minardi, renamed Scuderia Toro Rosso or 'Team Red Bull' in English. I knew Christian Horner, the Englishman appointed to head up Red Bull Racing trackside, from my F3000 days. He used to race himself but was honest enough to recognise he didn't have the talent to make it to F1 and so did the next best thing and set up his own race team, Arden, with his father, Garry, who helped fund it.

I knew Christian well enough to have the odd conversation here and there and it was obvious he had a big passion for the sport. However, I had no idea then just how lofty his ambitions were, nor the motives that inspired him to become such a force in F1. In later years I got to know him a lot better as we flew to races together. Ann and Garry went into business together with a GP3 team and we socialised regularly with the Horner family. Initially Christian did well to keep his feet firmly on the ground as he started to mix in supposedly higher circles, but inevitably you could see him being seduced by the trappings of an F1 lifestyle.

It wasn't all negative: he's ambitious, a good politician and he has worked hard to be accepted in the right places. But, because he likes to keep everyone happy and doesn't like confrontation, over time he's become less than consistent and I eventually found I couldn't rely on what I was being told.

So Red Bull Racing came into F1 in 2005, the phoenix out of the Jaguar ashes. In their second season, 2006, they had scored more points than Williams, which admittedly wasn't all that hard. The real lure for me at Red Bull Racing was Adrian Newey. He was, and has remained, one of the real technical geniuses of the Grand Prix world; his cars had won umpteen races and many championships for Williams and McLaren. While my time at Williams had been barren, that was in the post-Newey era, as he had already moved to McLaren.

It had been a real feather in the cap for Red Bull to attract him. He joined the team early in 2006 but such is the way F1 works that the 2007 machine, the RB3, was to be the first of 'his' cars for his new team. Not only that, but it would be powered by Renault in a new long-term partnership after RBR's one-season arrangements with Cosworth in 2005 and Ferrari in 2006.

F1 tweaks for 2007 included the move to a single tyre supplier, Bridgestone. The FIA had mooted this possibility some time before and Michelin had decided that, as a company whose entire philosophy was built around racing and the competitive edge, they didn't want to be in a formula that had no competition . . . On the wider F1 scene, Fernando had left Renault for McLaren, where his teammate would be British whiz-kid Lewis Hamilton

– but not for long. And McLaren would find themselves embroiled in one of the biggest controversies in F1 history, with a very large sum of money at its end.

Interestingly, it was another year when that recurrent theme, team orders, enjoyed the headlines, albeit briefly. As a season-long fight between Ferrari and McLaren developed, the FIA investigated the possibility that, in Monaco, McLaren had instructed Hamilton to slot in behind Alonso to protect him from the threat of Räikkönen's Ferrari. No action was taken, but once again it was clear that there were racing situations that could place considerable strain even on the oldest-established teams on the grid. So much so that McLaren's two drivers ended up virtually at war. Fernando's relationship with Ron Dennis at McLaren broke down beyond repair and after one year with the Woking team he was off back to the Renault team where he had obviously felt so much more comfortable.

As I prepared to go racing with Red Bull, there was one small nagging question in the back of our minds. It wasn't a deal-breaker at the time but I wanted to know what the situation was with Helmut Marko. The name will figure prominently in the coming years so it will be useful to know that he is Austrian, he was a schoolmate of 1970 World Champion Jochen Rindt and co-drove a Porsche to victory at Le Mans in 1971. He tried to make the step up to F1 but had his career cut short by an accident at the 1972 French Grand Prix in which a stone pierced his helmet and blinded him in the left eye.

He went on to establish a team of his own, RSM Marko, in F3 and F3000, and for many years was a major contributor to the Red Bull Junior Program and a consultant to Dietrich

Mateschitz. Let's just say he didn't command unquestioning respect around the junior categories because of the ruthless manner in which he dealt with young drivers. Although I was never on his radar or he on mine as our paths never crossed before Red Bull Racing, everyone knew someone he had upset along the way. In fact, I later made a point of asking people from across the generations, including those he used to race against in the 1970s, whether I had simply got it wrong about him and they assured me I hadn't!

Annie and I asked Red Bull Racing Sporting Director Christian Horner about him and he said, 'Just humour him and you'll be fine. He's only involved with the young driver program and you're not a part of that.' Mateschitz–Marko–Horner: how could I have anticipated the influence that this unlikely Anglo-Austrian triumvirate would be exerting over my life for the next seven years?

There was another plus to joining Red Bull Racing: 'DC' was going to be my teammate. David Coulthard had added his own chapter to Scotland's fine record in F1, claiming 13 Grand Prix victories while with Williams in 1994–95 (he picked the right time to be there!) and McLaren, to whom he gave yeoman service from 1996 to the end of 2004. He had been a founding member of the Red Bull team back in 2005 and he deserves enormous credit for his contribution in those early years, particularly in helping persuade them to bring Adrian Newey on board. I knew David and that we could enjoy a really good relationship racing alongside each other.

And so it turned out: the biggest thing I learned from David was how strong and purposeful you have to be in your directions to the team. It's not about building cosy friendships, it's about saying what needs to be said to get the job done. It was good for me to see how direct he was on the professional front, because that side of my driving life had taken such a battering at Williams. DC is also a product of the Jackie Stewart school of charm and grooming! His whole life from a very young age has evolved around motor sport; he doesn't take much interest in other sports. He was surprised, I remember, when I got involved in my Tasmanian adventure race while still active in F1. At the back end of his racing career he launched himself into media work and became a seasoned pro at it. He's just a bloody good bloke to be around. He's a straight shooter and we have a lot of respect for each other.

It was also very refreshing for me to come out of Williams when I did. The initial feeling in my new surroundings was one of relief. Being part of the Red Bull family, I was going to have the opportunity to do lots of fun stuff away from the track, although of course Christian had insisted that the Red Bull Racing focus was firmly on the circuits, where the important work was taking place. Christian had the knack of giving you a bit of a Chinese burn, knowing what you needed to work on without getting carried away with it. He knew the little trigger-points you needed to touch to improve as a driver, but he knew I was pretty self-analytical as well. It was such a different flavour, and it brought renewed drive and motivation.

But when all is said and done, there was one overriding consideration in my decision to go to Red Bull: I didn't really have any other option. F1 treads a fine line between success and failure, and I was teetering on that tightrope as my sixth season as a Grand Prix driver approached. Within a short space of time I got on good terms with the boys at the team, both the factory-based staff and those travelling to the tests and races, many of whom had been there in my Jaguar days. I was living 25 minutes away from the factory and spent a lot of time there. I used to encourage the guys to get into their fitness, organising some mountain-biking as we had done at Jaguar and competing in a few events together. There were occasional excursions to soccer matches, or to Cardiff to watch my fellow Australian Jason Crump in the major speedway events. It wasn't just 'my' boys, either – quite often some of the guys who worked on the other car would join us. If you haven't lived in the UK, it's hard to imagine how long the winter nights can be. They're even longer if you are working late or on the night-shift, so I used to stop in, if I was on the way back from a function, say, and have a chat, or arrange for some pizzas to be delivered.

The smile was back on the dial. But there were a few frowns around the Red Bull camp as pre-season testing unfolded, with Christian confessing in the first week of March that we were about four weeks behind in our preparations. This was largely due to a defect in our wind-tunnel work that Adrian had picked up on and begun to correct, but that four-week time lag complicated our lives because the first race was only two weeks away.

The team's stated aim was to be the leaders of the midfield pack behind the usual big guns, which in 2007 were Ferrari, McLaren and BMW. We would be in the race-within-a-race, the second tier, if you like, which would pit us against Renault, Toyota and Williams. But four races into the season Christian's tone changed: he was fired up about the reliability issues affecting the RB3's early performances that had the media talking about our quality control systems.

My home race weekend in Australia – always something of a test of endurance, both for me and my car – began well enough but a good start was compromised by a poor pit stop when the fuel flap wouldn't open, then wouldn't close. In our high-tech F1 world the boys had to resort to a screwdriver to pry the bloody thing open! It may sound like a trivial problem, but so sensitive are these F1 beasts that the flap staying open meant a 7 per cent loss in down-force at the rear of my car, which pretty much killed my rear wing, and I finished 13th. But at least I made it to the end, which is more than could be said for DC, who chose to demonstrate the inherent strength of a Formula 1 car by taking off across Alex Wurz's Williams in spectacular style at Turn 3 on the opening lap, happily with no harm to either driver.

I reached the heady heights of P10 in Malaysia, then the fuel-flap fiasco hit me again in Bahrain in the third round, where I posted my first Red Bull DNF with gearbox problems to boot. In the circumstances David's fifth-place finish in Spain was a bit of a breakthrough, but it came despite the car rather than because of it as he lost third gear at a crucial stage and had to nurse it to the line. A second DNF in Monaco was another disappointment for me following an engine sensor glitch, an early spin in Canada cost me several places, but then came a breakthrough of my own in the United States. At Indianapolis I enjoyed a race-long duel with Jarno Trulli's Toyota and emerged with seventh place, my first points for my new team at last.

Although I didn't realise its significance at the time, that race was also a landmark for another reason. In

Canada Robert Kubica had survived a stunningly fast shunt in his BMW Sauber, which was great testimony to the work we had been doing through the GPDA and the FIA to improve safety, but medical advice saw him sidelined for the next race as a precautionary measure. Into his seat came a young German who had come through the Red Bull ranks and had competed in Formula BMW. His name was Sebastian Vettel. Born in Heppenheim in south-western Germany, he began go-karting at the age of seven, and with Red Bull funding he had impressed in the junior categories. He made his F1 debut at the ripe old age of 19 years and 349 days and scored a World Championship point by finishing one place behind me in eighth at Indianapolis. In doing so, he became the youngest driver ever to score World Championship points until another Red Bull junior driver, Daniil Kyvat, superseded him in 2014 – one of many record-breaking firsts that Red Bull have made a conscious habit of collecting. In the 2015 Malaysian Grand Prix, 17-year old Max Verstappen lowered the record again when he finished seventh for Toro Rosso!

Indianapolis wasn't the first time Seb and I had crossed paths. I first met him when he did his initial F1 test for Williams at Jerez in 2006. He struck me then as being very young and not yet physically strong enough to hang on to these cars. They were what I call real cars at that time, with massive power on tap, and very tricky to hold in that performance envelope of within a tenth or two on every lap. During that test session, when I asked Sebastian his first impressions, his answer was: 'This is not for me – it's just way too quick!' Jerez is a tricky little circuit with some quick corners, and he was a little bit of a rabbit in the headlights. But a 20-second time differential per lap is a big shift, mentally, for anyone and that's what he was finding out that day.

*

Not long after the start of my first season with RBR, I had to manage a bit of a family upset. When Ann and I moved to our present home at the end of 2004, we bought one another housewarming presents – two 12-week old puppies! Ann's was a Weimaraner she named Shadow and mine a Rhodesian ridgeback which I called Milo after the iconic Aussie chocolate and malt drink! I had been around dogs all my life, but they had been essentially working dogs and I never formed a close attachment to them. Milo and Shadow, in stark contrast, quickly became cosseted and fully signed-up members of the Webber household.

We had come home from the early season 'fly-away' races and noticed that Milo was limping quite badly. Initially we thought it was just a harmless strain, but after numerous tests and X-rays he was diagnosed with cancer in one of his front legs. He was only two and a half years old. Annie and I were at Magny-Cours for the French Grand Prix when the vet phoned to tell us the news. That night we were both a mess and barely slept. When the vet suggested that Milo's life could be saved if we had the affected leg amputated, we didn't hesitate. The week between the French and British Grands Prix became a blur, travelling between home, the vet and the animal hospital where Milo was to have the operation. It went well and he recovered to become the fastest three-legged dog in Buckinghamshire. However, we were warned by the vet there was a slim chance the cancer could return as a secondary tumour in the lungs and that the tell-tale sign would be a cough, so that was always on our radar.

Meanwhile, Silverstone brought some good news with the announcement that DC and I would team up again for Red Bull in 2008, but we weren't able to build on our Indianapolis points for another three races, so it took us until the 10th round of the season to achieve a really significant result.

It came at a place that was becoming quite important in my F1 résumé, the Nürburgring, where I had finished sixth and seventh in my two Jaguar seasons. It was the scene of the 2007 European Grand Prix, where I claimed the second podium of my career and my first for Red Bull Racing. I was helped by the fact that the two BMWs hit each other on the opening lap in the rain. As always seemed to be the case up there in the Eifel Mountains it was wet or drizzly a lot of the weekend and it was all about being on the right tyres at the right time. I put in a long second stint on the dry-weather version and slotted in behind Fernando Alonso's McLaren and Felipe Massa's Ferrari, which had a massive battle for the win. I wasn't all that unhappy to see Kimi's Ferrari retire, either, as that gave me a reasonably clear run home. In terms of pure results, that was the highlight of my debut year with Red Bull, but I should say in passing that the very next race, in Hungary, was one of my best. It was a two-stopper, an epic fight with Heikki Kovalainen's Renault lap after lap, on the limit all day – to finish ninth. A long day at the office for no reward.

Spa-Francorchamps in Belgium is another of the greatest tracks in F1 history. Even though it's now only half of its original 14.8-kilometre length, it still rises, swoops and swerves through the beautiful forested landscape of the Ardennes, close to where the Battle of the Bulge took place in the Second World War. Spa has always been a favourite of mine, and in 2007 I reached the milestone of my 100th Grand Prix there.

However, the world was less focused on me than on McLaren: the news had just broken of their staggering $100 million fine over the spying case involving Ferrari 'secrets'. Not only that, but my Scottish teammate was very low after the death, in a helicopter accident, of his compatriot, friend and rallying superstar Colin McRae on the Saturday of the Spa weekend.

Where we traditionally stayed for Spa was a small family-run hotel called Le Roannay in Francorchamps. It's a quirky place but everyone in F1 would stay there, especially in the days when there wasn't much in the way of decent accommodation available so close to the track. It's convenient, it has its own helipad and right up until my final year in F1 we stayed there and flew in and out by chopper to Liege. That evening, David and Karen Richards (David ran Prodrive, the team with whom Colin enjoyed much of his WRC success) had flown in for the weekend only to be greeted by the terrible news. I heard it over the phone from a distraught Bernie Shrosbree, who had worked closely with Colin when he drove for Ford and was one of the first on the scene when he suffered his huge rallying crash in Corsica. So was my physio Roger Cleary, whom Bernie had recommended to me and who joined Team Webber in mid-2006. David and Karen were so distraught that they left first thing in the morning; unbelievably they had a nasty scare themselves when they had to crash-land their own helicopter in a field in Essex on the way home.

It was hardly any consolation, but back on track I put a good move on Heikki Kovalainen on the uphill run to Les Combes on the third lap and DC did a good job as my tail-gunner against Robert Kubica, so seventh place was mine. It was pleasing to beat the other Renault team but the feeling persisted that we simply weren't quick enough, which had been underlined by mediocre showings in Turkey and Italy. The Spa result was the last real on-track highlight of my first season as a Red Bull Racing driver.

If you want a low-light, look no further than the very next race, at Fuji in Japan. It was a very tough weekend for a number of reasons. One of those was a dose of food poisoning. I'm a great fan of seafood, which we had enjoyed for dinner the previous evening, but by three the next morning I was in big trouble. I was dehydrated and weakened by the time we went to the grid. I couldn't keep anything down and I rang Roger to ask him to come and offer any assistance he could. We took the decision not to tell anyone except Christian, which we did at the track. I was so drained, and it was only shortly before I got in the car that I tried some soup to see if I could keep that down. I couldn't – and the fans nearby must have been shocked by what they saw as I emptied my guts on the grass. I know the Renault mechanics were! The stop–start jolts behind the safety car in the race didn't help either, and I can tell you on good authority that being sick in a racing helmet is not an experience to be repeated.

The other reason why that Fuji weekend was not a brilliant success was Sebastian Vettel. By this time the new

German Wunderkind had switched from BMW Sauber to drive for the rest of the season with our sister team, Toro Rosso. But what he did to me in Japan wasn't very brotherly.

The track itself was treacherous because of heavy rain. There were rivers across the circuit everywhere. The race started behind the safety car and remained that way for the first 19 of the scheduled 67 laps. Once we were allowed to race, I led laps 32–36; shortly after that the safety car was out again because Fernando aquaplaned off on lap 42, hitting a barrier at Turn 6; that left me in second place behind race leader Lewis Hamilton's McLaren with Vettel next in line behind me. We were looking at a podium or even a win, which of course would have been Red Bull's first and a genuine milestone for the team.

I thought if I put pressure on Lewis he might start thinking about the big picture, championship-wise. He was being a bit of a smart-arse behind the safety car, which still had its lights on. The field was yo-yoing back and forward behind him as he worked his car's tyres and brakes. Apparently he was on the horn to his pit wall, asking them to tell Red Bull Racing to instruct me to back off. At one point he veered over to the side, and I drew alongside him to see what he was up to. Vettel had already been a bit wild behind me during the first safety car period, but that hadn't prepared me for what happened next. BANG! It seems he had been watching Lewis's car – and forgotten about mine, so fairly predictably he ran right up the back of me and we were both out on the spot.

After the race I had to go to the medical centre because I was so dehydrated, and deflated because a great opportunity had gone begging. The boys back in the garage took a long time to get over that. I did nothing wrong, and yet I got no reward. I heard later that Sebastian was in tears. I think he was quite frightened to see me the first time after it happened! He got his apology out pretty quickly, and I didn't hesitate when I was asked for my view of proceedings.

'It's kids, isn't it?' I replied. 'They haven't got enough experience. They do a good job and then they f#*k it all up. A little bit of day-dreaming cost both teams a lot of points.'

It wasn't the last time Sebastian would fall foul of safety cars . . . and for our team it was nothing short of a disaster.

I was fifth on the grid for the final race in Brazil but I was out after just 14 laps with another transmission failure. The five points we needed to beat Williams didn't materialise, which was a disappointing way to end that little battle, one I would have enjoyed winning. But at least we found some late-season pace for the people at the factory to latch on to for the winter ahead.

I now had 103 races under my belt and another podium to my record, finishing 12th overall, two places higher than the previous year. But neither I nor Red Bull Racing had set the world on fire. We were still a long way from where we wanted to be.

10

A Challenge of a Different Kind: 2008

AT THE START OF 2008, THERE WAS MORE THAN JUST FI ON my mind when what Ann and I were fearing came true. While I was away testing at Jerez in southern Spain, Ann detected our dog Milo had developed a chesty cough and sure enough, a visit to the vet and an X-ray revealed cancer in one of his lungs. I'd never really understood what it was like to form that special bond with an animal. In fact when I was younger I could never understand why my sister Leanne got so upset when she lost one of her pets. I barely paid any attention, never mind giving her any sympathy. Now it was happening to one of my own dogs. Milo and Shadow were a massive part of our home life; they were my mates and my training companions. I would seek them out as soon as I arrived home from a race and take them for a long walk, just the three of us, as I unwound from the stresses and demands of a Grand Prix weekend.

Arriving home from the test and seeing Milo so over-joyed to see me ripped me apart. He didn't look ill but we knew his condition wasn't going to get any better. Ann and I agreed we couldn't put this brave dog through any more trauma and so we made the heart-breaking call to Anne, our vet, and asked if she would come to the house to put him to sleep. I will never forget that day: the sound of Anne's car on the gravel outside and Milo wagging his tail madly at the thought of a visitor to the house. Totally oblivious to the reason she was there, he was still wagging his tail as she injected the drug. I'm not ashamed to admit I bawled my eyes out as I felt his head going heavy in my hands. His life slipped away and I remember I closed his big brown eyes. It was the worst day of my life. We had him cremated that afternoon and when we returned home, I took myself off for a long run in the dark with some of his ashes in a bag. When I got to certain places he used to enjoy, I stopped to scatter a handful of the ashes. I'm sure if anyone had seen me, they would have wondered what this tearful grown man was doing. I was saying goodbye to a mate.

But the world of F1 stops for nobody and it was only a matter of a few days before the next F1 pre-season test beckoned. I was back on the F1 treadmill, which was probably as good a way as any to manage the emotions I was feeling at that time.

Going into my second season with Red Bull, the top brass at the team were making predictions about finishing fourth in the Constructors' Championship, which would be one better than we had managed in 2007. At that early stage in the team's history Christian was very big on continuity, and that was one thing we did have, not least in the cockpit, where DC and I would be teaming up once more. Pre-season testing suggested the removal of some of the 'driver toys' like traction control might make life challenging for us all, especially on wet tracks. The RB4 had a new gearbox to counter the unreliability of the previous year's, and its weight bias was shifted towards the front. If we wanted to finish fourth overall it was logical to think we were targeting top-eight race finishes; as I tried to point out in an early BBC column, it was hard for people outside the sport to understand that coming sixth or seventh would be a bloody good result as far as we were concerned. It would be like winning the B-class race behind the front-runners, which once again were tipped to be Ferrari, McLaren and BMW.

We were a long way adrift of that ambition in Australia, which again staged the opening race of the season. I qualified a lowly 15th because a brake disc failed on my first run in Q2. It was a shame, because I had run in the top six in all three free practice sessions. I observed that we were lucky we didn't build aeroplanes, or the consequences of our failures might be much more severe, and I was firmly hauled over the coals for saying so.

After a goodish start to the race itself I became caught up in a bit of a Japanese sandwich: the Super Aguri of Anthony Davidson and Kazuki Nakajima in his Williams. My car broke a track rod despite the lightest of touches and I was ready for an early shower.

Things got worse. In free practice in Malaysia David suffered a bizarre suspension failure when the adhesives on a steering arm failed and the suspension simply fell apart when he hit a kerb. Meanwhile I suffered an engine failure on my car and the FIA actually asked for a report on Red Bull Racing's safety, which was not an encouraging start to the year's racing.

Luck seemed to turn our way slightly when I inherited sixth on the grid after the two McLarens were demoted for misdemeanours in qualifying, but I had to work hard to get round a fuel pump problem in the race that cost me as much as 15 seconds on my way to the first points of the season in seventh place.

I spent most of the Bahrain race absolutely on the limit in pursuit of another of those seventh places, then had to fight back from a difficult day and a half with a throttle actuator in Spain to qualify seventh and race to fifth, my personal best since the Nürburgring the previous year. If the car had been letting me down here and there, the tables were turned in Turkey: it was the driver who made a mistake in Friday practice on the Astroturf at Turn 6, which was still wet from an earlier shower. I dropped a wheel and ran out of talent, as we say. It was the first time I'd bent the car for quite a while. My race wasn't one of the most exciting I've been involved in and another seventh place was duly racked up.

And so to Monaco, for the first time without traction control. The week was difficult for a personal reason when a close friend I was cycling with was hurt in a road accident and had to have almost 100 stitches in his wounds. I had organised a cycling camp in France late in the week before Monaco, with Lance Armstrong, his good friends Morris Denton and Mike Scott, Troy Bayliss and my Renault engineer Pierre-Emeric Benteyn. We were out for one last ride on the Wednesday before the Monaco weekend got underway. Out near Menton there were some road-works in progress, which meant there was a one-way system in place. We tried to pedal up to the front of the queue, with Morris fourth in line. He was too far out in his lane and had a head-on with the car coming away rather too quickly on the other side. I heard the hit and it was a sickening sound. That was my first experience of thinking something terrible might have happened.

We turned and rode back to find Morris was in a shocking state with deep lacerations from the windscreen glass, injuries to his legs and hip and a massive shiner. You could tell how bad it was by the way he was moaning: 90 kilos of Texan muscle in distress. Lance was in a tailspin and didn't want to go anywhere near the scene, for reasons I have never understood. I tried and failed to get hold of an FIA medical delegate, but eventually we managed to have Morris taken to Monaco rather than going all the way to Nice. He didn't need surgery but they did put in 100 or so stitches. Troy took him a slab of beer, and to cheer him up even more we told him that if he thought he was in a bad way he should check out the 110-year-old bloke in the bed across from his! Riding with Lance was awesome. I'd watched him so many times in the Tour on TV and it underlined my fascination with that sport. After all he had endured it was doubly disappointing to hear him confess to being a drug cheat. He did a very good job to get the most out of his personal history, he put it right out there: he wasn't the only guy who's ever had cancer but he was trying to help other people. If only it had stayed that way.

Perhaps I was fired up by that episode, because I drove to a very hard-earned fourth place in Monaco in what was one of the most mentally draining races I've competed in.

When I opened the curtains on Sunday to a wet track I knew
it was important to show some patience and keep my nose
clean. As the rain came and went and I was fuelled only as
far as lap 48 I didn't really want to come in and bolt on dry-
weather tyres, but by that stage I had no option. I lost time by
the spadeful until the weather eventually relented, and I got
my fourth place back when Kimi hit Adrian Sutil. Take what
you can get and look happy about it . . . But by this stage, six
races into the season, we were joint fourth with Williams on
15 points and 37 behind third-placed BMW Sauber.

*

Back to Helmut Marko. My first glimpse of the behaviour people had warned me about came in Montreal. It
was around that time that DC began thinking seriously
about calling a halt to his long F1 career. In Canada he
told Christian in confidence that he might be making an
announcement at his upcoming home race in Britain. Next
morning Marko joined a gathering of people that included
DC and promptly congratulated him, very publicly, on his
retirement. Diplomacy is not one of Marko's strengths.

Meanwhile that weekend gave us a very popular new
Grand Prix winner in the shape of Robert Kubica. Just a
year after his massive shunt in Montreal he won for BMW,
the first Pole ever to do so. But sadly that remains his one
and only Grand Prix victory, because in 2011 Robert injured
his arm so severely in a rally crash that he has not been able
to return to F1 since. It's the sport's loss.

DC officially announced his retirement in the week
leading up to the next race, the British Grand Prix, and on
the eve of race weekend Sebastian Vettel was confirmed as

his replacement and my teammate for the 2009 season as I had re-signed for a further year. I said in the official release that I had realised as early as the middle of the previous year how much I enjoyed working with the team, I felt we had made good progress in recent months and it was an easy decision to make.

The promotion of Sebastian to the senior Red Bull team was to prove a pivotal point in the success of Marko's Red Bull young driver program. Up until then the results had been patchy, to say the least: three of the casualties included my former Jaguar teammate, Austrian Christian Klien, Italian Vitantonio Liuzzi, the 2004 F3000 champion with Christian Horner's Arden team, and American Scott Speed. Ultimately all three failed to live up to expectations and fell by the wayside. Seb, on the other hand, had been on Red Bull's books since 2000 and was making his way very nicely through the junior categories, all the while being effectively groomed by Marko for F1.

I put the car on the front row at Silverstone but blew it with a spin at Becketts on the very first lap and another one at Luffield much later in the race, but DC was out on the opening lap and stayed out, which was a bitter disappointment in his final home Grand Prix. Low finishes at Hockenheim and Budapest meant Red Bull Racing had gone three races without adding to our points tally.

By the time we finished the next race on the new Valencia street circuit in Spain we were scratching our heads and wondering where all that early-season pace had gone. That European Grand Prix was one of the worst of the 215 in my career, a totally pedestrian affair after our worst qualifying session of the year apart from the accident in Australia.

I spent the better part of the race trundling along, thinking about getting back home and taking the dogs out for a walk. And yes, I do means dogs plural as Annie and I had bought a new teammate for Shadow, another Rhodesian ridgeback named Simba who has featured prominently in our lives ever since.

We had now slipped to sixth overall. To make matters worse, our sister and supposedly 'junior' team, Toro Rosso, was now on a surprise roll with Sebastian Vettel in sixth spot and Sébastien Bourdais in 10th. Twelfth for me and 17th for David suggested Red Bull Racing was a holed ship . . .

We started patching her up in Belgium, thanks to a bit of good fortune on race day. From seventh on the grid I ended up ninth but was promoted into the points when Timo Glock was given a time penalty for passing me under yellow flags on the final lap. It's something every one of us out there has suffered at some stage, so I was happy to take the point and run, especially as I had made a personal promise to Dietrich Mateschitz that I would get myself off the 18-point mark where I had been stuck for what seemed like forever.

The Spa-Francorchamps race was interesting for another decision by the stewards, but this one came two hours after the finish and was, I felt, a bit harsh. Kimi and Lewis were in a terrific scrap for the win and the closing stages illustrated the decisions we have to make in the cockpit in a split second. Lewis tried to force his McLaren past the Ferrari at the chicane before the pit-lane entry, then did the right thing by handing back the position he had gained by cutting the corner. But he got enough momentum off the last corner to pass Kimi at the first, La Source, and went on to win – until the stewards in their wisdom decided to take it away from him two hours later for allegedly gaining an unfair advantage. The whole incident caused a media uproar, with most of the 'real' racers – men like Niki Lauda, for example – insisting that Hamilton had done absolutely nothing wrong. He could have made the move on Räikkönen at a number of places, but he felt he had the opening and decided to do it where he did. Split-second timing . . .

I had a moment of my own in Lewis's company at Monza when I had to take to the escape road at Turn 1, but my eighth place was small consolation as we contemplated another historic moment in the sport: the first and only victory thus far for Toro Rosso – once 'my' team when it was known as Minardi. It was also the maiden Grand Prix win for one S. Vettel of Germany. At the tender age of 21 years and 73 days he became the youngest winner in World Championship history and put another record in the bag for Red Bull. I am happy to acknowledge that it was an incredible drive from pole position. I said at the time that Red Bull was one big family and I was pleased for both teams, but in all honesty it was not one of the allegedly 'senior' team's better days. And now we were seventh, a point behind the 'other' Red Bull outfit.

Next stop: the Lion City, Singapore, for another new street circuit, but this was no Valencia. Not only was the Marina Bay street circuit a brand-new venue, it was also a brand-new concept: the first night race in F1 history. Something like 1500 lights on gantries all around a 5-kilometre layout with 23 corners: this was going to be different, to say the least! I made a point of getting down there early, and I ran the track with Roger. Before we got out there for real I had done

100 laps of the place in my head and I wasn't too unhappy with what I had seen. Sadly that didn't stop me having a Friday 'off' when I nosed the car into the wall at the 90-degree Turn 18, trying to wrestle it round when I should have realised the corner was gone and used the escape road instead. Still, although I could only qualify 13th after hitting traffic – always worse on street circuits – during my last throw of the dice in Q2, the race was promising for a while.

Renault's Nelson Piquet had a strange crash. I dived in for fuel and was going to be able to run longer than Piquet's teammate Fernando Alonso, so a podium was looking good until the halfway point, when my car somehow contrived to engage fifth and seventh gears simultaneously, a bizarre occurrence which was later put down to the surge of electricity from a tramline under the track! It proved terminal, if you will pardon the pun, and when DC broke one of the pit crew's ankles during a pit stop another below-par weekend was complete.

That strange accident of Piquet's eventually turned into 'Crashgate', the scandal over the alleged fixing of the Singapore race result that cost Flavio Briatore and Renault Technical Director Pat Symonds their place in the F1 paddock soon afterwards. Although the full story took a while to emerge, we all knew it looked pretty suss that Piquet's Renault had crashed where it did, and when. The team did all the homework on the best corners to crash, there's no question about it: there was a plan and it included an accident at a place that would guarantee the emergence of the safety car.

Why? Fernando had qualified down in 15th in the other Renault; normally that would prompt the driver to take on a heavy load of fuel and make just one stop if he could.

Renault's strategy was to start him on a light fuel load to try to recover track position. The ideal time for Fernando to have the safety car deployed on that strategy was within those 60 or 90 seconds when his teammate crashed. Staging a crash is not a good idea, although by selecting the 'best' place to have it happen you can eliminate many of the inherent risks and get the result you're after. But for someone to put the idea forward, then go out and execute it? That's an entirely different matter.

Alonso was first to pit after 12 laps; on lap 14 Piquet spun coming out of Turn 17 and hit the concrete wall at a point which was extremely awkward for car recovery and triggered the safety car. At that time its emergence meant pit lane was closed; I was one of three drivers to dive into the pits before that happened. As the subsequent pit stops played out, Fernando moved through the field. The plan to recover track position had worked: he won the race! If he had finished fourth or fifth as the team probably had envisaged, perhaps they would have got away with it. But when the race started coming towards Fernando, he was like a dog with a bone. Give him a sniff and he'll win, because all of a sudden he goes to that next level. He might have thought . . . 'I'm going from 15th to fifth or maybe fourth . . . I'll feel a bit rough if I get on the podium . . . Bloody hell, I've won!'

Many months later the upshot would be swingeing suspensions for both Pat and Flavio but it's equally important to remember that in 2010 the Paris courts rejected the lifetime ban that had been imposed on Flavio by the sport's governing body. He had always maintained his innocence but accepted moral responsibility because he was the man heading up the team at the time of 'Crashgate'. And Pat has now also been restored to the F1 paddock as the man in charge of matters technical at Williams.

For me the whole Crashgate saga was another eye-opener: was there really so much at stake that a respected team would risk losing its hard-earned reputation to secure a result? My thoughts flashed back to Adelaide, a kid climbing trees to catch a glimpse of the passing cars, and his own crazy dream to do what they were doing one day. Another example of Australian naïveté: clearly it's not just about jumping in a fast car and going racing. Especially when you graduate from a small team like Minardi, whose owner was happy to share all the difficulties with you, to a race-winning and potentially title-winning outfit that feels it can stop at nothing to achieve its targets. Not for the first time I felt the guys in the cockpit were simply pawns in a bigger game.

How do you deal with that? The immediate answer was: with difficulty. As the political infighting provoked by the Singapore race developed, there were threats of drivers having their vital super-licences revoked if they opted to stay in the Briatore management camp. Some of the younger, less experienced guys caved in; Fernando and I stayed loyal to the man who had already done so much to shape our respective careers. But the question – how to deal with all the behind-the-scenes stuff – would recur throughout the remainder of my F1 career.

Red Bull Racing's own form dipped for the remainder of the season, largely due to the team switching focus to 2009 and a new car for new regulations. A point for eighth place in Japan was my last visit to the scoreboard for my second year at Red Bull. Brazil, as is so often the case, brought a dramatic conclusion to the season. You had to feel for Felipe

Massa: for just over 38 seconds he and his family thought he was the World Champion. He had just won his home race in front of those passionate Brazilian fans, and his chief rival Lewis Hamilton was seemingly too far adrift to score the points he needed to spoil Felipe's day. That all changed in the last few corners when Lewis clawed his way past Timo Glock's Toyota, which was all at sea on dry-weather tyres on a wet track, to finish sixth, 38 seconds behind Felipe – but now one point ahead and the new champion. Felipe let all his Brazilian emotions show through but he handled what must have been a heart-breaking disappointment very well.

The best thing to happen to me in Brazil was a compliment from DC. His final race was a disaster when he retired on the opening lap but he still had the grace to thank me for making his decision to retire an easy one. 'I just couldn't live with you,' he said. What had helped me through my less successful F1 years was the ability to out-perform my teammates on track, and I had done that with 13-time Grand Prix winner DC as well.

Now I had another teammate to deal with in the form of Sebastian Vettel being tipped not only as the new Michael Schumacher but also as the driver who would finish my career! So said a certain Marko before we had even raced together. I found it an odd statement for him to make, and it sure as hell wasn't calculated to enhance team spirit. But I didn't believe for one minute the whole team management thought that way; this must be some personal axe that he was grinding.

*

The date was 22 November 2008. The new Formula 1 season was due to begin on 29 March 2009. Before that we had a test scheduled at Jerez in southern Spain, starting on 11 February. The experts were all telling me that the arrival of my new teammate, Sebastian Vettel, would present me with the biggest challenge of my career. And I was lying on my back in Tasmania with a broken leg . . .

The one thing the Mark Webber Challenge was not supposed to do was leave its founder unfit for duty! The accident happened on the fourth day of the Challenge. It had started with a 22-kilometre run near Port Arthur, and I had to obey the call of nature before we set off. I had the mandatory orienteering dongle on my finger, which competitors use to clock in at the various waypoints. By the time I got back to the starting line there was no time for reflection – it was 'Go!' About a kilometre into the run I realised I didn't have my dongle, but I knew exactly where I had left it and had to bolt back for it.

Later in the day sea conditions meant the kayak leg had to be rescheduled. Instead we had been on our mountain bikes for about three-quarters of an hour. We were on a typical Australian bush road, about one-and-a-half lanes wide, on a downhill section with a corner at the bottom. I was out in front; the four-wheel-drive coming towards us was probably on the wrong side of those one-and-a-half lanes when I saw it. I couldn't see its driver because the forest canopy had turned the windscreen into a mirror. Not being able to see where his eyes were looking or the position of his hands on the wheel, I was lost: no visual cues to work from. And as I got really close to him I knew I was in trouble because it was too late for me to take the avoiding action I had hoped he might take himself.

My partner on the Challenge was Dan Mac – that's Daniel MacPherson, who will be familiar to many readers from his early roles in *Neighbours*, *The Bill* and other popular television shows. I was lucky Dan was there, because he dealt with things superbly. We had a satellite phone with us but unhelpfully it was in my backpack, which was underneath me on the road. I didn't know what sort of condition I was in and so I didn't dare move to try to retrieve the phone. We decided to wait for the next team to arrive so that we could use theirs. Dan had had a bit of a shunt of his own a few years before, so he stayed pretty calm, apart from getting stuck into the photographers covering the event at one stage in proceedings. He got me warm and helped me make the right decisions, particularly about protecting my spine.

When I hit the front of the car, my right leg bore the brunt of the impact, which sent me spinning down the road. It was Dan Mac who told me how high in the air I went! The driver was unhurt but quite distraught, as you would expect, but when Dad arrived on the scene and came over to me, all I could say was, 'Mate, I'm suffering . . .'

All sorts of thoughts were flashing through my mind as the ambulance people set about straightening out my leg so they could get a pulse going in my foot. Never mind the F1 career everybody was talking about. What if I were to lose my leg? What about damage to my pelvis, my spine?

Mercifully the drugs kicked in pretty quickly and my last memory of the immediate aftermath is asking the helicopter pilot to fly faster as we headed for the hospital. The surgeons inserted a rod in the lower part of my right leg. While I was lying out in the bush Dan had cracked the odd joke, but in hospital he was hilarious. I'm lying there off my face with the pain relief medication and Dan's sitting beside my bed, acting like a loveable rogue. I needed that in the ward – there was a good spirit in there, and it bonded Dan and me pretty tightly.

Not long after my accident – I had just returned to the UK – I received news that put my plight in perspective. I enjoyed a friendly relationship with Pierre-Emeric, the Renault engineer who came on the cycling camp with us before Monaco. I used to joke that we got on well because he had a twisted mind-set like mine. He was a real free spirit who loved giving things a go even when they looked pretty daunting – like the time he had a crack at Mount Fuji in Japan and got pinned up there for a while.

Late in 2008 Pierre-Emeric decided to go climbing in the Andes, with Mount Aconcagua in his sights. Aconcagua – the 'White Sentinel' – is in the Mendoza province of Argentina. At almost 7000 metres it's the highest mountain outside the Himalayas. Pierre-Emeric was climbing solo; he never came back and to this day they haven't found him.

Renault contacted me from Paris to see if there was any help I could offer. Jackie Stewart was the obvious man to call: he knew Nando Parrado, one of the men at the centre of one of the most famous survival stories of recent times. Nando was one of the survivors of a plane crash in the Andes on Friday 13 October 1972; it had been carrying, among others, the Rugby team he played for. After two months trapped up there he and Roberto Canessa set off on an ultimately successful attempt to fetch help. Their story was the subject of a movie, *Alive*, in which Nando was played by Ethan Hawke. Nando wrote his own account of those events, *Miracle in the Andes*, and is now one of the world's finest public speakers. He has given tremendous support to mountain search and rescue services in South

America. But even he was powerless, in the end, to find Pierre-Emeric. Renault left his desk as it was when he left; during my first few Grand Prix victories he was one of the people uppermost in my thoughts.

As for Tasmania, it wasn't until four days later, when I tried to get out of my hospital bed for the first time and felt the incredible pressure in my leg, that I realised just how long the road back was going to be. I had survived with 'only' a broken leg, an open compound fracture of the fibula and tibia. There was also the small matter of a broken shoulder that wasn't diagnosed until I got back to Canberra in the early stages of my rehabilitation.

My career was at stake. The only thing on my side was that when I hit that car I can truly say I was the fittest I have ever been in my life, but that's not what was running through my mind right then. In Formula 1 we hate finding ourselves out of position on the track. Here I was, completely out of position in the world!

I wasn't able to fly for five weeks. I managed to get back to my UK home in time for Christmas to continue with my rehab program there. Roger Cleary, my personal physio, became pretty much the central figure in my life at that stage: he was as keenly aware as I was that the career was on the line and he organised a careful but very intense schedule of work in the swimming pool and on the static exercise bike as well as other specific exercises.

Much to Ann's chagrin, the kitchen at home became a makeshift treatment room with the massage couch permanently set up in front of the Aga oven! I spent most days there dressed in shorts and T-shirts in the middle of winter, having regular treatments from Roger or being strapped to or zipped into various pieces of apparatus all intended to aid my recovery. To speed up the recovery process I also did short, sharp sessions in a cryogenic (low-temperature) chamber.

In January I went to see Dietrich Mateschitz at the extraordinary Hangar 7 at Salzburg Airport. I was still on crutches at that stage so goodness knows what sort of figure I must have cut in the eyes of the team owner! My whole life long I will be grateful for the way he and his team handled me throughout a time which was testing in more ways than anyone had anticipated. Dietrich was the one who led the way. He could have taken quite a different tack, but the way he handled it was awesome. Mind you, I got the basic message loud and clear: 'Mark, what are you doing?' he asked me. 'This is your event! This is not supposed to happen!' He immediately told me they would wait for me to recover, but it would be 'good' if I could be ready for that first Jerez test. He knew me well enough to understand that I would be doing everything I humanly could to get there.

Before mid-January I was able to drive a road car for the first time, although I wasn't actually walking unaided yet. Roger handled an impatient, wounded F1 driver with immense tact and patience. My attitude wasn't a self-pitying 'Why me?' What was hurting me most was the disruption. It's tough enough as it is, preparing for an F1 season, making sure you're happy with the new car, getting to know any new crew members, ensuring you're involved in decision-making processes about car development and generally showing everyone you're ready for another year. Normally at this time of the year I'd be at my physical peak; this year things were very different.

Meanwhile Vettel was settling into the team in my absence; the press were saying this was a turning point as

Red Bull would now put their car development work in his hands rather than the more experienced pair that belonged to me. The psychological games were on for young and old, you might say, and for the time being it was the 'young' who had the upper hand. To tell the truth, all the 32-year-old 'old hand' could focus on was the second week of February and being able to get into the new RB5 for that test session in Jerez. If I couldn't do that, my season might well be shot before it even started. Confidence would be undermined – not only among the people around me, but perhaps even in my own mind.

The 11th of February duly rolled around, and I was not in good shape at all. By now the doctors had removed the top screw from the main pin inserted in my leg and I was in considerable discomfort. Essentially the leg was still broken; the bones weren't knitting because the screws were sitting proud and keeping them apart. There was no way I was going to let anyone else see that, though, so I gritted my teeth and tried to walk as normally as I could towards the car, surrounded by key people like Adrian and Christian. The crucial moment had arrived.

Eleven weeks and four days after my Tasmanian mishap I was back in the cockpit of a Formula 1 car. On the installation lap my first concern was to test my ankle: with so much of the strength in my lower leg gone, could I modulate the throttle satisfactorily? Answer to question 1: yes. Next up: could I cope with the bumps and the kerbs without too much discomfort? It was a little bumpy heading into Turn 1 under braking, and I felt it, but the answer to question 2 was: yes. Next, the bigger picture: was my general level of fitness up to the job in hand – the neck and the G-forces, the aerobic condition? Answer to question 3: yes. Last but not least, the big question: could I do the job I was being paid to do, go flat out and put a Grand Prix car on the limit? Answer to question 4: yes. On my second run I was not only very quick, but I also completed 83 laps. That's more than any Grand Prix we compete in.

Normally we drivers enjoy the adrenaline rush that goes with what we do. This time it was pure, unadulterated relief that swept through me as I climbed out of the RB5, grinning like the Cheshire Cat. With the help of Roger and many other people I had kept my focus and got myself into the condition I needed to be in to pass the first test since my accident. I knew now that I would be on the starting grid for the first race of 2009 back in my home country. Tasmania had left me with a personal challenge to overcome; now another one lay ahead. It would be with me for the remainder of my career in Formula 1 . . .

11

Yes I Can: 2009

I HIT 2009 DETERMINED TO PROVE THAT I COULD PICK UP MY racing life where I'd left off. Before the season got underway, however, I had the chance to see exactly what having to start all over again meant. Australia has a great deal to offer, but our country has one permanent and dangerous enemy: nature. Every now and again she issues a devastating reminder of what she can do. On 7 February 2009 bushfires swept through the State of Victoria on a day that has gone down in history as 'Black Saturday'. On that date 173 people perished, as well as countless birds and animals; 5000 more people were injured; more than 2000 homes were lost; 4500 square kilometres were burnt out. While I had been trying to rebuild a sporting life, people in places like St Andrews and Kinglake were trying to rebuild their entire lives, literally from the ground up.

Once we got back to the relatively insignificant business of Grand Prix racing at Albert Park we quickly saw evidence of some pretty impressive rebuilding of a quite different kind. Brawn GP arrived on the scene and dominated the Australian Grand Prix with a 1–2 finish courtesy of Jenson Button and Rubens Barrichello. Brawn GP was not a new team but a rebranded Honda, which had pulled out of F1 at the end of 2008. Ross Brawn, the mastermind behind Michael Schumacher's successes at Benetton and Ferrari, was the main man and the team ran under his name. Their dominance that weekend was a clear signal to the rest of us that the fight was well and truly on.

When I say 'fight' I can't exactly include Red Bull Racing in the battle. Once again Melbourne was a bit of a grave-yard for the only Aussie in the field. Things were already looking shaky on Friday morning when a driveshaft issue kept me in the pits far longer than I would have liked. Then in qualifying I got a bit greedy under braking at Turn 9 in Q3 and threw away a few grid positions, starting 10th while Sebastian was on the second row.

Worse was to come: on lap 1 Rubens got things wrong at the start, suddenly found a gear and dived under me. That pushed me into Heidfeld's BMW, knocked off my car's nose and cost me a lap. In the end I tootled around at the back of the field to get some mileage on the car and was last man running by the finish. Sebastian picked up a 10-place grid penalty for Malaysia for allegedly triggering a fairly spec-tacular accident with Robert Kubica in the other BMW. Things could only get better, but at least I could report that I was pretty happy with how my recovery from injury was progressing.

Next stop Sepang, Malaysia, where we made a little bit of history as the first F1 race to be stopped since the very wet Adelaide Grand Prix back in 1991. The drivers had already been in two minds about Melbourne's decision to switch to a twilight race with a 5pm start: the light was very marginal and the sun was just so low. It was a very different set of conditions for us. When you've got all day to have a 90-minute race and you pick the worst hour-and-a-half to have it, you have to ask why. We knew exactly why we did it: because of commercial rights back in Europe and the television audience. But next up we were taken aback by the Malaysians' decision to have a late afternoon start of their own, for the same commercial reasons. It's pretty obvious to anyone who has ever been there that there's a decent chance of rain around that time of day, and so it turned out. Not right at the start: we got away under a very threatening sky, but the rain only began around lap 22 of the scheduled 56. Fernando immediately went off the track and most of us dived for pit lane and wet-weather tyres. Within a few laps it was clear that 'inters' were the tyres to be on rather than full wets, so I pitted again, only for the rain to intensify, prompting another unscheduled call to the pits to change tyres yet again. The downpour began on lap 30 and three laps later, when it was clear that the weather had gone beyond F1 cars' capacity, the race was suspended.

That's when the most intense action of the day began – on the starting grid. TV viewers may remember seeing me moving from car to car, talking to some of the other drivers. In my role as a GPDA director I was making sure that we were all on the same page, because very often the guys talk a good game when there's no pressure, no big decisions to be made, and then promptly crumble under the pressure from their teams. But my feeling was that even though there was going to be potentially a very, very good result for me at the end of it – I was fourth when the red flag came out – if any of us lost the car on the straight there was a disaster waiting to happen.

Fans will ask, and legitimately, why the best drivers in the world are not prepared to go out and race in the rain when they pay their money and stand there to watch us. All I can say is that when you can't control the car in a straight line, never mind through the corners, because the aquaplaning is so bad – your car is sitting on a film of water, not the tarmac – then even the best drivers in the world simply can't race each other. Skill is taken out of the equation; luck comes in, and even those of us who take risks for a living see no reason to tempt fate.

I have raced in some horrendous conditions and enjoyed the challenge, provided it was in one or two sections per lap, but this was quite different. So I asked some of the guys their opinion.

'It's crazy,' they said – they were with me.

'Well, what are you doing sitting in your car?' I asked. 'It's just not sending the right message. These guys will override us if we don't take a bit of action. We don't have to go crazy – let's just see if it blows over and we can go from there.'

A few of the drivers got out of their cars.

'It's not about your team, it's about you,' I told them. 'Is it safe? Can you race? No, of course you can't, let's just wait a little bit.'

Lewis Hamilton was right behind me, in fact they pretty well all agreed. We had to come up with something better than sitting there like lambs, then before we know it we find we're out behind the safety car and then we're racing again because no one took a stance. I wanted to make sure we took control of the situation. Fernando and I were both out of our cars, intending to wait until the rivers cleared on the straight – which they never did – because if you're not in your cars what are they going to do? I remember speaking to Dietrich on the phone. 'Tell them, Mark, tell them: you can race another day,' were his exact words. It was good to hear, since he was the guy who paid my bills. It was so obvious: there are other days to race, it's not that desperate. But the drivers get almost brainwashed by other people into believing that we have to do it. In the end we didn't have to race because the weather took another turn for the worse, but I still wonder what might have happened if it hadn't. I ended up sixth, because the result was called according to the race order on lap 31. For only the fifth time in F1 history and the first time in the 21st century, half-points were awarded.

Sadly in 2014 we saw exactly how badly things can go wrong in such conditions when Jules Bianchi crashed at Suzuka during the Japanese Grand Prix. He lost control at Dunlop Corner and his car collided with a tractor crane removing a car that had crashed at the same spot a lap earlier. While some tragic accidents in motor sport can be attributed to sheer bad luck, others have contributing factors: the race start, the pressure to finish the race before sunset, worn-out intermediate tyres in increasing rain, and one of the toughest corners in the racing world. Scenarios like that have made the drivers take a strong stance and that's why I was so vocal in Malaysia that day.

As things turned out, Sepang was good practice. The next race in Shanghai was also wet, and this time we made history of a quite different kind. To start with we qualified in a Red Bull Racing best-ever pole position for Sebastian and third for me. When it rained, we spent the first six laps behind the safety car and curiously enough Sebastian, who had punted me from behind in similar conditions two years earlier in Fuji, was lucky to escape undamaged when Sébastien Buemi's Toro Rosso did the same to him. As the race unfolded it became obvious that in those conditions it was only ever going to be between the two of us. Sebastian stopped for tyres on lap 36 and I followed him in a lap later, after which the instruction came to hold station and run to the finish. We secured the first 1–2 finish in the team's history and I can tell you it felt great to get the 'real' Red Bull team up onto that podium. It was an incredible day for the team and a great reward for the people who had shown faith in me and stood by me in those difficult close-season days. 'Now I've just got one more step to go,' I said after the race. My pace all weekend had been terrific. I knew I wasn't a million miles away and that my day would come.

*

In sport, momentum is everything. After that historic Red Bull 1–2 in Shanghai, JB and the Brawn team went on to win in Bahrain, Spain and Monaco. But while the juggernaut rolled on, we were building up a pretty decent head of steam in our own right. Sebastian claimed second spot in Bahrain, which was consolation for the team after Adrian Sutil compromised my weekend in Q1. The German driver thought I was on an 'out' lap, which his Force India was on at the time. He was penalised for baulking me, but the

Above Even with a broken leg I had to keep the conditioning up. At my peak on the rowing machine I could pull 1.53 average split for 10 kilometres and a 2.03 split for 25 kilometres.

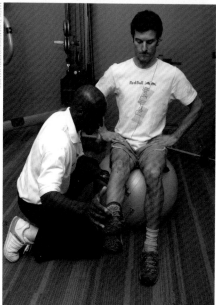

Left The 2009 season began as a race against the clock with my physio, Roger Cleary. We had two months to recalibrate my right leg after my accident in Tasmania.

Above The 2009 Malaysian Grand Prix served up horrendous conditions and visibility levels that were extremely dangerous. On days like this drivers have to make their opinions known to officials.

Above My first Grand Prix win – the 2009 German GP at the Nürburgring. It had been 21 years since Alan Jones's Australian flag had flown from the middle of an F1 podium. I was immensely proud, not only for myself but for Aussie motor-sport fans.

Above Racing over the ragged edge. The Grand Prix circuit at Silverstone in 2009 was heaven for a Formula 1 driver. Real aero, real tyres!

A great shot from a good friend of mine, Mark Thompson of Getty Images. I jumped into the Monaco harbour after my win in 2010. When I surfaced Thommo shouted out 'Mongrel'! I looked back up and he took the shot!

Above A crap moment. When Seb and I touched at 300 kph in Turkey 2010, he retired on the spot. I managed to get my wounded car home in third place.

Above Mum and Dad celebrating my British Grand Prix win in 2010. If only you could bottle the pride in this photo.

Above My first Grand Prix win at Monaco was made all the more special for Sir Jackie and Lady Stewart being at the presentation.

Above The British GP win in 2010 was one of the most powerful victories in my career. It had been a tough week and a hugely satisfying comeback after the Valencia crash.

Above My fury at the 2010 British Grand Prix post-qualifying press conference was for the reason I missed out on pole position and, oddly, not to do with Seb. The breakdown of trust with Red Bull Racing had begun.

Above The middle step was familiar to me at Silverstone. I won there in Formula Ford, Sportscars, F3000 and, for the first time in 2010, F1.

Above A pretty handy bunch but I'm the only non-World Champion! Left to right: Lewis Hamilton, Fernando Alonso, me, Bernie Ecclestone, Jenson Button and Sebastian Vettel. I loved every minute of my five or six years fighting these guys!

Above Left to right: Christian Horner, Adrian Newey, Seb and me. Following the 2010 Championship decider that delivered Seb and not me the Championship, a private flight took us from Abu Dhabi to Red Bull's Hangar-7 at Salzburg airport. I did not want to be here!

Left A defining moment and job done for the Red Bull Junior Driver Program. Helmut Marko shares the Abu Dhabi podium with Seb in that pivotal first world victory in 2010.

Above Team Webber Christmas card 2010. A bit of a mickey-take on the season!

Above Opening the Red Bull Ring with Seb in 2011. This was a moment where we were both genuinely proud for our boss, Dietrich Mateschitz.

Above A very tight move past Fernando Alonso at Eau Rouge, Spa Francorchamps in 2011. I enjoyed making statement moves like this until the end of my F1 career.

Above Jenson Button and I sharing a light-hearted moment with Sir Frank Williams on his 70th birthday at the 2012 Spanish Grand Prix. Sir Frank's wife, Ginny – an edgy lady whose company I always enjoyed – is in the background chatting to Bernie Ecclestone. Sadly she passed away in 2013.

Above One of my greatest victories – Monaco 2012.

Left My final Grand Prix win – the 2012 British Grand Prix.

Right After the 2012 British GP win at Silverstone, my rock, Ann Neal, gave me a big pat on the back – she doesn't hand them out lightly!

Above An interesting aside on the podium at Silverstone in 2012. Fernando 'The Fonz' Alonso asking me whether I'd really said 'No' to Ferrari. I told him 'One more year at RBR, then I'm off to Porsche'.

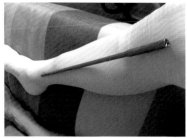

Above Four years after the crash in Tasmania, the last bit of metalwork was removed from my leg in Brisbane in 2012. Nice to have it out at last!

Left On the podium following the infamous 'Multi 21' moment in the 2013 Malaysian Grand Prix. Here's Seb telling me he had f***ed up and could he ring me to talk during the week?

Right Competing on the world stage brought Australians together. Former Wimbledon champion Lleyton Hewitt joined Team Webber in the trenches at the 2013 British Grand Prix.

MARK THOMPSON/GETTY IMAGES

Right Bernie Ecclestone asked me at Spa 2013 if I was sure about my decision to join Porsche. He was pushing to sort me out a Ferrari seat in 2014.

XPB IMAGES

Below Fernando Alonso gives me a lift back to the pits after the 2013 Singapore Grand Prix, burning my right arse cheek! The fans went ballistic, but the race stewards gave me a penalty for the next race. My final remarks to the race stewards were not pretty!

PAUL GILHAM/GETTY IMAGES

Above Even this sensational photo from the 2013 Italian Grand Prix at Monza doesn't convey the emotion of the podium. I stuck up for Seb at the post-race press conference.

Left Left to right: Jenson Button, me, Lewis Hamilton, Nico Rosberg and Felipe Massa at Suzuka 2013 after a huge night out in Tokyo a few days earlier.

Left Triple champion Sir Jackie Stewart visits me on the grid at Abu Dhabi in 2013. He has been a colossus of F1 racing and, having lost many friends to it, has made the sport much safer for us.

Above My final few metres in a Formula 1 car. Taking off my helmet on the in-lap made my goodbye to the sport and the fans all the more genuine.

Left Hanging up my helmet after my last Grand Prix in Brazil 2013.

Right A big day for me – returning home with instructor Al Gwilt after earning my helicopter licence in 2013.

Below Famous brand, famous backdrop. My Porsche 919 LMP1 car at Eau Rouge, Spa in 2014.

Above A blusterly selfie with Annie in the Scottish Highlands, 2014.

Above The biggest crash of my career – the final race of the 2014 WEC championship in Brazil. I was so dazed I only woke up properly on the way to hospital. After such a ginormous impact, I was lucky to escape with my life.

Left Family holiday in Finland.
Left to right: Jemma, Abbey, Mum, Ryan, Ann, me, Dad, Leanne, Dean.

Right Chilling out with 'the boys', Shadow and Simba, at home in Buckinghamshire in 2015.

damage was done: starting 19th on the grid is no good anywhere and Bahrain was no different as I finished 11th.

In Barcelona I qualified fifth but a strong middle stint in the race saw me come through for third place and my fourth F1 podium. A landmark of sorts loomed when we headed for Monaco, and this one really was quite special for me. It was my 127th Grand Prix start, which meant I would be Australia's longest-serving F1 driver: Sir Jack took part in 126 World Championship races, while our second World Champion, Alan Jones, started 116. The problem from my perspective was that they had won 14 and 12 World Championship races respectively; my 126 starts so far had not yielded the victory I was so hungry for. The hunger wasn't satisfied on the beautiful Mediterranean coast, either. A single run in Q3 was a tactical error and meant I started eighth on the grid, but another good middle stint earned me fifth place.

In Turkey next time out I qualified fourth, with Sebastian on pole again, then equalled my best-ever F1 result with second behind Jenson. Again the second stint was the deciding factor, then I was defending well against Sebastian when we got the call to save the cars as I was the faster driver and we duly came home for a 2–3 finish.

Looking back now, there was a taste of things to come even at that 2009 race in Turkey. Sebastian was on pole but finished third; he made a mistake by running wide on the opening lap and letting Jenson into the lead; he was fuelled lighter and made three stops to my two. Seb came in after 15 laps; I set purple sectors galore (when you are the quickest driver in a session or race in a particular sector of the track, the timing screens show your time in purple) and came in on lap 17. When Seb pitted for a second time after 29 laps I pushed hard again before making my second and last stop after 43 laps. Seb was back for his own last stop after 48 laps and then closed the gap to me to just over a second before the telephone call came.

I had laid the foundation for my second place in that middle stint and all the signs were that he wasn't too happy with how the race had panned out. That race brought a first test for the Red Bull Racing engineers when it came to having their two drivers on different strategies, and managing the driver reactions. On this particular occasion, Sebastian was furious that his strategy hadn't worked and it was to become a trend. Whenever I was on a different strategy, especially when it had worked to my advantage, he would ask incredulously, 'How is this possible? How is Mark ahead?' or even, 'How is Mark quicker?' It seemed the thought of me simply being quicker was not one he could entertain! There always had to be another reason why. Over time I realised his meltdowns came when he thought he had done enough when in reality, he hadn't. To my way of thinking, if you get done fair and square on the day you should take it on the chin, but Seb's arrogance meant he simply couldn't comprehend how it had gone wrong and would take it out on the team or, rather, want the team to do something about it.

Guillaume Rocquelin, aka Rocky, Seb's engineer, was the only man in the team who would tell it to him straight. I'm sure some of Seb's behaviour was down to his youthfulness, but the team's executive management repeatedly allowed him to get away with it. No one was ever big enough to pull him into line, tell him that kind of behaviour wasn't acceptable. He was treated like a favourite son, which meant he would throw his toys out of the pram from time to time when he didn't get his own way. Even so, I couldn't help but try to cut him a bit of slack because I got to know his family a little and I liked them. Despite the language barrier, you could tell they were decent people with a good set of values. Essentially he was a good kid at heart but the team allowed him to behave like a spoilt brat.

At the height of Red Bull Racing's success our post-race debrief would involve up to 25 people plus another 10 or so back at the Milton Keynes factory linked up by video stream and radio. Everyone would listen as we gave individual breakdowns on how our race had gone before the race engineers and other departments contributed. The meeting could take between 90 minutes and two hours – often longer than the actual race! Seb may have become a four-time F1 title-winner but he was also a world champion at talking! His ability to recall and relate fine details post-race to key personnel was certainly a strength of his, although I did get the occasional kick under the table from some of the engineers as he could be patronising! The meeting would end with Christian and Adrian giving their take on the race, Adrian clearly with an engineering focus. What I loved about Adrian was his attitude. The race result was generally invisible to him; even if we had dominated with a 1–2 finish, fastest lap, pole position and fastest pit stop, he was still always pushing the team to improve and that's why we were as good as we were.

Looking back on it now, neither Seb nor I knew at the time how significant Istanbul Park 2009 would be for our relationship within 12 months. For the moment we had a good rapport and enjoyed a professional relationship. The key ingredient was that we shared a common goal to lift the team's performance and I thought the chemistry among us all was exceptional. In fact we were on a rocket-ship, and it was on the launching pad.

The rocket really started to lift off when we went to Silverstone and claimed Red Bull's second 1–2 finish of the season. Seb did a good job in qualifying to take pole but I had an awkward moment with Kimi Räikkönen when I caught him on Hangar Straight as I was trying to commit to Stowe Corner. It cost me a front-row start as Rubens pipped me to second. Kimi and I went chest-to-chest in an alpha-male moment on the drivers' parade lap the next day as he hadn't found my comments about him perhaps having drunk too much vodka all that amusing! My race was jeopardised as well: I was bottled up behind Rubens for the whole first stint, only a good first stop letting me get ahead of the Brawn and set off in pursuit of Sebastian, but by then it was too late. I have to be honest, I was disappointed. It really grated on me that Seb had won the British GP because victories were now on the table and he had won what I considered to be my 'other' home race.

Still, it was a second Red Bull Racing 1–2, and this time it was in the dry and totally credible. Ann and I joined the team and celebrated wildly at Christian's Oxfordshire home, where he and his long-term partner Beverley always threw a team barbecue after the British GP. One of the lasting memories of those annual get-togethers was the sight of Adrian tearing up the perfectly manicured lawns by performing donuts in one of his or Christian's exotic cars, usually with a drink in hand. Adrian might be F1's biggest geek but ply him with a few drinks, and you'll see another side of him! He's great fun when he's off-duty.

On 11 July 2009 my Queanbeyan mate Brad Haddin scored a century for Australia in his maiden Ashes Test in Cardiff. I wasn't there: I had urgent business of my own in Germany. But I did follow the boys' progress on the television in my hotel room, and maybe I drew some inspiration from what they were doing in the baggy green caps of Australia, because that day I went out and claimed my first pole position in Formula 1 at the Nürburgring, the home of that year's German Grand Prix.

The track lies adjacent to the famous 22-kilometre long Nordschleife or 'Green Hell', as Jackie Stewart nicknamed it. Built in the 1920s, the Nordschleife is still to this day arguably the most dangerous and treacherous track in the world and was the scene of Niki Lauda's horrific fiery crash in 1976. The modern Nürburgring may not share the same place in history as the original, but it has been the setting for some classic races. It's a nice undulating track tucked into the Eifel Mountains where the weather often plays a deciding part in the outcome. I always enjoyed racing there.

That Nürburgring weekend was the first time I out-qualified Sebastian Vettel as my Red Bull Racing teammate, and it's difficult to overstate how significant that was in itself. Ahead of that weekend I had done some of my best physical training sessions, just me and my road bike on the hills in the south of France. Ann and I had also paid a visit to Dublin for a few days with Mum and Dad and my auntie Pam and uncle Nigel, who were on their first European trip. In the end I decided to go home early because there was no gym in our hotel and the weather was dreadful. Before I left

I thought it was essential to try some of Dublin's famous black velvet – a pint or two of Guinness! There were some workers on the local road who recognised me and yelled out that I was going to win the next race . . .

It was critical for me to take some of the wind out of Sebastian's sails, not only in terms of the championship but in the context of the team we both drove for. Once a driver starts to gain a bit of momentum, it's only natural that other people will gravitate towards him, so it was important to try to get my own winning campaign underway. It wasn't until Q3 that the top 10 got to see a dry track for the first time in what seemed quite a while. It all came down to my last run: I was the first of the front-runners to post my final flying lap and two purple sectors put me on top with a 1:32.320. Both Brawns and Sebastian had still to go: my teammate went second-fastest, was demoted by both Jenson and Rubens, but none of them could beat my time. After the sheer elation had passed, I commented that I would really like a nice, boring GP next day to cash in on my maiden F1 pole position.

Race day dawned, and it was wet. It rained before seven in the morning but had dried by 11. Rain was forecast for later in the race but a dry start would be something. Within seconds of the start I was in a spot of bother: where the hell was Rubens? The little Brazilian had got the jump on me off the line and as I tried to fight back I lost sight of him momentarily. It wasn't until I hit him that I realised where he was. It looked quite dramatic from the outside: the two cars seemed to cannon off each other like billiard balls. I've spoken to Rubens about it and he said he was adjusting something on his steering-wheel. I've looked at the on-board camera footage and he wasn't, but he said he was about to and was distracted for a split second. The contact was minimal, both cars were undamaged: I wasn't squeezing him, it was in the middle of the track.

My troubles weren't over: Lewis had also made a quick getaway in his McLaren, good enough for him to attempt a pretty daring move on me into the first corner. My front wing clipped his left rear tyre and the inevitable happened: he got a puncture. While the World Champion dealt with that little problem Rubens and I started putting some distance between us and the rest of the field. I was comfortable enough being behind, as I knew he was on a lighter load and was sure to be three-stopping. Then the call came: the race stewards had studied the start, decided they didn't like the dramatic coming-together they had seen, and given me a drive-through penalty for the offence of 'causing an avoidable collision'.

That was it: all the hard work that went into getting that pole position counted for nothing, the first five seconds of the race had squandered any advantage I had, and now the law-makers were on my back as well. All I could think was, 'It's just not meant to be.'

So I came in to serve my sentence, as it were, on lap 15, but first I made sure I put a gap on Heikki Kovalainen, who was doing a useful job of bottling up the likes of Jenson and Sebastian behind his McLaren. Once I got back out there I had Ciaron Pilbeam, my race engineer, trying to reassure me and tell me I could still win this thing. My first scheduled stop arrived on lap 19 and I rejoined eighth, which quickly became second again as the others went in and out of pit lane. When Rubens made his second stop that put me in the lead.

Two threats remained, one called rain, the other Vettel. The rain never came; Sebastian led after my second stop on lap 43 but still had his own stop to come and I was back in front. I was now closing out the win, everything was absolutely under control, but I remember asking Ciaron to confirm that I was starting my last lap. I wanted to triple-check as Roger, who doubled as my pit-board man for a couple of years, was liable to be the odd lap out because he sometimes forgot to hang out my board! It usually happened when I was racing in a pack and he was excited. I could see him looking at me over the wall, cheering me on, but he didn't have the pit board, which made me laugh! But this time the laps had been counted correctly and after 130 races, and 232 days after breaking my leg on a Tasmanian bush road, I was a Grand Prix winner.

Maybe there's something in what they say about the luck of the Irish after all because those blokes in Dublin had been right! The journey had led me down several blind alleys, I had hit several unexpected obstacles, yet here I was: on the top step of the podium at one of the most famous racing circuits in the world, the famous Nürburgring.

I hadn't won a race in a long, long time, and finally winning a Grand Prix was very different from my previous visit to the top step. People's perceptions of me instantly changed: Mark Webber, race-winner in F1 . . . and the most important thing of all for me was that I absolutely deserved to win. The race may have been a mirror image of the stop–start career that preceded it, but we were always going to win on that day. It meant so much to me that it was a genuine victory, not one of those races handed to you by sheer force of circumstance.

There were two people with me that day that I really wanted to hug. One was my dad, who had guided me away from Australia and into single-seater racing in the first place and backed me every step of the way. He injected a comical note of his own into the proceedings – one of his front teeth had fallen out that very morning and he couldn't crack a decent smile for the rest of the day! But he well remembers that first win: 'Something I had never told Mark was that in my many years of following motor racing I had formed a great admiration for a New Zealand driver called Chris Amon. The general consensus about Chris was that he was a very talented but unlucky driver. I watched him quite a bit: he contested 96 Grands Prix but never won one. He was second three times, third eight times, but never first. Well, at one stage I thought, "Mark's going to be a bit like Chris Amon, all that talent, but never quite in the right place at the right time – he's just never going to jag one." But finally he did, I was on the pit wall – minus a front tooth – and it was a fantastic day.'

The other person I had to hug was Ann: her plan had got me here, her support had kept me going through all the ups and downs. This wasn't my day, it was ours. And while Dad was having his problems smiling, Flavio came out with the comment that it was the first time he had ever seen Annie smile!

I was also looking forward to hearing the Australian national anthem – for me. I love sport, I'm very patriotic to our flag and about us as a sporting nation, which is how most of the rest of the world perceives us. I had been to watch Jason Crump winning in speedway in front of a full house, and even Dad had goosebumps when Crumpy won and we heard the national anthem.

I thought then, 'I want to do that one day . . .'

I was a Grand Prix winner at last, the first Australian since Jack and Alan who had had a chance to fly the flag. I had done it my way, and perhaps a little bit differently. I shared the podium with Felipe Massa and Seb, and I will always remember Felipe looking across at me and saying, 'It's a good feeling, isn't it?'

Most of all, my own question – 'Can I do this?' – had been answered. On my slow-down lap after crossing the line I gave vent to all those pent-up emotions. It went something like this: 'Woo-hoo! Yee-hah! Yes! Yes, yes, yes, yes, yes! Ha-ha! Yes, yes, yes, yes, yes, yes, yes, yes, yes, yes!!'

I think it meant: 'Yes, I can.'

There was just one little cloud on that memorable day. It drifted over when a well-known television commentator came into the Red Bull hospitality area in the immediate aftermath of the race. As he looked around the place at other members of the team he asked Ann, 'Why the long faces?' Then the penny dropped: 'Ah, I see,' he added. 'The wrong driver won!' It was a telling comment and although it did nothing to spoil our pleasure, we realised later that it went right to the heart of the matter. There was a bit of celebration and showbiz for the cameras but it was clear some of the senior management weren't all that happy that I had turned the tables and won in Seb's own backyard.

After Germany I felt I had got through another stretch of uncharted waters: pole position and a Grand Prix victory. Clearly a lot of other people thought the same! My first pole attracted something like 90 messages, and that figure seemed to double after I won the race. I didn't realise so many people had my bloody contact details but I was blown away to receive messages from world champions like Sir Jack Brabham, Nigel Mansell, Jody Scheckter, Valentino Rossi, Troy Bayliss, Casey Stoner and so many of my racing colleagues and friends.

Twenty-four hours later I was enjoying the company of the Australian Test team, who had been such an inspiration to me and were in the UK on an Ashes tour. Ricky Ponting was hosting a foundation dinner for the charity he had established and it was phenomenal to be with some of my cricketing heroes. But they seemed to think I'd done something pretty heroic in my own field and I was given a heart-warming reception. Luke and I went to Lord's again to watch some cricket later that week and I was overwhelmed by the response of people around me on the train heading into London and then at the hallowed ground.

A funny moment happened when the Aussies invited Luke and me down to their dressing-shed. Luke's a massive cricket fan and devoted to the Baggy Green, but he was completely overawed and speechless when he was introduced to the Australian captain. Ricky was great, Luke was silent. He'd met the likes of Fernando Alonso, Lewis Hamilton, Jenson Button and Sebastian Vettel over the years but cricketers were on another level as far as he was concerned. He'd seen so much of them on TV, they were pros, the real deal. We spoke to Ricky and the rest of the lads, and of course we had a lot in common, but Luke came away as if it was his first date with a supermodel – he should have said and done a lot more! 'That was crap,' he grumbled as we were going down the stairs. 'I had so many questions to ask Ricky but I froze.'

Another happy memory of that day in Germany was that my buddy Bernd Schneider was there to see me win.

He never managed it himself in F1, but he played a role in helping me get there and he sent me a nice message after the race to say how happy he was that he was so close to me on such a special day. Soon after I got home there was another one: a telegram from Bernie Ecclestone. It was pretty special, not only for the kind words: it was made entirely of silver.

The next step was to keep the momentum going but after another podium in Hungary our charge stalled. Valencia, Spa, Monza and Singapore came and went without any more points, but the prospect of returning to Suzuka for the first time in three years helped lift the spirits. The circuit has always been one of my favourites and I felt sure we could pull off a great result there.

'We' did, in the sense that a Red Bull Racing car won the race. Unfortunately it wasn't mine. A free practice 'off' meant I missed qualifying, started from pit lane – and had to come straight back in when my headrest worked loose. Out again, same thing, in again. A puncture on the fourth lap meant all I could do was treat the rest of the afternoon as an unscheduled test session. I was the last classified finisher in 17th place. When that happens, not even the satisfaction of another fastest lap is enough to redeem the weekend. That was the first time in 2009 where I felt there was a very good result to be had and I wasn't there to get it. Suzuka was a low point, no doubt about it.

I had never scored a point in seven attempts at Interlagos in Brazil, but I had to stop beating myself up and move the bar up another level. As a result I went to Brazil better prepared than ever. Heavy rain made qualifying very long – two and three-quarter hours, to be precise – and very dangerous, and in the end a small mistake meant I couldn't quite match hometown hero Rubens Barrichello as he took his third Brazilian pole position. Still, I knew we were in good shape to give Brawn a run for their money the following day. To ensure we did, I was rather harsh and leant on Kimi Räikkönen at the start and took his front wing off. It was crucial he didn't come past me; he had KERS and I didn't, so passing him later would have been hard.

I came through unscathed as the safety car came out. When it retreated after four laps Rubens opened up a handy little gap, but he pitted after 21 laps and lost ground when he came back out in traffic. His absence freed me up to reel off some quick laps, including fastest race lap for the third time that season, and I was still ahead when I emerged from my own first stop. My second was as well executed as the first, I got out just ahead of JB, a puncture cost Rubens any chance of a home win, and I was home free: a second win to go with the big breakthrough in Germany.

It had felt like playing chess, where we had the advantage of knowing all the moves that were coming and being ready to counter-punch. It also confirmed the runner-up spot for Red Bull in the Constructors' Championship, and my green-and-gold chest was puffed out even more when my good mate Jason Crump took out the World Speedway title that same weekend and Casey Stoner won the Australian MotoGP down at Phillip Island. After the Brazil race Valentino Rossi sent me a text: *Two is double of one!* which I think was Italian for *There's a lot more to come.* Whatever the translation, it meant a great deal to me and helped me realise that when you achieve at sport's highest levels, you have a natural affinity with people who have also competed on the world stage.

The celebrations started in earnest when I caught up with DC and a few of the others in the bar at the hotel post-race. Somehow, we managed to screw up logistics with too many people going to the airport, which resulted in four on the back seat and DC sitting on the centre console between the driver and front seat passenger. Brazilian roads aren't the smoothest so I think DC spent most of the trip head-butting the roof. He probably never felt a thing! We carried on drinking in the airport lounge and when we had boarded and levelled out, we were at it again. Two hours later we couldn't work out why our fellow first-class passengers were pissed off with us so we decided to take ourselves off to business class and wake up as many passengers as possible. I seem to remember we played a little game with the non-F1 personnel on the flight who were asleep and fell victim to a few of our shenanigans!

One race to go. It took us to another spectacular new venue for the F1 calendar, the Yas Marina Circuit in Abu Dhabi. It turned out to be, slightly disappointingly, a track of two halves: a nice first sector with some high-speed stuff, but a lot of corners packed into a tight space in the second half of the layout. Lewis took pole for McLaren, with Sebastian alongside him and me in third spot. Lewis's race finished early with brake problems on the McLaren and with Sebastian proving just a little bit quicker on the day – or night, as we raced into the darkness – I was left to fend off a late challenge from the new World Champion, JB himself. I admit to struggling to have any real feel for the option tyres in the closing stages as Jenson closed in, and I knew it was going to be pretty tight by the end of the race.

Isn't it funny what pops into your head at the strangest times? As JB was reeling me in, it came back to me that after Tasmania he was probably the only bloke among the drivers that I have a good relationship with (and still do) who didn't get in touch with me, and that had left me feeling a little disappointed. Looking back, in late 2008 he was under a bit of stress himself, unsure about his own destination for 2009 after Honda's withdrawal from F1, so I shouldn't be too hard on him. But I confess that right then I was thinking, 'Righto mate, this is going to be interesting . . .'

The aim was to be totally accurate with my braking-points and leave no room for error when he attacked. That long straight was definitely a window for him to create some pressure and we knew the Brawn – or the Mercedes engine – had a little more top speed. Sebastian had it won, this was down to a race for second between the two of us now, so I had to make sure I caused as much havoc as I could getting onto the straights. On the last two laps it got very tight: he attacked, I defended, it was a lot of fun. I was pretty pleased with my defensive drive, especially when it secured Red Bull's fourth 1–2 finish of the season.

What a roller-coaster ride 2009 was. High anxiety through the European winter of 2008–09 after my accident in Tasmania . . . Low morale for a while as I felt the pain of driving the car again . . . High expectations dashed at Silverstone . . . The penalty in Germany followed by the incredible high of my first Grand Prix win . . . The dip from Hungary onwards offset by another taste of success in Brazil . . . 18 points out of 20 in the final two rounds.

In the end I got from the year what I believed I deserved. I was fourth in the drivers' standings on 69.5 points, the odd half coming, of course, from our abbreviated race in Malaysia early in the season. From a team perspective too, 2009 was special, a unique season when Red Bull Racing ticked a great many boxes.

It was nothing compared to what 2010 had in store.

12

In High Places

My early F1 years took me to base camp at Everest. In 2010 I would learn what it was like to attempt K2, which most serious climbers agree is the toughest mountain of them all.

In his autobiography *In High Places* the great climber Dougal Haston said that the climber has to control self-doubt and fear; that climbing happens as much in the mind as in the battle of body against mountain, and sometimes the challenge seems unreasonable. But then Haston asked a pertinent question: what could be more reasonable than finding out about yourself?'

Switch 'mountain' and 'F1' and you have a pretty fair summing-up of where I was now in my career: in high places. The year ahead would bring incredible highs like Monaco, moments of fear when my life seemed to have been taken out of my hands, and moments of self-doubt.

Could I go higher still? Climbers start out quite often as a large group; they build camps at key positions on their route up the mountain; as they go higher the group gets smaller; in the end only the climbers capable of making the final push for the summit remain. And to make that push they need all the help they can get from the people behind them. That's how it was in the 2010 Formula 1 World Championship. By the end of the season we were down to four title contenders, two of us from the same team. The summit was within reach.

Going into 2010 the Webber stocks were higher than they had ever been. I was an F1 race-winner now, in a front-running team, and I felt I belonged there. But the bar had been raised higher again: could I go on and win more races and, if so, what else might come my way? Could we – the whole Red Bull Racing team – continue on this steep climb and put ourselves in World Championship contention?

In 2009 we had a quick car in the shape of the RB5, but it was found wanting on a number of tracks. Adrian Newey's priority for 2010 was to come up with a successor, the RB6, that would be quick on every track – and that meant 19 of them, because 2010 was scheduled to match 2005 as the longest seasons in F1 history to that point. While the team considered a switch to either Mercedes engines (vetoed by their other partner, McLaren) or Cosworth (ultimately short on development), we stuck with the Renault units that Adrian thought were somewhere around 4 per cent down on the German engines' power. As the season loomed I was pretty optimistic. The key performance ingredients that make these things go fast were not really changing much for the new year, Sebastian and I had finished first and second in the last race of 2009 so we clearly had a great base to design the RB6 on, and we had developed the RB5 quite well in-season, so looking at a 24-month cycle there was nothing to suggest that progress shouldn't continue. As a unit we were one of the most stable teams over the break, and that continuity was only going to help our cause.

Most crucially of all, I believed Adrian had the hunger back again. We flew down together to Valencia for the MotoGP race at the end of their 2009 season along with two of my bike racing mates, Jason Crump and John McGuinness, and you could tell that he was excited by the potential of his latest design.

For 2010, quite simply Adrian had designed the best car. He had come up with a system at the rear of the RB6 where the engine's exhaust gases were channelled through a slot in the car's bodywork into the central section of the diffuser. That would boost the down-force and increase cornering speed: it would prove a valuable aid in the early part of the year.

The one regulation change of note was that refuelling had been banned, meaning we would have to run the cars heavy from race start. My feeling was that 2010 would be all about tyres because the additional weight in the car would affect their reliability. That meant there was room for a bit of tactics on the fuel burn – how to do a Grand Prix with the minimum amount possible.

Setting off with around 160 kilograms of fuel on board, the cars would get quicker through the whole race to the tune of about four seconds per lap as the fuel load burned off (each litre weighs around three-quarters of a kilogram). But the driver's job wouldn't change massively: every corner is on the limit, to a point. People think that when the cars are heavier they're at their worst but I think they're easier because the lap time's slower so the G-forces are lower, and the car's less nervous, more docile in the driver's hands.

As for this driver, I was in pretty good shape too, although not without a minor alarm. I had been hoping to have all the remaining metalwork in my leg removed in one hit but the recovery period from that would be too long. The screw inserted in my leg had a small cap in the top and this had been giving me quite a bit of discomfort since the original surgery 12 months earlier. It had been cross-threaded and was sitting proud, and that's why it was causing me pain. The start of December 2009 was the only window I had to allow my new case surgeon Dave Hahn to put things right. It required a full incision at the front of my knee and Dave couldn't guarantee the recovery period.

It was a relief to get the work done but I infuriated Dave when I resumed training way too soon. I thought the knee might have become infected; I remember being at the Red Bull Racing Christmas party a week later in excruciating pain and on crutches. I panicked and drove up to Nottingham to see Dave the next morning. He said, 'You stupid bastard, you've been doing too much on it and not enough on the crutches. When I say rest, I mean rest.' He got a syringe out and withdrew a lot of fluid, knowing full well it wasn't infected. I did what I was told this time and the leg was happier and better. I was back in light training again just four weeks post-op.

The 2010 season marked the return of one Michael Schumacher. He had been tempted out of his three-year retirement by the prospect of teaming up again with Ross

Brawn, who was now in charge of the born-again Silver Arrows. The Mercedes F1 team were coming back into the sport in their own right, rather than as engine suppliers to other teams, for the first time since 1955. For Michael it was a case of 'full circle', as it was Mercedes who had really launched his career in their sports-car program in the late '80s and early '90s. His teammate would be compatriot Nico Rosberg.

I was all for it: we all knew only too well what Michael had already achieved, but comebacks are something else. You don't hear of many absolutely phenomenal comebacks. You hear a lot more about the ones that haven't gone to plan – think Björn Borg, for example – because generally the people under scrutiny have had phenomenal careers first time around. They left on a slightly higher level than everyone else in their chosen sport; they think they can come back, have a crack and be right back where they were.

Personally I didn't think Michael would be the same driver he once was. Still bloody awesome, but the hunger, the willingness to go the extra mile and then some, all those things he used to take in his stride . . . Would he still have it? I reckoned he would be half a yard short in a few areas here and there: like a footballer short of match fitness or a boxer who's been out of the ring too long. But hats off to him for coming back and having a crack, because the young guys still knew where their right foot was and he wasn't about to be given any preferential treatment. He wouldn't want it anyway.

His return meant we would have seven German drivers on the grid, a mark of how powerful their nation had become in our sport. And one of them was in the car right next to mine.

I totally agreed with some of the tweaks that had been made to the 2010 regulations, such as the ban on in-season testing: I was all for that because I hated driving round and round doing 15 Grand Prix distances on top of all the racing. I wasn't so happy with the decision that had been taken on World Championship points though, with the introduction of an inflated 25 points for a Grand Prix win and a sliding scale of 25–18–15–12–10–8–6–4–2–1 for the top 10 finishers in each race.

Why? As a sports fan I can relate to however many runs Bradman made, or his batting average, or how many goals Eric Cantona scored. To my mind it showed scant respect for the tradition of our sport. Compare my points to Jack Brabham's now and the picture is skewed. I'm a tradition-alist and I like the way tennis, cricket or golf have stayed consistent. It's a shame that the powers that be in F1 keep tweaking the small things instead of looking at the big issues.

*

For Team Webber, four Grand Prix victories in 2010 were like those camps mountaineers set up at various altitudes. Each win took us higher, each meant our focus had to be adjusted upwards again. But as we kept climbing higher, other incidents cast ever-lengthening shadows across our path.

My third F1 win and my first of 2010 came in Barcelona in round five and it was one of those weekends where the car was quick throughout. It's hard for people outside a Formula 1 team to appreciate the amount of work that goes into putting two cars on the starting grid, but the Barcelona performance level was testament to what the people at

Milton Keynes had achieved in the three weeks since the preceding race in China.

Before qualifying in Spain Christian told me to go out there and enjoy myself because I probably wouldn't get too many chances to drive a car like ours around that track. He was dead right: he had driven there himself and he knew that for Barcelona – a track we all know so well – you have to be confident in your car because it has so many fast corners. In Friday's practice we were already looking pretty strong.

During our briefing that night we knew qualifying in this car in Barcelona would be something else. Being flat out in sixth gear through Turn 9 at Barcelona is quite a feeling, I can tell you. It's a spot where you usually had to lift off a little, maybe brake slightly or perhaps even downshift. Not in this car. It was so good I could go through Turn 9 at full throttle. Christian was right to warn me not to take it for granted, but he also knew there weren't many better men than me when it came to fast corners. I still remember it to this day. The boffins in the garage see the telemetry, they know your foot didn't come off the throttle and that's a hugely rewarding moment for them as well. It certainly helped me put the car on pole.

Translating that into a race win meant getting off the line cleanly, being as precise as I could into Turn 1 after the long, long run down there and then settling into a rhythm of my own. The option tyres had to be cycled through as quickly as we could, but in the end everything fell my way. It's not often the serious journalists in the racing magazines write about 'the perfect drive in the perfect car' so it was very gratifying to see such comments alongside my name.

I could have done a thousand laps that day and I was still going to win.

Ann and I then drove to our holiday home in Vence in Provence, so there was another 600 kilometres on the clock that same night! We did some TV and radio interviews in the car and it felt so rewarding to have the first win of the year under the belt. Not only that, but I had kept a personal promise. When I left home I said to the dogs, 'Hopefully, boys, I will bring home quite a big chunk of points for you,' and that's how it worked out. It was another very special day. Another one was waiting at the end of the very next week on the Mediterranean coast between France and Italy.

For eight years I had thought 3 March 2002 in Melbourne, my F1 debut, was my greatest day ever. That changed on 16 May 2010 on the other side of the world. That day I experienced the unique thrill of winning the Monaco Grand Prix. The jewel in the crown, the *crème de la crème* – use any cliché you like, but I knew when I crossed the line that this was the single greatest thrill a Formula 1 driver could ever have.

A look at the winners' list should help explain why: Fangio wove his way around the chaos caused by a freak wave back in 1950 to win Monaco's first World Championship Grand Prix . . . Moss won back-to-back races there in 1960 and 1961 . . . Stewart won Monaco three times and made a brilliant documentary, *Weekend of a Champion*, about it with Roman Polanski . . . Prost was a Monaco winner four times, Graham Hill and Schumacher five and Senna an astonishing six. More importantly to the Webber clan, the man who ignited Dad's passion for racing, Jack Brabham, took his own first Grand Prix victory there in a

Cooper on 10 May 1959 – 51 years before my own day in the Monaco sunlight. That is quite some company for any driver to be keeping.

If they were starting a new World Championship today, would they keep Monaco on the calendar? A racing driver's every instinct screams, 'No!'

It's too narrow, too tight, there is virtually nowhere to go if you start to lose the car. It's a ridiculously short lap, it inflicts the severest strains imaginable on car and driver – and yet it is the most eagerly anticipated race of every season. It is, too, the only venue on the calendar that Formula 1 needs more than the venue needs Formula 1. For the driver, it's just you against the track. It doesn't matter if you make a minor mistake or a major one, the end result is the same – and it's not good.

But going there less than a week after taking my third career Grand Prix victory in Spain meant I arrived with my confidence high. We didn't have the best of Thursdays (Monaco starts a day earlier so they can open up the streets for Friday shopping). I got limited running in and I was never quite comfortable in the car. But we made changes on Saturday morning and knew we were in the hunt.

That feeling only grew when I took pole position for the second week running. In fact I could have taken it twice: in Q3 I did just the one four-lap run and my third and fourth times were good enough for top spot on the grid. My final lap of 1:13.892 was the only one under 1:14 all weekend. That day it felt like I found another gear in terms of confidence in the car. When you are concentrating so hard and putting everything on the edge your heart rate soars, and then you have that horrible wait to see if what you've done is good enough. Someone in the post-qualifying press conference reminded me about Jack winning there all those years ago; I said that it was an honour to get pole but it would be the biggest highlight of my career if I could join him on the Monaco winners' list the next day.

For a little while on Sunday the omens weren't good. I managed to break the pit-lane speed limit during the pre-race installation laps and collected a €2200 fine for my trouble. More worryingly, I thought I had let all the hard work on Saturday go to waste when I made an average start. I don't know if it was my fault or my guys hadn't set the clutch up correctly, but that was my only alarm, and I recovered from it well enough on the short run off the line to be P1 at Ste Dévote, that familiar first corner before the uphill surge towards Casino Square. Once I came out of that first turn in the lead I knew this Grand Prix was mine to lose. But if I thought I'd got the hard part of the job done, I had another thing coming.

We had got through just one of the scheduled 78 laps when the safety car made its first appearance. Nico Hülkenberg had crashed his Williams in the tunnel. I got going again nicely when the safety car went in after six laps and was still leading after my pit stop on lap 23, then out came the safety car again on lap 31 when the other Williams came to grief.

In *Weekend of a Champion* JYS talks about the centimetres (or inches in the old money) he had to keep up his sleeve to avoid the Monaco manhole covers. Well, in 2010 he should have reminded his former driver Rubens Barrichello: it was a loose drain cover that came up and destroyed the Brazilian's right rear wheel. Just 10 laps later another menacing drain cover was spotted and the safety car came out until that was fixed; and with just four laps to go it was out for the fourth and final time when Jarno Trulli's Lotus climbed all over Karun Chandhok's HRT on the way into La Rascasse. This was the only really worrying one, because I was right behind them.

As I saw Jarno lunge for the inside, interlock wheels with the HRT and go up in the air I was praying there would be enough room left for me to go through on the inside, and sure enough, there was. It was a help to me that Seb struggled on the restarts: it meant I was able to impose myself on the race again each time and start the hard work all over again with a bit of a cushion. Actually I had expected Robert Kubica to be the main opposition. His Renault had been very quick throughout the build-up to the race, so it was something of a relief to see Sebastian get ahead of it at the original start.

On days like those – and there aren't many of them – you understand what it means to be lost for words. As a Formula One driver all you want to do is win races; if you could choose, then the Blue Riband event on our calendar is very, very special for any driver. My name was up there alongside Jack's now. All the basic questions a Grand Prix driver can be asked were flung at us that day and we had an answer for every one of them. All things considered, jumping into the swimming pool on the Red Bull Energy Station was a pretty conservative reaction!

My journey really was different now: not only had I got to F1 from Queanbeyan, I had got to the top step of the podium in Monaco to receive the winner's trophy from a prince. Although the special thing about that podium was

having Sir Jackie and Lady Stewart up there as well –
I wasn't really worried about the other guy! The end of
my race brought a slight hiccup just as the start had done:
I jumped up in my exuberance, hit the trophy on one of the
steel beams overhead and put a dent in the lid!

Not only had I damaged the trophy, I had also failed to
pack a suit. Jackie had told us that he always used to travel
with a dinner suit in his luggage just in case it was ever
needed. To me, that sounded a bit like tempting fate, so
mine stayed firmly at home. That was inconvenient, because
at Monaco there is a gala ball on Sunday evening at which
the winning driver, among others, has to make a speech.

As luck would have it, Grand Prix racing's best-dressed
man – JYS – was on our table and he gave me hell. He was
still on about it on the telephone the next day! I duly apol-
ogised in my speech but really I was too busy enjoying the
fireworks (I'm a bit of a pyromaniac), enjoying the company
(there were members of Grace Kelly's family on our table),
and basking in the glory of that day to care about what I was
wearing.

Red Bull put together a nice bash at one of Monaco's
night-clubs. Everyone was there, and there were people on
the dance floor, the Monaco Grand Prix winner included,
who shouldn't have been! I don't think I will ever erase the
image of Red Bull Racing's Rob Marshall, who could not be
described as a small man, doing belly-flops on the floor . . .

Next morning I discovered that Rob had popped a note
under my hotel room door that said, *Lost the Ashes again –
but won Monaco Grand Prix! Fair dinkum*.

It was nine years since my last Monaco success, in the
F3000 race in 2001. How far we had travelled in those

intervening seasons, and how much higher we were about
to go!

*

Monaco 2010 – perhaps the greatest day of my F1 career –
is a perfect example of the two faces of Red Bull Racing that
I was having to come to terms with. Something happened
in Monaco, which couldn't take the gloss off my win there
but, looking back, said a lot about what was going on at
the heart of the team. Somewhere in the post-race mix
there was talk that Sebastian wanted my chassis. In the end
Christian Horner took me aside and told me that he had
given Marko the opportunity to tell Sebastian that he had a
cracked chassis – which he didn't – to help him rationalise
the fact that he had just been well and truly beaten, for the
second race in a row, by the old Aussie in the other car.
It seems it had been affecting his confidence, and to Seb
that's everything. As with Turkey 2009, it seemed beyond
his comprehension that I could beat him fair and square: for
him there had to be another reason why.

It was really the remarkable four-race sequence in the
middle of 2010, from Istanbul through Montreal, Valencia
and Silverstone, that signalled the beginning of the end
of my positive feelings for Red Bull Racing. F1 fans will
remember Turkey that year and the infamous coming-
together between Seb and me as we tussled for the race
lead. The day before that happened I got wind that matters
might be conspiring against me.

At this stage of the season I was the championship leader
by virtue of my two wins to Vettel's one. I had led every
lap of the previous two races from pole position, so I may

have reasonably expected that to be enough to give me the edge in the pecking order when it came to new components for our cars. But on Saturday morning in Istanbul it was Sebastian who was given a new rear wing; mine arrived only minutes before the qualifying session got underway that afternoon. It was touch and go whether it would even get on to the car because we had so-called F-duct rear wings that year, with a device that allowed the driver to alter the airflow and increase speed, and setting one of those up was no five-minute job. But it was done, just in the nick of time. On Sunday the two Red Bulls clashed on-track and Sebastian's retired on the spot. In the lead-up to that unfortunate moment Ciaron had come on the horn to tell me I needed to turn the engine down to manage the fuel load. I did, but I made a point of asking about Sebastian's status on fuel. He was fine: I had been leading for so long that the guys in my slip-stream were able to save their fuel slightly and buy back some kpl (kilos per lap). It was one of the few F1 races I can remember where there was Formula Ford-style slip-streaming going on. I was the guy who led, and who suffered; that's what Seb had in his top pocket and he planned to use it when he could get a run at me.

When he did, I held my line and kept him on the inside for as long as possible. As the corner approached he flicked his car over to the right where I was and high-speed contact was made. Seb retired on the spot and spent some time making weird gestures meant to indicate it was all my fault. I managed to limp back for repairs, rejoin the race and claim third place. Immediately after parking my car I had to go into the mandatory FIA press conference before I had any contact with the team; I dealt with the questions as straightforwardly and professionally as I could, went back to the paddock – and found that I was being blamed for what had happened.

Annie had been watching the whole situation unfold. In the blue corner, Horner seemed to be managing things well enough and like the vast majority of people who had witnessed the incident he appeared to know where the blame lay even if he was being diplomatic. But in the red corner Marko was surrounded by the German/Austrian media and blaming me. Since Sebastian had moved up to Red Bull Racing from Toro Rosso, it was evident Marko was taking more and more of an interest. Now, here in Turkey at a highly controversial moment, he had apparently become a spokesperson for the team as well!

On hearing what Marko had said, Christian seemed to perform a 180-degree turn and ended up siding with Marko. As sections of the British media reported, Horner was 'initially equivocal but later moved towards Marko's view'. I couldn't believe what I was walking into when I returned from the press conference. Later, when I saw on TV the hugs Sebastian got on the pit wall from the team, I began having serious doubts as to who was really pulling the strings at Red Bull Racing.

The team was sheepish to say the least. We had a 60-strong workforce at the race, one of our cars was in the fence and the other had gone from the lead to third place, and no one really knew how to handle a scenario that had been played out in front of a global TV audience.

The post-race debrief was interesting: we were minus one driver as Seb had been excused from attending! I was quite happy he wasn't there as it gave me the higher moral ground. I was the one with the team. To this day I still don't know why he missed the debrief, which is the essential conclusion to a race weekend. It's a time for everyone to face the music from the various departments and that includes driver performance. I don't think team management was particularly happy with either of us. After all, we had committed the ultimate sin in motor sport – colliding with your teammate.

Next morning, when I switched on my phone, I was inundated with SMSs and voicemail messages; by the time we got home my inbox was swamped with emails, not only from fans but also from well-known figures in the motor-racing world who were outraged by what had happened. One well-respected captain of industry took time out to call me and strongly recommended that I should put my thoughts down in writing for Dietrich Mateschitz. That struck me as a pretty good idea, and this is what I wrote:

1 June 2010

Dear Dietrich

I know we have already discussed the events of the Turkish Grand Prix and will continue to do so over the next few days. However, now that I've had time to consider my position and view what happened on Sunday as objectively as possible, I believe it is also important to express my thoughts in writing.

What strikes me is that there are two very separate issues that need to be addressed and I hope we can do so as professionally and as quickly as possible to prevent any further damage being done to the Red Bull brand and

*Red Bull Racing's reputation. By doing so, I also
hope we can move forward from here in a positive
manner and concentrate our efforts on winning the
world championships.*

The two issues are:

1. *The very public outburst and apportionment of
   blame in my direction following the on-track
   collision between Sebastian and me while I was
   leading the race.*

2. *The build-up to the collision.*

Point 1
*I have always tried to conduct myself properly as a
professional sportsperson and a team player and I believe
I continued to do so on Sunday, both on and off the
track, in the aftermath of what happened. I participated
in the post-race press conference as I would after any
top three finish and without any briefing from the team
and not knowing the full extent of the picture, I was
diplomatic and measured in my opinions and represented
the team to the best of my ability. I have been widely
commended for maintaining my composure and for the
way I handled the questions repeatedly put to me.*

*Therefore, I was disappointed to find out later that
I was on my own. While the rest of the world – having
seen for themselves what took place on the track – were
unequivocal in their opinion as to where blame should
lie, factions within the team had adopted an immediate
stance and had spoken to the media apportioning
blame for the incident firmly on me before the facts had*

been established and discussion had taken place with those involved. I find this to be very unprofessional and believe the whole matter could have been controlled and managed much better out of earshot of the media.

Regrettably what's been said will remain on the record and I'm disappointed that some people showed their true colours amid the pressure and a lack of team spirit. Now I believe we need to reinforce the reputation of our team. I appreciate that it is not easy but I feel I am entitled to an apology from the team for the hasty and inaccurate comments which would not only help to restore my confidence and demonstrate that I enjoy the full support of the team but would also go a long way towards restoring the team's integrity and alleviating the mass condemnation it has received by so many. The team's own website has received more than 1000 complaints.

Point 2
At the time of writing this letter, I still don't have a full understanding of what happened in terms of the discussions that took place on the pit wall.

I had been under immense pressure from Hamilton for the whole of the first stint as he was incredibly fast on the soft tyres. I felt I had soaked up this pressure well and was clearly focussed on building a gap over the rest of the field. My holding Hamilton out for the first stint gave Seb the chance to jump Hamilton at the first stop (which worked well) as Seb wasn't quite on our pace during the first part of the race.

Maybe I was naïve in thinking that we were trying to control the McLarens from the first stop to the flag but this is what I set about doing. Yes, at times there were surges in pace from all three of us for the next 23 laps but keeping in mind that I was the leader, I was the first car to arrive to clear backmarkers and also the first car to arrive at corners where it was spitting with rain; it wasn't easy. And last, but by no means least, as the lead car I was giving a very good slipstream at certain sections of the track.

However, from the cockpit everything felt fine and repetitive (i.e. the status quo was being maintained) until lap 38/39 when the alarm bells started ringing after obeying instructions from the pit wall to change my fuel mixture. I radioed the team immediately to ask what Seb's engine situation was as I was now concerned about 'friendly fire'.

At this section of the race, Seb was certainly under pressure but no more or less than he had been from Hamilton in the previous 23 laps.

I was thinking 17 more laps of this . . . yes, admittedly tough but I strongly felt that the top four positions would not have changed in the race. All four of us had pushed very hard up until that point. It was true that at that particular point of the race, Seb's car was the fastest out of the four but only by a sniff.

Let's not ignore the fact that I had led the last 180-odd Grand Prix laps (combining the three GPs together until the point of contact in Istanbul) and I wasn't leading the Turkish GP by any fluke. So, I felt that after the first part of the race when I had dealt with severe pressure from Hamilton, and Hamilton and I had both edged a small gap over the rest of the field, I had earned the right and was capable of finishing the job off by leading home a RBR 1–2. Yes, there was a lot of pressure from McLaren but I don't believe it had reached a critical point as Hamilton wasn't attempting any overtaking moves into Turn 12 at that stage.

In the future, there should be more communication between drivers and the pit wall about how they see the race. We shouldn't be paranoid about talking and using our radios during Grands Prix in fear of people eavesdropping (i.e. TV networks) because at the end of the day, we have people who are well able to control Grands Prix to the very best advantage of the team.

It's a fairytale what has happened to our team in the last two years, and I say 'our' team because I have certainly felt a part of it. We have to recognise though, how difficult it is to get two cars into first and second place in the closing stages of a Grand Prix. We have had many 1–2s in the past under no pressure and we have proved we can handle it. But this was the first time that we were under severe pressure trying to execute a 1–2 and we caused ourselves extra pressure from within our own troops.

The stakes are high for us as a team as our own performances and commitment to Red Bull Racing have lifted the bar to a very high level. We are a unique team and I believe this remains a huge strength in our quest for the world titles.

Kind regards,

That was my letter in its entirety. Dietrich was fine about it – but Christian went apoplectic!

After Turkey, as much as the team denied it, it became slowly but painfully evident that Marko was pulling the strings. More than that: there was an agenda – his. I had been assured by Christian that as long as he and Adrian were at Red Bull I would be looked after. They said they wanted me to win races; they even wanted me to win the title and I believed them. I did wonder, though, what would happen if they weren't there!

That summer my management and I tried speaking to Christian and asked him as bluntly as we could to abandon his pretence of even-handedness and just tell us exactly where I stood within the team. Not that we were going to trumpet it to the outside world: behind closed doors, we said, just level with us and be straight. If there was an agenda, we needed to be told clearly what it was.

We tried to make him understand that he was doing a great disservice to himself by allowing himself to be undermined by Marko. On the other hand, it's important to see that Marko was already a very useful conduit between the Red Bull Racing team and Dietrich, with whom Christian had little rapport. Marko had positioned himself between them, which helped Christian bypass bureaucracy and go straight to the top when important decisions had to be taken. In a sense, Marko had made himself indispensable. I have no doubt that Christian was put in a very tricky situation as that 2010 season unfolded. Not only did he have two drivers capable of winning races, it was looking more and more likely that they would also be in contention for the greatest prize in the sport. I'm sure he must have been asking himself, 'How do I keep them both happy? I've got to keep Marko happy as well . . .'

To him it perhaps seemed the lesser of two evils if his down-to-earth Australian was the one upset, not the blue-eyed boy from the Red Bull Junior Program in the other car, and he played that game all the way through, right to the end. Ultimately siding with me and upsetting Marko wasn't an option for him. To maintain harmony within the team (and you've got to remember there were 800 people involved), the focus had to be on keeping Marko happy, which meant making sure Vettel's side of the garage was happy.

Team Webber was old enough and ugly enough to understand that, but Christian insisted on keeping up the pretence that everything was even-handed, despite growing evidence that it was anything but. All we wanted was to be told the truth but he couldn't do that, and for me that was a sign of weakness. It was at this stage that I began losing respect for him. It must have been uncomfortable for him to be a front-line spokesperson for the team without enjoying any real power within the hierarchy.

The long and the short of it is that we read the whole Red Bull Racing team situation like a book, none more so than Flavio. After my back-to-back wins in Barcelona and Monaco he told us this situation wouldn't be allowed to continue. Not for the first time, he was absolutely right. Having a washed-up old Australian dog take the title was not part of RBR's plan!

13

In Rare Air

ALTHOUGH THE BAD SMELL FROM ISTANBUL STILL LINGERED, I re-signed with Red Bull Racing for the 2011 season just before the next race in Canada. My driving contract renewals and negotiations generally began around May or June of the preceding year and concluded, but were not always announced, by the end of July at the very latest. I was well and truly in the championship hunt with my teammate as well as Fernando and Lewis, so I wasn't about to write off my own chances by announcing to the team I was off to pastures new in 2011. I already felt things were starting to be stacked against me but they would have turned the tap off quick-smart and the momentum would have swung firmly in Seb's direction.

In Montreal I qualified on the front row alongside Lewis Hamilton but overnight my car suffered a gearbox problem and the boys had to change it, so I was hit by a five-place grid penalty and started seventh. Towards the end of the race Sebastian too had a problem with his gearbox. If that was a normal competitor ahead of me, like a McLaren or a Ferrari, you'd smell blood – but not when it was Sebastian. I wasn't free to attack my teammate.

Ciaron had to be incredibly reserved on pit wall: from that year on there were coded messages between us so I knew when it was 'not him' talking to me. Clearly I could have caught and passed Sebastian if I'd known about his gearbox issue. Instead they elected to shut the race down from there and not push his car that hard.

There were two reasons for their call. They knew he couldn't deal with being passed by his teammate; and if the car was nursed home Sebastian would avoid any risk of component failure leading to a grid penalty for the next race. Instead of saying, 'Sebastian, let Mark through,' or 'Mark is quicker,' they wanted him to do a certain pace at the end of the race which I then had to match. I could have raced at a totally different pace, but that would have meant me going past him at some stage, and that really would not have gone down well.

So what's the best solution for them? Turn both of us down. An engineer from Renault came to me at the end of the race in a fury and said, 'This is ridiculous. You need to do something, it's just going too far.'

The same Renault engineer also said that when engines were routinely tested on the dynamometer, the unit showing the higher readings – the strongest engine – would systematically go to Vettel's side of the garage, rather than alternating as had been the practice previously. The crux of it was that we were always free to race when my teammate was behind, never free to race when I was behind.

Canada had come just 10 days after Turkey so I bit my tongue. After the race Annie and I were sitting with Christian in the Montreal airport lounge and Sebastian's name cropped up. Christian commented that the problem with Seb was that he read straight from the pages of the Michael Schumacher manual.

As I said, it's on-track happenings that matter most, but there was another little off-track episode in Canada that left us nonplussed. At the time of the Malaysian race Seb had hosted a team dinner. I offered to do the same at the next suitable fly-away race, which would be Montreal. Everyone agreed; we booked a restaurant and paid a deposit. But after all the goings-on in Turkey the Red Bull Racing team manager, Jonathan Wheatley, called Ann to tell her that Christian no longer felt it was appropriate for me to host the evening. Jonathan added that Renault would be more than happy to take the team out to dinner in Montreal, but they had a particular restaurant in mind. Ann explained that cancelling our booking would cost us a bit of money, as we had paid the deposit. Jonathan went off to check with Renault and see if they would simply take over our booking. By the time he rang back to say they would rather not, Annie had come up with a compromise. Since we were so keen to present a united front, why not have Sebastian and me jointly take the team out and share the costs as a sign of team harmony? Of course that idea went down a treat with the senior management at RBR and the evening duly went ahead. We made a point of ensuring that the whole team thanked Seb as well as me. Ann and I settled the balance of the bill on the night – but it took until November for Sebastian to stump up his share. It probably wasn't his fault, though: we got the distinct impression the team had never actually shared the news that he was going halves with me!

I left the next race in Valencia battle-scarred and with no points after the biggest accident of my Formula 1 career. I had endured not one but two terrifying moments at Le Mans eleven years earlier; I'd also had a fairly major moment in the wet in Brazil in 2003. But what happened in Valencia was in a different league to any previous F1 shunt I'd been through.

My first lap was poor, so I had embarked on a comeback drive and pitted early. When I came out I was told I had to clear Heikki Kovalainen in the Caterham as quickly as possible. I cruised up into his slipstream – and Heikki started to defend his position. Clearly I was a lot quicker, so for every corner I found myself still behind him I was losing time to the guys who were now starting their own round of pit stops. I thought he had started to open up the line for me, but there is such a tunnel effect between those concrete walls in Valencia that it's easy for a driver to lose his reference points on the track and there was slight confusion about the braking-points for the next corner. His car became a launching-ramp – and my RB6 was the missile being flung into the sky.

Shades of those trees at Le Mans: as the car went up I had it in my mind that there was a bridge over the track somewhere nearby. 'Jesus,' I thought, 'if I hit something up here . . .' But the car came down, landed on its roll-hoop and thankfully righted itself. There was no deceleration process – the grip was non-existent. By this time, like Interlagos 2003, I'm no longer in a racing car, I'm on a bobsleigh: no steering, careering towards the wall.

As the car strikes the track, instantaneously you hear it starting to break up. However, the violence of carbon fibre disintegrating quickly becomes a second thought as you try to hold your body in the right position: the hits will inevitably come, but you don't know when they will happen. At this point you want speed and inertia removed but you can do little about that as you're only a passenger. When the car comes to rest, the initial feeling is relief that you're okay. Of course the adrenaline is high, as is the shock, but very quickly you're thinking that it's a lost result. It's amazing how the mind works.

It certainly must have looked dramatic – 'fourteen seconds of hell', my dad called it – but the car was strong and my belts did their job. Just as bloody well because I moved the concrete barrier several metres back, snapping the brake pedal in the process, which meant the pressure had been up around 250 kilograms! In an accident of that force your body stretches a lot, but ironically all I suffered was a fair bit of toe-bashing. Still, in the scheme of things a sore toe is nothing. I had always made a point, if I was involved in any kind of accident, to move as quickly as I could in order to reassure my girls, Mum, my sister and Ann, that, as Dad puts it, I've 'still got two arms and two legs and my head is together'. But the first thing on my mind this time was that some championship points had gone begging. This time, unlike Brazil seven years earlier, I was taken to the medical centre and quickly given the all-clear.

One of my mechanics wrote on the wreckage, *Thanks for taking care of my mate*. By the way, I wasn't thinking about it at the time of the accident but I was in the car which had carried me to those race wins in Barcelona and Monaco and it was supposed to be mine at the end of the year!

After Monaco my third victory of 2010 came at my adopted home track, and the British Grand Prix pretty much summed up my entire 2010 season. It was a bittersweet weekend, one that started with a very angry Australian and finished with another victory at the home of the World Championship, a circuit that had been very kind to me over the years. I had already won there in Formula Ford, in F3000, in the FIA GT Championship. I only had the big one to add to that list. But in F1 in 2010 Silverstone would be where I learned that despite the company motto, Red Bull Racing didn't give us wings – at least not both of us.

My team, I felt, made the task of adding a British Grand Prix victory to my Silverstone record unnecessarily hard for me. They discovered after practice that they had been left with only one example of a crucial new component – the front wing. The one they had was already on my car at that point. Sebastian's had been damaged and was no longer usable. So they decided to take the new wing off my car and give it to my teammate for qualifying and the race. I was furious.

The logic the team tried applying to the situation was that Seb had been quicker in the final free practice session, so he should have the sole remaining wing. That was all well and good but I had been forced to concentrate on long-run work rather than focusing on pure performance after my car had problems in Friday's second free practice. Likewise, their reasoning that Seb was ahead in the championship was flawed: if that was the case, then why, in Turkey, when I was ahead in the standings, did I still have to play second fiddle and wait for my new rear wing to arrive in time for qualifying? It seemed to me the goalposts were forever shifting.

If truth be told, neither Sebastian nor I particularly liked the new wing, but our Friday end-of-day briefing had shown that factory data suggested there was a gain to be had from using it, so the team wanted us to persist with it. I was a bit bemused when a story was leaked to the media, allegedly by a senior RBR engineer, saying that I didn't want the new front wing as I didn't find it any more effective than the old one and I only asked for it when there was only one of them!

At Silverstone, experts said the new wing was worth around two-tenths of a second on a quick lap; Sebastian beat me to pole by 0.143.

In the post-qualifying press conference it would have been obvious to Blind Freddie that yours truly wasn't thrilled with what had gone on, and slamming my glass of water down on the desk would certainly have helped to get that message across! A respected F1 scribe called it 'quite possibly the unhappiest team front row of all time'. Later that evening I headed home to Aston Clinton – one of the joys of the British GP was that I could commute from home – and watched my Aussie mate Crumpy win the British Speedway Grand Prix. Next day Mum and Dad came to the race, but Annie didn't. She was so incensed she decided to stay well clear of Silverstone. She didn't even watch the start on TV, but she told me afterwards she knew it must have gone all right because of the flood of text messages she started receiving just a few minutes later!

I was utterly determined to win the start, and I did. Seb bogged down, I got away beautifully and although he tried to squeeze me I was having none of it. The first corner was mine; so was the race. I beat Seb off the line fair and square and simply stood my ground. Perhaps it was inexperience on his part, perhaps it was something else entirely, but he didn't back off and inevitably his car ran over the kerb just as he was having to turn his attention to the man behind him. That was Lewis Hamilton; when the two touched it seemed at first the Red Bull – new front wing and all – was unscathed, but it had picked up a right rear puncture and Sebastian had to make an unscheduled call to the pit lane.

From where I sat it was all pretty straightforward. I made a good start, I was pretty keen to make it my corner and it worked out well for me. Monaco had taught me a lot about resuming behind a safety car so I wasn't unduly worried when it appeared in the aftermath of a shunt between Adrian Sutil's Force India and the Sauber of Pedro de la Rosa on pit straight. The safety car is always a threat because it means the unexpected has a chance to happen, but on the other hand I had a gap for a reason – I was quick – and although I had to start all over again I was quick enough to build that gap once more. I had a better car than anyone out there, I used it as it was intended to be used and the result was the logical outcome. And by the way, after my own car was destroyed in Valencia, the chassis I used to win at Silverstone was the one discarded by my teammate earlier in the year so there couldn't have been too much wrong with it!

There have been a few moments throughout my F1 career when radio communications played a significant and highly public part, and Silverstone 2010 was one of them. As my anger abated and the delight of winning my 'home' race set in, I made a comment that was meant to sound like typical Aussie irony, a laconic little dig at everything that had gone on that weekend and my feelings about it all. As the congratulations came over the radio into the cockpit, my response was, 'Yeah, not bad for a number 2 driver!' The team was always saying everything was kosher and Seb and I had equal status. But sometimes I had conflicting reports from the troops on the floor and saw evidence myself. At this point I simply didn't know who to trust. Adrian is a person I really struggle *not* to believe, and as was well documented towards the end of my career, he (and Dietrich) were the reasons I stayed at RBR as long as I did.

I should have fired in a bit of unprintable language and made sure that my comment wouldn't go to air, but of course it did and the whole world latched onto it as a sign that I was well and truly ticked off. I had been, but the comment wasn't intended to keep the feud going, it was meant as a wry Aussie slant on the day. In the context of mid-2010 it only drove another wedge between Team Webber and Red Bull Racing.

The German Grand Prix was race 11, the pivotal point on the calendar on our 19-race 2010 journey. From here on in, the climb would become steadily steeper. In such a strong year, Germany was not one of our better races. The race went to Alonso but only after Ferrari gave a very public display of team orders by radioing Felipe Massa: 'Felipe, Fernando is faster than you.' Everyone knew what it really meant and sure enough, the Brazilian slowed to let Fernando through. It was a season in which team orders were illegal so Red Bull Racing was quick to use the media to slate the Italian team, adding that RBR's drivers were free to race one another.

Really?

Still, the second half of the racing year began well. You couldn't get a much more blatant contrast than Silverstone and the Hungaroring, but the second race after the British Grand Prix the tight, challenging circuit outside Budapest brought my fourth victory of that remarkable season – and in a fairly remarkable way. Once again the safety car played a crucial part in the proceedings. The Hungaroring is a notoriously difficult circuit for overtaking: just ask Thierry Boutsen, the surprise winner back in 1990 when his Williams kept Ayrton Senna's faster McLaren bottled up for virtually the whole race. Knowing that history, it was disappointing to me when Sebastian claimed pole by the fairly large margin of 0.411 seconds, partly because I couldn't get a clean run and partly because he put in a bloody good lap. The car actually surprised us. We couldn't believe how phenomenal it was round there. It was a bit like Barcelona: we knew the other guys weren't going to get a crack at us so whichever of the two of us did the job would most likely be on pole.

Being out-started by Fernando's Ferrari, however, was not part of the plan and when he got between me and Sebastian off the line I thought, 'Here we go, bloody Budapest again . . .' We were happy to see Fernando pulling away from his teammate because that meant I could take him on one-on-one in the stops and not have Felipe trying to undercut me in turn. I was just looking after my car and tyres, waiting for a round of pit stops to try to do something different from Fernando.

But then along came a nice little safety car to turn the race on its head.

Tonio Liuzzi's front wing parted company with his Force India out at Turn 11, so the race was neutralised while they cleared the debris away. While most of the other drivers dived for pit lane, Seb included, Ciaron was yelling, 'Stay out! Stay out!', so I kept going.

I saw Fernando go into the pits and thought, 'Fantastic! Righto, now we can do something different because Seb's going to be in second position and I need to do 40 laps from hell – really quick ones.'

But would my tyres get me there? Nine seconds, 12 seconds, 15 seconds: that didn't help me at all: the magic number we needed was 18 seconds and a bit. Once we got the gap out to there or thereabouts we could win the race.

That thinking too went out the window when the safety car went in after 17 laps. Sebastian seemed somehow to have lost concentration briefly. Instead of observing the mandatory 10 car lengths maximum distance behind me he had fallen further back. At first I thought he must have a gearbox problem, then for a fleeting moment I thought he was trying to screw Fernando, backing him up massively and giving me a flying start to try and help with the pit stop. Then I thought, 'Shit, he'd never do that!'

In any case the stewards take a dim view of teams using one driver to shield the teammate ahead of him from attack. Sebastian's mistake was compounded when they handed him a drive-through, which he completed with his arms waving out of the cockpit in indignation. My race had changed dramatically. Now Fernando was the enemy and we had the luxury of going a few extra laps longer so the boys weren't panicking about my final pit stop. Imagine if I had done all that work for 30–40 minutes to help my pit crew, come in with the win in sight, then one of them fumbled a wheel-nut . . . He'd have gone and hanged himself.

The plan now was to pull off a delicate balancing act: find the limit of driving the car flat out but without falling off the edge, either of the circuit or of the option Bridgestones on my car. In the end I did 43 laps on a set of tyres the engineers thought were good for a maximum of 30, and half of those were like qualifying laps. I needed a gap of around 20 seconds to be able to contain Fernando when I stopped, but I wanted to try to give the crew that buffer if I could. I got the margin out to 23.7 seconds, pitted and cruised home. A bit of a gift, I had to acknowledge, but who was I to look a gift horse in the mouth?

The good thing about that day is that I did something different to the rest of the field. Everyone else had pitted and I had to come up with something else to win it. It was a new scenario for me but I had been optimistic about taking it on. It was Red Bull Racing's 100th Grand Prix, but it was also my own 150th, and what better way to celebrate that landmark?

We had left base camp far below us; the summit was in sight. There were only seven races to go and my name was at the top of the Drivers' World Championship standings.

*

Going into the August break as championship leader it was hard to imagine that Hungary would be my final visit to the top step of the podium for 2010. But this is a game of fine lines. There would be other highs in those final seven races, and the first of them was next time out when we visited Spa-Francorchamps, always one of my favourite circuits, for the first race after the break. We felt this and the race after, at Monza in Italy, would be two of the tracks that suited our car least well but once again I put the RB6 on pole, thanks mainly to some sensational advice from Ciaron in Q3 when he told me not to build up to a fast time but to fire in a quick one on my first lap.

Problems, though, had begun on Saturday morning with a hydraulic glitch. When it reared its head again on Sunday the boys were pretty nervous and I was asked to break with habit and do two full laps on my way round to the grid to check the systems. Their fears were well founded: getting away from the 'dummy' grid on the formation lap the car bogged down and though I played with the settings again on the way round to the 'real' grid the same thing happened at the race start. Upshot: from pole to P7 as I exited La Source, the famous right-hander which is Turn 1 on the Spa layout.

But all wasn't lost. On a rainy day, as this was, there were going to be safety cars, there were the pit stops to work on, there would be parts of the race when it was wet, so I felt I just had to hang in there and see what came of it all. Sure enough, events began playing into my hands, not least when Sebastian earned himself another drive-through for hitting Jenson at the chicane before the main straight. Fernando then fell off all on his own. That left me in P3 behind Robert Kubica, who then obliged by over-shooting at his pit stop as he fiddled with his settings on the way down pit lane. While Lewis's win was very impressive, second place was an excellent result for me and though it cost me the championship lead I was still just three points behind the McLaren man. Red Bull Racing were now a point ahead of McLaren in the Constructors' stakes as well so there was everything to play for.

One more log on the fire: at Monza we arrived with my name second in the Drivers' Championship with 179 points alongside it; Vettel's, meanwhile, was 28 behind mine in third place. But Monza brought further evidence that Marko was calling the shots; he informed us that if I was 28 points clear of Sebastian in the title chase after Monza, then the team's weight would be thrown directly behind me.

That was another weekend when it felt as though the pendulum had swung the wrong way. I had a water leak and an air-box fire in free practice, and by the time qualifying began I still hadn't tried the option tyre. Long story short: no Red Bull on the front row for the first time in a year, and a Ferrari there in the shape of Fernando Alonso for the first time in 22 months!

My start was average but I got done by Nico Rosberg, was out of shape at the first chicane and was murdered by a whole group of guys and down to P9 before I knew it. I got stuck behind a mobile chicane called Hülkenberg (who cut the first real chicane deliberately on two separate occasions as that was the only way he was able to stay ahead of me) and apparently the team's approaches to Race Director Charlie Whiting about the German's erratic behaviour didn't carry any weight. When we left Monza the gap between us had narrowed to 24 points, but I was back on top of the table while Sebastian had slipped to fifth.

Another good result in unlikely circumstances came about in Singapore, which had never been a happy hunting-ground for me. I figured I had to improve the way I was getting through that twisty final sector but in qualifying, ironically, it proved to be my best and I ended up on the third row. At the start I was boxed in behind Jenson's McLaren, but there was a very early safety car for Liuzzi's damaged Force India. I confess to being a bit nonplussed when the team called me in to change tyres. That meant I would have a long stint on Bridgestone's medium compound – but it turned out to be an inspired decision. I cleared Kamui Kobayashi, who was doing some kamikaze stuff on the Singapore streets, but got to Rubens and couldn't get past him. Then the safety car intervened again because sure enough, Kamui had overdone it, gone into the wall at Turn 18 and been collected by Bruno Senna's HRT.

Once we got going again I had Lewis chasing me and we had both Virgin race cars in our way. When Lucas di Grassi, in one of them, held me up through Turn 5 Lewis was all over me but I held my line through Turn 7. As the McLaren came across on me I was doing my best to get away from it but we touched and Lewis was out on the spot. The stewards had a look and declared it a racing incident, so I was free to carry on. My concern now was that my right front wheel was in a spot of bother: I had a huge vibration through it and only the bead was keeping the tyre on the wheel rim, but we made it to the end. Fernando won in Singapore again, keeping Seb at bay, and for me third place was a good salvage job. I now had 11 points in hand over Fernando; Lewis was 20 behind me and Seb 21.

Next stop: another favourite, Suzuka in Japan. This time I made the going tough for myself. Before the race I went back to Australia, hopped on a mountain bike for the first time Down Under since my accident in Tasmania – and broke my right shoulder when I went straight over the handlebars in one of the slowest accidents imaginable! It was a skier's fracture, as they call it, and it meant I needed pain-killing injections over the course of the next weekend. Christian Horner later complained that he hadn't been told about my injury, but I honestly hadn't felt it was worth mentioning. I was certain it would have no effect on me in the cockpit, even though Suzuka is one of the most physically testing tracks we have to contend with. The other reason I didn't say anything was because I knew it would be seized upon as a means to undermine my championship campaign and I wasn't prepared to give them that opportunity. In the end I was grateful that the Japanese weather intervened and gave me a little extra time to recover. After a pretty seamless Friday, track activity was washed out on Saturday and the mechanics occupied themselves building model boats instead of racing cars.

Sunday was unusual with qualifying and race on the same day, but it was back to situation normal for Red Bull Racing, a front row lock-out as we had become used to earlier in the season. The car really did work very well in Japan. Sebastian took pole by just 0.068 as the bee's dick syndrome continued, and the alarm bells started ringing again when Marko came out with another of his classic comments. 'That was a bit close,' he told me, meaning he felt I had pushed 'his' boy a little too hard for comfort.

Robert Kubica's start from third on the grid was phenomenal. It was a relief when he lost a wheel early on and was out, otherwise he would have been very difficult to catch. Seb headed up another Red Bull 1–2 finish, but while my first Suzuka podium was very welcome I felt I really needed to win another race to put me out of reach. Still, I had pushed Seb over the line at Suzuka with just 0.7 seconds between us at the flag, and I now had a 14-point cushion.

But there was another name in the equation as the final races loomed. Fernando Alonso had 206 points – and so did Sebastian Vettel.

*

History shows that my last three races of the 2010 season yielded just 22 points out of a possible 75. Sebastian scored 50. The figures become even starker when you remember that neither of us scored any points at all in Korea the first time F1 visited those far-off shores. We locked out the front row once again, for the eighth and final time in 2010, but Sebastian was out when his Renault engine expired and as for me . . . Well, this was the one unmitigated disaster of my 2010 season and it came at precisely the most damaging time. The race began in pouring rain – Fernando radioed that they were the worst conditions he had ever driven in – and the red flag was out to stop us racing after just three laps.

We restarted just over three-quarters of an hour later, though I couldn't see much difference in the conditions, but this time we were behind the safety car. It was in again after lap 17, but two laps later it was back in action once more – and this time it was because of me. The previous time around I had gone wider through Turn 12 to see if there was any more grip out there. This time I went too far, got the wheel tucked in behind the kerb and spun out of the race, collecting the luckless Nico Rosberg as I went. With Fernando coming home ahead of Lewis the tables had been turned; Alonso now led on 231 points from Webber on 220, Hamilton on 210 and Vettel still on 206.

So two races would decide the outcome of the 2010 World Championship. The first was in Brazil, a circuit I usually enjoyed. This time was a little different. As the title chase reached its closing stages, some people were starting to question Red Bull Racing's wisdom in allowing the drivers to keep racing each other rather than throwing their full weight behind one of us. What was being said in public didn't chime with what was being done in private: in Suzuka team management had shut down the race ahead of our 1–2 finish, while Sebastian was ahead. When we asked why, we were told it was because Adrian didn't want to risk seeing the two of us wipe each other out again. When it was suggested they should know me better, we were left with the very clear impression that it was the other driver they couldn't trust.

Since around the time of the Hungarian Grand Prix, Flavio and Bruno had been doing their utmost to get Christian more actively involved in the debate about the drivers, and to back my championship campaign wholeheartedly. Christian later admitted that he had approached Dietrich Mateschitz during that period in 2010 and told him that in his view RBR should throw all their support behind me. According to Christian Dietrich agreed, but then Marko got in his ear and advised him otherwise. The story changed: it became, 'We're going to support both drivers' campaigns until it's mathematically impossible for one of them to win the title.'

*

The furore in Brazil could hardly have come at a worse time in the fight for the 2010 world title. It was sparked by me saying that I didn't seem to enjoy the emotional support from Red Bull Racing that my teammate did. In fact I had asked for a clear-the-air meeting with team management ahead of the race. My concern was that I seemed to be going to Brazil on the back foot even though I was ahead of my teammate in the title chase. My boys sensed that something was going on, and I didn't want them to lose motivation if they felt I didn't have the team's full backing. I was keen for that clear-the-air meeting to happen as soon as possible after we arrived in São Paulo, and away from the circuit. I heard nothing back on Friday, nothing on Saturday: in fact nothing until Sunday morning, not long before the race.

The timing seemed bizarre to me. On Sunday, I walked into our meeting followed by Christian and Adrian, then Sebastian and Marko arrived. Marko wasn't normally in those meetings, but this time not only was he there, he and Sebastian ran the whole bloody show!

What if we were running 1–2 again at the end of this penultimate race, was the key question. My teammate's response was that 'we' – he and Marko, I assumed – wanted to keep the title race alive for as long as 'we' possibly could. My concern was that rather than backing one of us, they were actually loading the dice heavily in favour of losing the title altogether. I felt Christian was trying, suggesting that decisions needed to be made in the best interests of the team, but Sebastian and Marko were very firm on their position. Ultimately they wanted to keep Sebastian in the hunt.

In that meeting it hit me straight between the eyes where the real power in that team lay. It was also clear how much we were still prepared to gamble, with Fernando poised to beat both of us to the title. Adrian said to me afterwards it was one of the most awkward meetings he had ever been in, but for me it simply confirmed what I had been thinking.

On the positive side of the ledger, that Sunday in Brazil in 2010 was a sensational day for Red Bull Racing as we clinched our first world title – the Constructors' Championship. It came about with another 1–2 finish, our fourth of the season, with Seb again leading me home. The 43 points put us 48 clear of McLaren with just Abu Dhabi to come, an unbridgeable gap for Ron Dennis's team.

On the way to our 1–2 finish I got the call mid-race to shut my engine down because of a water pressure issue and conserve it for Abu Dhabi. I short-shifted my way to second place, moving through the gears more quickly than normal to reduce engine stress. I enjoyed a very strong rapport with the Renault engineers and in a case like that I simply had to trust them: I had been out to push Sebastian all the way, as I did in Suzuka, but what if I did that and the engine failed? We'd had everything thrown at us in 2010: protests over ride-heights, protests over flexing wings, and at the end of it all we had won the title. It was a very big achievement, not least for all the unrecognised people back at Milton Keynes who had slaved so hard to put us in a winning position in the first place.

First place was what I needed in that final race of the season in Abu Dhabi if I wanted the second title – the drivers' – to be mine. I went to the final race eight points behind Fernando and with seven in hand over Sebastian. Had the Red Bull Racing positions in Brazil been reversed I would have had a yawning 21-point advantage over my teammate. Lewis was an outside chance, 24 points behind Fernando and 16 adrift of me, while 2010's 'Big 5' was now a 'Big 4' as Jenson's hopes had gone. If I won the race and Fernando didn't come second, the crown would be mine.

In less than two seasons I had gone from being a 130-race winless veteran to a multiple Grand Prix winner; this season I had led the World Championship for longer than any other driver on the grid. My career had not been ended by the young fellow on the other side of the garage, instead it had blossomed; and now I was one of four blokes looking up at the summit of that mountain.

In the car it felt like a normal weekend, but there was so much more at stake. Lewis and Fernando had been in that fraught but happy position before; neither Sebastian nor I had. No need to dwell on it: Seb did the best job. He put his car on pole and drove it to victory. For some reason I couldn't get to the lap time I needed in Q3; in fact I qualified fifth, my worst effort since that first race in Bahrain, and was therefore out of position from the word go.

The consequence: eighth place, only four points, my worst result, DNFs apart, since China back in April, just when I needed my very best. This time the safety car didn't come to my rescue. It did come, as early as the first lap, when Tonio Liuzzi was left with nowhere to go as he came round and found Michael's Mercedes ahead of him and pointing straight at him.

Some drivers pitted under the safety car; I waited till lap 11 then made the switch to different rubber so I could go looking for the speed I needed. Jaime Alguersuari had other thoughts: I got stuck behind his Toro Rosso, found myself behind Fernando when he pitted four laps later, then both of us got bogged down again behind Vitaly Petrov. The Renault was quick in a straight line, we couldn't pass and so that's where we stayed. Ferrari, trying to cover me, had forgotten about Sebastian. The only time my teammate led the World Championship was when it mattered most: after the final race.

Despite my disappointment, I went to see Seb after the race and spent 20 minutes with him in his room, which he seemed to appreciate. I was hurting badly but I had always been brought up by Mum and Dad to play hard yet fair and display sportsmanship even when you had been beaten. So I had to go and shake his hand. But I was in a bad way, as Dad will tell you: 'I've known quite a few top-line sportsmen, played with a few and been around many others, but I've never seen a man so gutted in all my life. There was nowhere to hide: media people came into the room, Jackie Stewart came into the room, Sebastian came into the room and he wasn't even smiling. He was probably ecstatic but it was difficult to show that in the room with Mark. It was as gutted as I've ever seen anybody without that person being physically hurt.'

As if that wasn't bad enough, the team asked me to attend a celebratory function back in Austria and I felt I just had to be man enough to do that as well. Going there was tough; it was painful to watch the celebrations when it was all still so raw, coming to terms with not winning the title and seeing how much it meant to my teammate. It was difficult to man up, especially when there had been so many undercurrents throughout that season. But the one positive was the reaction from the Red Bull staff: they gave me a standing ovation, a nice touch that helped soothe the wounds.

It's very important for me to get one message across very clearly. At the end of 2010 I was *not* pissed off with Sebastian Vettel. It was hard to swallow the fact that my teammate had come through on the line and won a photo-finish for the biggest prize in our sport, but I could handle that.

If I was unhappy with anyone, it was with the Red Bull Racing management. When the kitchen got hot they didn't handle it very well, and that's what got to me. I felt there were constant attempts to devalue what I had done, even when I was winning races for the team and leading the championship, and the job's hard enough without having bricks put in your backpack and feeling that you are being constantly undermined. Unfortunately that feeling would only intensify through my final three years with Red Bull Racing. To many people, I know, it must seem as if the infamous 'Multi 21' message in Malaysia in 2013 was the beginning of the end for me as a Red Bull Racing driver, but our relationship had started to disintegrate long before that unhappy day.

Despite their protests to the contrary in 2010, I think recent history has proved that Red Bull were driven by a desire to produce the youngest-ever World Champion from the ranks of their Junior Driver Program. It would have been a failure for Helmut Marko otherwise.

Every picture tells a story, as they say. Just how much this all meant to Marko was laid bare in one rather poignant shot of him, sitting on the top step of the podium in Abu Dhabi after going up to collect the team's race-winning trophy and to share the podium with Seb. If you look closely at the apparent tears on Marko's face you have to wonder why he is crying. Is he remembering his friend Jochen Rindt, the sport's only posthumous World Champion? Is his commitment to Vettel some kind of throwback to his own career, which was cut short? Had he been living vicariously through the young German driver all this time? Or was it none of these reasons, but just the sheer relief at finally turning one of his Red Bull protégés into a World Champion?

Whatever the reason, it was clearly an emotional moment for him and I have no problem with that. Ann understood too: she had been close to someone who had all the talent but never got the chance to fulfil it, Paul Warwick, who died at just 22. I never met Paul, of course, but I knew what happened to him was part of Ann's reason for moving to Australia, and the foundation of her motivation to drive my career so passionately. After everything she and I had been through we'd been beaten to the winning-post by a power structure that influenced the final decision, and nothing was ever going to change at Red Bull Racing.

Still, none of this should detract from the job Seb did. I can say with absolute honesty that he is a better all-round F1 driver than I ever was. He has some sensational qualities. There were things he did and you just had to take your hat off to him. He has a computer-like approach to executing race weekends, and he was a Red Bull driver through and through, whereas the hardest thing for me at Red Bull Racing was to get some momentum going on my side. I always suspected Seb was just as much a pawn in the game as I had been and the pressure on him to deliver must have been immense. I'd just like to have had a crack at him 10 years earlier.

One of the greatest challenges in Formula 1 is to have two drivers at the top of their game going for the same prize within the same team, especially when they aren't the only ones in the title race. This wasn't like 2014, when Mercedes had zero opposition in the championship, so once they had wrapped up the Constructors' Championship they allowed their two drivers, Lewis Hamilton and Nico Rosberg, to slog it out for the Drivers' Championship. In 2010 Seb and I were battling hard with Fernando, Lewis and Jenson for the ultimate prize, so I think everyone was a bit surprised that Red Bull Racing elected not to follow accepted F1 practice and throw their weight behind the man in the lead at the appropriate stage of the season.

The well-respected F1 journalist Mark Hughes summed it up succinctly in his *Autosport* column immediately after Abu Dhabi 2010. Reflecting on my position, and the position Felipe Massa found himself in at Ferrari, he wrote:

> *Red Bull, the Austrian soft drinks company, now has the perfect world champion for its marketing aims. Sebastian Vettel is nonetheless a sensationally good racing driver who has been caught in the middle of the conflict between those aims and those of the racing team that represents it. In both situations, Ferrari's and Red Bull's, it has left only a small space for the other driver. Not in terms of racing hardware or available resource, but in psychological terms. Neither can feel as wanted as the guy on the other side of the same garage . . . With Mark Webber it's as if feeling he's the underdog has brought out some of his greatest performances.*

To end on a wry note, as soon as Seb took the chequered flag in Abu Dhabi to win the title, the team handed out *Sebastian Vettel, 2010 World Champion* T-shirts. A couple of days later, assuming they would have produced similar T-shirts with my name on them, my office phoned the team to ask if it was possible to obtain a couple of the *Mark Webber, 2010 World Champion* shirts. After a bit of to-ing and fro-ing, the answer came back that they had already been thrown away! Maybe they could have saved on such wastage by producing a generic T-shirt that either driver could have worn – as Mercedes did in 2014.

14

One Day You'll Look Back

ONE OF THE TOUGHEST THINGS ABOUT CLIMBING MOUNTAINS is that you have to come down again, whether or not you made it to the summit. And when you have come so close to the top of K2, it's a long way down, as I found out in the aftermath of Abu Dhabi 2010.

At the start of 2009, after my accident in Tasmania, I had been in no real physical shape to take on the start of a new season. As the start of the 2011 campaign loomed, I wasn't mentally ready. My work-rate, my attention to detail just weren't what they should have been. I had geared myself to win the title in the previous season and then retire, partly to put an end to all of the negativity in my racing life, but also because there would have been a sense of having reached my ultimate destination. I would have been ready to come off the mountain. When that didn't happen, I'm willing to admit it knocked the stuffing out of me. Ayrton

Senna knew a thing or two about winning titles – and losing them. He once said something that summed my feelings up pretty well: 'Anyone who prevents an athlete from going to the highest place strikes a major blow to his mind and motivation. In that situation everything goes against you in your heart.'

It was a bit of a struggle early on in the year, and that was a combination of the team's reaction to 2010 and my own. The team were pretty good with me but the shift was obvious: it was as if I had lost the championship in 2010 by 400 points rather than losing it by a handful of points at the final round. As for me, the new season came too quickly and it was hard for me to find the motivation from within. I was finding it harder to keep the fire alight, and it was very tempting to stay at home and walk the dogs. But once I was back in the car the competitive juices started to flow again. It was all about me now: dig deep, show what I was made of off-track as well as in the cockpit. My target for 2011 was to get the absolute maximum out of myself. The plan was to do what every athlete says you must: break it down into its component parts, go and get the best out of every single Grand Prix. The thought of stopping had already crossed my mind, so the idea was to treat every race like a footballer's last match. It was important to keep going back to the whole journey and see things in perspective.

Adrian's latest brainchild, RB7, was launched in Valencia early in February of that year. It was the first Red Bull Racing car to incorporate KERS, which was reintroduced for that season; we had a new gizmo called the Drag Reduction System (DRS), supposedly to help drivers overtake on designated sections of each circuit; and, most importantly in my view, the sport had switched to Pirelli as sole suppliers of tyres.

In the final years of my F1 career the Pirelli tyres posed the biggest challenge as far as I was concerned – and at the same time they helped take Grand Prix racing in a direction I didn't particularly like. Throughout the season we were troubled by intermittent KERS failures, but it was the speed with which the Pirelli tyres degraded that plagued my car most. 'In years gone by,' I said somewhat ruefully, 'you could race hard when you were behind people, but that's not the case in 2011 due to the tyres.' They 'went off', as we put it, losing their performance edge quite dramatically as soon as you found yourself in the dirty air behind another car. It would be a theme song throughout the year. On top of my disillusionment with things at the heart of Red Bull Racing, I was growing a little disenchanted with the sport itself and the departure from what I suppose you would call good, old-fashioned racing. There was a kind of long goodbye taking place.

Mind you, someone clearly would have preferred it to be a short and snappy goodbye. In Melbourne, ahead of the opening race, Marko came up to me and said it would be good if I could let them know as soon as possible what I planned to be doing in the future. Obviously he just wanted to make me feel even more at home than I already was!

Ironically, despite not being in the right state of mind to start with, I demonstrated exceptional consistency throughout 2011. I racked up the most World Championship points in my whole career: 258 to be precise, or 16 more than in the 'nearly' year of 2010. As in 2010, I was on the podium 10 times but unfortunately there was just one visit to the top step, not four, and it had to wait until the final race of the season in Brazil.

By the time we came back to Europe for the Spanish Grand Prix I had posted fastest race laps in Malaysia, China and Turkey. I was fourth at Sepang, then third in Shanghai despite qualifying 18th after electrical and up-shift problems. Despite being KERS-less I finished second in a Red Bull 1–2 in Istanbul. For Catalunya I put the car on pole for the first time since Spa-Francorchamps in 2010. But I was caught on the long run into Turn 1 by both Vettel and Alonso and spent over 30 laps behind the Ferrari.

In Monaco I qualified third, was beaten off the line by Fernando and struggled with the rear tyres again. I seemed to be searching for sheer pace in the early part of each Grand Prix when the cars were bloated with fuel, although in the streets of Monte Carlo I was also hamstrung by a radio failure that caused a fiasco in the Red Bull pits in the first wave of stops. Confusion over Sebastian's choice of tyres meant his own stop took longer than expected. I came in – and there were no tyres waiting for me at all! It cost more than 15 seconds and dropped me to 14th. It took a good pass on Kamui Kobayashi at the chicane to finally seal a top-four result. Curiously enough, it was only after that Monaco race, and its disappointing performance levels, that one of the guys told me I had been driving a different chassis from the one I was accustomed to. Why? And why wasn't I told before I got in it? Christian Horner's response: he didn't think it was important.

Ann and I began to call incidents like these the one-percenters. They were the sorts of issues that, in the main, shouldn't have mattered, but they started to occur more and more frequently and each time they added a little more to our frustration.

An example was the way in which the PR commitments were loaded in my direction. No driver enjoys having his race weekend preparations and procedures disturbed by PR appearances, but when you have sponsors investing big bucks in your team it just goes with the territory. However, there were times when Seb simply cancelled these appearances and, because no one was willing to confront him, he was able to get away with it. Red Bull Racing knew that they were pushing my patience and I'd get a call to say that because Seb hadn't shown up for his Paddock Club appearance, they felt it was only fair that I had the opportunity to do the same when it was my turn the next day. On one occasion Seb informed the team that he wouldn't be going to the annual filming day. It was the only chance for the team to get all its trackside filming and photography done for the year at a private test day. Christian felt that it was only right that I knew and could decide for myself whether I wanted to attend or not. Although I felt bad for the team, I declined too, on grounds of principle. The day went ahead with the Toro Rosso drivers subbing for us and wearing our helmets!

These one-percenters lowered everyone's morale, and I know Ann had to battle not to allow her feelings to affect me. I'm grateful she did, because I was in the thick of it all and I had to stay focused on the job – the 2011 F1 season.

Not long after Monaco, Red Bull reopened the old Osterreichring/A1-Ring racetrack, the picturesque Styrian circuit that had hosted the Austrian Grand Prix from 1970 to 1987 and again from 1997 to 2003. It was renamed the

Red Bull Ring and both Seb and I were part of the grand opening. It was there that I met Wolfgang Hatz, a member of Porsche AG Board of Management, who told me that the famous manufacturer was returning to motor sport in 2014. He was interested in having me join the test program which was commencing in 2013. I still had a bit going on in F1 but we agreed to keep in contact. I went to see him in November 2012 in Stuttgart; we shook hands and agreed to continue talking about a deal for 2014 and beyond.

Also sniffing around at the same time in 2011 were Ferrari! I'm not really sure how serious they were at this time but knowing how much I loved my motorbike racing, they invited me down to Mugello for the Italian MotoGP in July.

*

Even if I wasn't going to join them, I was certainly enjoying an exhilarating series of tussles with Ferrari on track. It started in Valencia in late June and the first battle only went Fernando's way in the final stops. The sequence continued at Silverstone, where I overtook Alan Jones with the 25th F1 podium of my career, but not without what seemed to have become the usual British Grand Prix drama and the next clear example of the growing rift between me and Red Bull Racing.

Do you like your F1 cars with cold blow or fired overrun? In the lead-up to the British Grand Prix there was yet another regulation change and the technical gobbledy-gook dominated the team managers' press conference. Only the engineers and technically minded will understand and that's certainly not driver talk.

My reaction? 'Seb and I are just here to drive: let's get on with racing.'

Trouble was, we weren't allowed to.

It rained at Silverstone that year. Nothing unusual in that, but it made qualifying a tricky game and I was both lucky and well advised to get a banker run in early in Q3. Pole position was the end result, but I lost all the benefit when I couldn't find any grip at the start, then ran wide at Brooklands a few laps into the race. Worse was to come: at my second stop, on lap 26, the front left wheel stuck and I was stationary for 10 seconds. A lap later Sebastian was in – and the jack broke, so he was delayed as well. In the meantime a certain Fernando Alonso took full advantage and blazed through from fourth to lead the race.

Sebastian and I were running third and fourth; then we both got past Lewis Hamilton, so we were second and third and we were racing, or at least that's what I thought. Fat chance: I got the telephone call from the pit wall telling me to maintain position. After everything that had happened in 2010, I wasn't impressed with the order, so it was a pretty one-sided conversation. They radioed about four times in all, but I kept pushing for a while before ultimately holding station as instructed. On this occasion, to his credit, Seb said we were simply racing and he saw nothing wrong with that.

During that 2011 season we returned to the Nürburgring, but on this occasion the memories would be slightly less glowing than in 2009 and had nothing to do with the race. Instead I need to 'fess up to another 'Mercedes moment', something that seems to be a recurring thread in this story! Mercedes are in the habit of hiring out the famous old track, the Nordschleife, on the Thursday of race week for some private running with friends and guests. Norbert Haug called me – as I said, our relations were always friendly despite the 1999 fiasco – and explained that they were a bit short of drivers to do those duties and would I help?

I had some friends over from Australia and I was happy to oblige. I split my invited passengers up over separate rides in the car, which was a C63 AMG. Soon enough I was beginning to grow a tad frustrated with the performance of this Merc and at one corner I just went in a bit too deep and ran out of room. To minimise the risk of injury I had to invent the softest possible way of making contact with the wall, which was to go in backwards, and in we went! I knew it was pretty bad, but I grabbed first gear and started driving again. After two kilometres I had to face it: the rear differential was gone, and this Mercedes was on its way to one place only – the scrapheap. Another car had gone in after a monumental tyre failure: not our finest five minutes on the famous Nordschleife . . . In the end I went to Norbert and asked him just to send me the bill this time. Once again he said, 'Look, we've been through plenty together, don't worry about it.'

* /

The series of on-track battles with Fernando continued when we went back to Spa-Francorchamps for the Belgian Grand Prix. Before the race Red Bull Racing announced that I had re-signed for a further year. The decision was harder in mid-2011 because I was struggling with my qualifying performance on the new Pirelli tyres, but I was still racing well and it was fairly clear that Adrian's cars would still be the ones to beat. In fact before that Belgian race there was also some fairly juicy debate over tyre safety – shades of Indianapolis in 2005, only this time it was an Italian company rather than a French one at the eye of the storm. Pirelli's soft tyres had blistered both on Seb's car and on mine in the closing stages of qualifying, but Pirelli were claiming we had been running outside their recommended camber settings on the front wheels. We stuck to our guns, and that meant we had to think hard about our race strategy, the timing of stops and so on. In my case the 'so on' included an atrocious start when the car's anti-stall mechanism kicked in and I trundled rather than rocketed off the line from the second row.

Within three laps I came in to switch to Pirelli's medium compound. When the safety car came out following a shunt between Hamilton and Kobayashi my teammate pitted; meanwhile, à la Monaco, my radio jammed and I missed the call to come in. At that stage Fernando stayed out and his Ferrari took the lead. When the restart was given after 16 laps Seb was quickly back in P1 ahead of Fernando and me. I came in for the last time after 31 laps and was soon on Fernando's gearbox in the fight for second place.

Now unless you have been to Spa-Francorchamps, stood on the outside of the track at the bottom of the old pit straight and seen it with your own eyes, you cannot believe how steep the run down to Eau Rouge is. You swoop down the hill and then the car just smashes into the bottom of the corner, which is in essence a left-right-left flick as the track heads uphill again through the Raidillon towards Les Combes. Going downhill with Fernando in my gun-sights, I had the momentum with me. 'I can make this work,' was the thought flashing through my mind. I was prepared to try because it was Fernando Alonso in the other car. I had the slightly better line as I pulled to the left; one of us had to lift, and in this case it was the Ferrari man who backed off. He is quite simply a world-class driver and he knew it was time to call it off, but it was one of those moments where I admit I held my breath just for a moment.

And what a moment it was! I knew instinctively that it was one for the scrapbook. I thought to myself quietly afterwards, 'One day you'll look back in years to come and think that's when you were at your peak, performing well, driving against the best and sometimes beating them.'

Ironically, what happened immediately after that moment with Fernando reminded me that there were things I didn't really like about modern F1 racing. One of them was the DRS, which the powers-that-be had come up with to allow drivers to open their rear wing, reduce the aerodynamic drag on the car and temporarily increase top speed. Fernando's Ferrari, with its wing duly open, blasted past me on the long uphill straight we call Kemmel before we got to Les Combes at the top. All that hard work for nothing!

As the last word on the subject of Spa 2011, I should add that Adrian Newey, who had been so concerned about seeing us start on blistered tyres, showed more emotion than I can ever remember from him when Seb and I met up on the podium after our 1–2 finish. 'Boy, am I happy to see you two!' were his exact words. He was actually in tears.

The podiums kept coming in Singapore and in Korea where Red Bull Racing and Seb retained both titles. The next two races, our first foray to India at a new track south of New Delhi, and Abu Dhabi, yielded little for me, but it all came together again – at last – in Brazil. It's another wonderful place to go racing: you feel as if you're a gladiator in an amphitheatre. The Brazilians love their F1, and why wouldn't they with names like Fittipaldi and Piquet, Senna and Barrichello in their history? They are always very vocal in their support and it gives the race a carnival feeling that you can't help but respond to.

I missed pole by the proverbial bee's dick again as Sebastian broke Nigel Mansell's long-standing record of 14 in a season, but in the race I felt comfortable towards the end of each of my stints, which had been far from the case in the rest of the year, and even though they said there was a gearbox issue on Seb's car I felt as if the day and the win belonged to me. In fact I posted the fastest lap on each of the last two just to prove a point.

Perhaps it wasn't my greatest season but then again I had three poles, seven fastest laps and 10 podiums including my second win at one of my favourite places. And while there weren't enough highs on-track, away from the circuits there was one I will never forget.

I took on one of the toughest stages of the Tour de France, L'Alpe d'Huez. Even better, I was in the company of one of the all-time sporting greats. His name was Alain Prost, my boyhood hero. I've never forgotten how bitterly disappointed I was not to see him race in Adelaide in 1991 because he had fallen out with Ferrari and had been dropped from the team. I was able to tell him about that let-down when he and I had dinner together the night before taking on the climb, which is more than 15 kilometres long and boasts an average gradient of around 10 per cent.

I have always enjoyed ascents on the bike, not least of all because it's so rewarding to look back and see how far you've come when you get to the top. I was curious to see how I would go against both the mountain and Alain. He was 56 by then, but to me he looked fitter than he had ever been. If age was against him, size wasn't!

A familiar problem from my four-wheeled racing career cropped up again on two wheels because Alain weighed only around 58 kilos, which gave him about 18 in hand on me. He took up cycling seriously after his F1 career finished in 1993 and by the time we got together he was riding five days a week and apparently had no fewer than 10 bikes to choose from! We set ourselves an initial and quite challenging target of an hour to make it up there and while I went well in the early stages, 'The Professor', as Alain was always known in F1, had got it right again and was ahead of me by the time we got to the top. He was gentlemanly enough to wait a few seconds so that we could cross the line together, the time being around 61 minutes and 55 seconds – just outside our target, but nonetheless respectable and rewarding enough on a day I will remember very fondly indeed.

*

A good break in Noosa and plenty of fitness training over the Australian summer had put me in a very good frame of mind as the 2012 season approached. Unlike the start of 2011, I felt refreshed, motivated and keen for it all to kick off again. Once again, it was all about me: I had no control over reliability issues with my car or bad decisions by the team, so I simply had to tick all the boxes in my own preparation. That was the mind-set that carried me through the back end of my F1 career and drove me to rise above the obstacles put in my way, either by the team or by certain individuals. It's all about digging deep and never letting yourself be ground down. So four fourth-place finishes and a DNF in the opening five rounds were misleading: I was quietly optimistic about the year ahead and again I was utterly focused on getting the best out of myself.

In fact the season began with a sequence of seven different winners in the seven opening rounds from Australia to Canada – and I was one of them. At first the same themes emerged as Red Bull Racing had seen in 2011: no KERS in Melbourne, aggravated by another start-line clutch issue, very testing conditions in Malaysia making it hard to have confidence in the wet-weather tyres, a worrying little moment when the front of the car lifted as I got on the grass in China, and defective KERS in Bahrain. Barcelona was a bit of a disaster: we chose not to do a second run in Q2 and failed to make it into Q3. An early stop for a damaged wing didn't help and 11th place signalled the first time I had completed a race distance without finishing in the points since back in 2009.

To me the whole thing underlined once again the frustrating nature of F1 racing at that time: if you started at the front you were free to drive your own race, but starting towards the back meant you would inevitably finish pretty much in the same place. You would find yourself stuck in traffic, take too much out of the Pirellis, and end up having to drive as slowly as you could to get to the end of the race. I'm not a big fan of racing like that.

By the time we arrived at Monaco in 2012 my Monte Carlo record included a Formula 3000 win in 2001, my first

F1 podium in 2005, a fourth place in 2008, and that wonderful day in 2010 when I won. There, more than anywhere, starting from the front is crucial, and that's what I did, for the second time in Monaco. It wasn't all down to Webber brilliance on this occasion: a bloke by the name of Schumacher beat me to it by eight hundredths of a second, but sadly for Michael at the place where he had set his very first F1 pole 18 years earlier, he already knew he was carrying a five-place grid penalty for his part in taking Bruno Senna out in the previous race. If you're going to enjoy a piece of good luck in securing pole position, then Monaco is the place to do it.

After an early safety car we were free to go racing. That meant managing my tyres very carefully: would supersofts last long enough for us to risk one-stopping or would we be forced into a two-stop strategy? The Pirellis hung on longer than we had dared hope and I made my one stop on lap 29. After that I had to manage the gap to Sebastian, who was leading but still had to stop again. He needed around 21 seconds on me to make that work. I managed to bring it back to 16 seconds or so and stabilise it there. It started to sprinkle with 10 laps to go, but luckily it got no worse and my second Monaco victory was in the bag.

It had been harder than two years earlier, not least of all because RB8 was less dominant than 2010's RB6 had been. To see your name on the Monaco Grand Prix winner's trophy is one of the most amazing things a driver can hope for in his F1 career; mine was there twice now. And by the way, this time I had taken a dinner jacket just in case . . .

Two days later I found myself back in Monte Carlo for an important meeting. At this point of the championship I was on equal points with Seb, both of us three points behind the leader, Fernando Alonso. My meeting was with Stefano Domenicali, the Ferrari team principal, on Flavio's boat in the famous Monaco harbour. There was now a very real chance I would be joining the Prancing Horse team. Flavio, Stefano and Fernando all wanted it to happen; contracts were sent but they were for one year plus an option for the second year, instead of the two years we were pushing for. At that stage I hadn't taken a final decision to leave F1 and join Porsche; I just wasn't interested in switching to another F1 team for 2013 when in the July of that season they might tell me my services wouldn't be required the following year.

Canada and another struggle with the tyres was an anti-climax after that Mediterranean high, then I enjoyed a dice with Michael in Valencia where he sniffed the one and only podium of his comeback years with Mercedes – he would retire for good at the end of 2012 – and wasn't about to let it slip. The next race was at Silverstone, where the Ferrari deal was still on the table. I remember driving to the track on the Friday morning and chatting to Fernando on the phone. We swapped a few more calls and although he asked me to wait for a bit longer, my gut was telling me that Ferrari wasn't right for me. Red Bull Racing were having a bit of fun talking to other drivers too, Lewis in particular, as they had clearly got wind of the Ferrari approach, so there had been no dialogue about extending my contract.

At Silverstone, however, Christian suddenly wanted me to sign a new deal for 2013, which we did a few days later. It would have been a change of scenery to go to Ferrari: it was also nice to feel a little bit wanted. Interestingly Bernie Ecclestone did a U-turn on that prospective Ferrari move:

he was against it the first time, but in mid-2013 he asked me if I was comfy with my decision and said he believed we could still make the Ferrari deal happen for 2014.

Although there was no way I could have known it at the time, Silverstone would bring my final climb to the highest step of a Formula 1 podium. Alonso figured prominently again, taking pole position with me alongside him on the front row.

That sounds pretty straightforward. It wasn't.

In Q2 Fernando came upon a pool of water at Chapel and demonstrated the reflexes that make him great when he caught the Ferrari and saved it from disaster. The session was suspended soon after. Then Q3 came down to the closing seconds, with Fernando and me in the hunt for pole. We delayed our run as long as we could, watching the weather, but as I was going for it the rain began again and I came up five hundredths of a second short. Fernando had given Ferrari their first pole of 2012: could I do anything about it on Sunday?

I have always enjoyed being the hunter rather than the hunted, and I am pleased that my final F1 victory came that way. Mid-race Fernando and I were running 1–2; I stopped for the final time after 33 laps, he came in to cover that move four laps later. Now he was on unused soft compound tyres, I was on the harder variety. There were 15 laps to go. At first it looked as if the Ferrari had too much of an advantage: Fernando was lapping under 1:36 to begin with, but soon he drifted back into the mid-1:36 range.

Meanwhile I was picking up speed and firing in laps in the mid-1:35 bracket. The hunt was on: I smelt blood. I was on his gearbox by lap 45 but bided my time before passing him as we went into the left-hander at Brooklands three laps later.

It felt like another special victory. Like Monaco, Silverstone has always been one of F1's 'Blue Riband' races. After all, despite all the changes to the track, it is still the birthplace of the World Championship. And, like Monaco, it was now a place where I had won twice in a Grand Prix car and it had taken me into second place in the championship. A year earlier at Silverstone, I had overhauled Alan Jones with my 26th F1 podium; in 2012 I overtook my second great compatriot, Sir Jack, with my 32nd.

*

The next three races in Spa, Monza and Singapore netted me the grand total of eight points, so two straight podiums in India and Korea were a welcome dose of better-tasting medicine. But I was disappointed in Korea when I took pole and set fastest lap but then couldn't make it the hat-trick by winning the race. KERS raised its unlovely head again in India, where I started from the front row but finished third behind Vettel and Alonso, but there was an enjoyable end to the Indian trip.

Seb offered me a lift on a private plane he had organised and we flew together from Delhi to Dubai. There were stories circulating in the media at the time about how we weren't getting on, I was refusing to help Seb with the championship and so on, so the press would have got a big shock if they had seen us travelling together. It was just Seb, his girlfriend Hanna Prater and me. We chatted about personal stuff we'd never had the opportunity to in our working environment, like our love of dogs, how private he is and how he doesn't much like the limelight. I always enjoyed Hanna's company too. She had her feet firmly on the ground and was great for Seb. She was fiercely loyal to him, a quality I admired in her.

In racing terms 2012 went downhill for me after that: a run of 23 straight race finishes came to an end in Abu Dhabi when I tangled with Romain Grosjean and F1's first visit to Austin in Texas proved an anti-climax when my alternator failed after 17 laps.

A great shame, that, as the Circuit of the Americas is one of the few new tracks that can hold its head high among the best F1 has to offer. We retained the Constructors' Championship that day, but Lewis went and spoilt the party by winning the inaugural Austin race and so denying Seb the drivers' title for the moment. Austin brought a defining moment for Ann. When she looked across the room and congratulated Marko on the Constructors' title he simply dismissed her. Clearly the only title Marko was really interested in winning was the Drivers' Championship.

I was immensely proud of my contribution to another Constructors' success. You may be on your own out there, you may want to beat your teammate more than anyone else around you, but F1 remains a team sport in name and there is an enormous number of people who make it possible for two drivers to go out and chase the glory on a Sunday afternoon.

At the final race in Brazil, Seb and I were out-qualified by the McLarens; we started from the second row and I did what a racing driver is supposed to do – try to get off the line as fast as possible, position the car for the first corner and start racing. That meant getting away in front of Sebastian as I was ahead of him on the grid, which I did, and then all hell broke loose a couple of corners later when the whole world sat in his cockpit through the magic of on-board cameras and watched as almost an entire Grand Prix field went past him – while he was facing the wrong way!

I had absolutely no part in his drama. He had turned across Bruno Senna's Williams, which was later called a first-lap mishap. But he claimed afterwards that the main reason he was in a position to have an accident in the first place was that he had been squeezed by me at Turn 1! 'The angle became worse and worse,' was how my teammate put it, 'I didn't want to lose my front wing so I dropped down to first gear and lost both momentum and positions.'

Red Bull Racing management took exception to the fact that I didn't let Sebastian come down the inside, but you just don't risk that kind of manoeuvre at that stage of a race. Never mind that Seb had fought back for sixth place and enough points to beat Alonso to the title, Marko spouted off about me in the Red Bull in-house magazine, *Red Bulletin*, over the winter break. Enough's enough: we told Christian that the man was now persona non grata and I don't think we ever spoke again! On the other hand, Mr Mateschitz himself told me I didn't have to move over for Sebastian – he should be able to look after himself.

While Sebastian was taking his third title the season ended in anti-climax for me when that chaotic Brazilian race finished behind the safety car and I was off the Interlagos podium for the first time since 2008. I was sixth overall in the championship, my worst finish in the final five years that I raced with Red Bull.

15

Finishing Strongly

BEFORE THE START OF MY FINAL SEASON IN F1, A FOUR-YEAR
marathon came to an end: in December 2012 the last piece
of metal was removed from my right leg, a 40-centimetre
titanium rod that forced me to relax the Webber training
regime for a brief period. Although it wasn't long before
I began to concentrate on my fitness once again, my thoughts
were increasingly turning away from Formula 1. Only those
closest to me knew it, but this was to be my last season.

I had concluded my negotiations with Porsche and signed
a contract for 2014 that would allow me to continue racing
at the highest possible level after Formula 1. Ann had left
the decision completely up to me. Perhaps if she had had
her way I would have called a halt altogether, but I wanted
to keep racing and she accepted that. While I wanted to
make the most of my last season, I was also looking forward
to life away from the goldfish bowl of the F1 paddock.

I set myself the task of learning to fly a helicopter, having had a fascination with aviation for many years. It was a daunting prospect at first: although I was always going to be fine with the practicalities of flying, studying for exams was another matter as it had never been my forte at school. I had to work hard to get the radio communications section of the licence right, and I have never done so much reading in my entire life! I was left wondering what might have happened if they'd taught this stuff at Karabar High. Thankfully I managed to get to grips with all the theory and I'll admit I was very proud when I eventually qualified. I have to say that flying helicopters is not a pastime that sits entirely comfortably with Ann and I think she'll always be a lot more nervous about me doing that than racing cars!

Another factor that had influenced my decision to leave F1 was the fact my parents weren't getting any younger. I was very conscious that Mum and Dad, my sister Leanne and her young family had taken a back seat for most of my adult life. I wanted to redress the balance and find the time to enjoy special moments and experiences with them. Of course Dad had mixed feelings about my retirement – we had come a long way from Queanbeyan together – but he understood that bringing an end to the F1 adventure was my call, and I know he and Mum respected me for bowing out with my head held high. In Dad's words: 'How could we be disappointed? Our son was the first Australian to win a Grand Prix since Brabham and Jones, he enjoyed a wonder-ful 12 years at the pinnacle of world motor racing and he took us along for the ride with him.'

*

Back in the goldfish bowl Marko was making some pretty unflattering remarks about Red Bull Racing's Australian driver. According to him, Red Bull had put me in a winning car, then a young kid had come along and beaten me to the prize. He suggested I had a couple of 'unbeatable' races each year but couldn't keep it up, and that I couldn't handle pressure.

All I could say to that was that everyone in our sport has their own agendas and it was clear I had never been a part of Marko's. In a script like that you can read all sorts of things between the lines, but as far as I was concerned it was of very little consequence. My decision was made; Marko's attitude would soon be a thing of the past. There was only one way to go about the season: do my absolute best.

As well as an old enemy, going into my 12th season I had a new colleague to work with. My long-time race engineer Ciaron Pilbeam had had enough of Red Bull Racing and was off to Lotus. In his place came Simon Rennie, so we needed to get to know each other's way of working pretty quickly. With a new suite of regulations waiting to transform the face of F1 at the start of 2014, the 2013 RB9 could be seen as the last in Adrian Newey's sequence of all-conquering Red Bull Racing cars.

Early in the season, with new Pirelli tyres using softer compounds all round, the car would struggle, perhaps because of its aerodynamic characteristics, although Sebastian managed to win four times in the period before the mid-season break. But when there was a switch mid-year to the 2012 constructions with the 2013 compounds it became practically unbeatable. Unfortunately Seb's car was beating mine as well! From the Belgian Grand Prix onwards

Seb embarked on a run of nine straight Grand Prix wins, a season's total of 13, and he won his fourth title by a country mile at Suzuka with four races to spare.

*

It didn't all start with 'Multi 21', but that's probably as good a place as any to finish on the subject of my differences with Red Bull Racing.

Sebastian arrived in Malaysia in 2013 after a podium in Melbourne, but in Sepang we were very concerned about our pace. Our Friday race preparation was slow, so we decided to use Saturday's free practice session to do long runs, which is unusual for us. Pirelli were very pessimistic about the length of the stints we could do: we were very hard on tyres. So we did those long runs on Saturday morning, and tried some highly unusual set-ups while we were about it.

Sunday's track temperature was six or seven degrees cooler. A shower just before the start meant we began the 56-lap race on Pirelli's intermediate tyres. Thanks to a good call from Simon I got my cross-over, switching to the right tyres at the right time, spot-on. Seb, who had started from pole, changed too early and soon we were running 1–2, with my car in the lead. I stayed there through the second round of stops but that's when the trouble started. As the third round of pit stops neared, I had backed off to take care of my tyres; I didn't know this at the time, but Sebastian was making a fuss over the radio and had issued an order of his own: 'Get Mark out of the way, he's too slow.'

The team asked if I could lift my pace before the final stop which is a normal request, and I obliged. This is where it got tricky for the team as they were trying to keep Seb ahead of the Mercedes, so they pitted him first. Normally the lead car, in this case me, would have priority over the pit stop sequence. Once the stops were done, Seb had not only gained time on the Merc but the powerful strategy of pitting earlier meant that he was straight into DRS range of me.

The team were happy that their strategy had protected him against the Mercs and so we got the infamous 'Multi 21' message to turn the engines down and bring the cars home. It wasn't always beneficial to us to race hard against each other because that was too hard on the tyres and in Malaysia we had had that very discussion beforehand. I knew within two laps that Seb was going to take matters into his own hands despite the reassurance over the radio that the race was mine.

I started defending, but as a result of our respective qualifying runs he had new tyres and I didn't. My attempt in Q2 was too conservative so I did an extra lap: that meant I was on a three-lap-old set while Seb's were brand-new. Maybe he felt he should be able to use those tyres to the best effect rather than be told to back off? Whatever his thinking was, when he overtook me I wasn't so much angry as very sad that the team had reached this sorry state.

With Seb's victory done and dusted, Adrian Newey came up to me saying, 'We told him, we told him.' Seb himself was very keen to talk to me before we went up to the podium but I didn't want to listen. When we got there the interviewer, Martin Brundle, found himself in a very awkward position. That was when I made my remark about Sebastian making his own decision to disobey orders and race and then being given protection, as usual, by the senior management at Red Bull Racing.

After the podium ceremony Sebastian said he wanted to give the win back to me: he said it had been a complete f#*k-up. We knew by then that the official FIA press conference was going to be very awkward for all concerned. The team PR people couldn't get to us before we went in there. Sitting next to Seb was very uncomfortable. He had executed the whole thing and now he had to deal with it. He said he would call me in Australia, where I was going after that race. But it was no surprise when I got a call from Dietrich Mateschitz instead.

He was furious about what had happened and what it had done to Red Bull's image. He asked me to give him both a verbal and a written account of what had happened, which I did. He also asked me to tell him what had gone wrong in Melbourne: he was very curious about the technical issues I had faced before the start of the race. It was clear he wasn't very happy about it, as Melbourne was a race he would have liked me to have won.

The next time I saw Sebastian was on the Thursday of the race weekend in China, and I said we needed to talk. The ensuing conversation was the most disappointing moment of our entire relationship. He said he was pissed off by what I had said on the podium in Malaysia, that while he respected me as a driver he had no respect for me as a person.

That was a heavy line for me. I simply said, 'Then our relationship is in trouble. That's it.'

I had clung to the belief that we might sort things out between us but I couldn't help thinking someone must have got in his ear to cause such an about-face. Christian later insisted it was all of Sebastian's own doing, his justification being that it was payback for Silverstone 2011 and Brazil 2012. I could have gone back a lot further than that!

From then on I knew the end of the season was going to be difficult. Drivers are such beacons within a team: the tensions between us would put stress on all the other areas of Red Bull Racing.

Perhaps Dietrich could have sorted it out, but he had plenty of other things on his radar and in any case he ought to have been able to trust the people he'd put in place to handle the situation. He had told me he would have liked to handle things differently even back in 2010. I trusted Adrian, but Christian was in an awkward position having to keep Marko happy, and it turned out that the protection for the other driver *was* there. It might have been different had we had really strong management. Sebastian and I both tested the system and when your drivers are fighting each other for race wins the pressure on all concerned is that much greater.

When Ann later pressed Christian about why the team had never reprimanded Seb or issued any punishment for the 'Multi 21' incident, he said that the team had received a two-page letter from Seb's lawyer a few days after the Malaysian race stating that they were in breach of his contract by giving him 'an unreasonable instruction/team order'. Red Bull Racing clearly felt they were in a very awkward position because they ended up paying first-place bonus money to both drivers and the figures weren't small either!

*

With the Malaysian mess behind us, saying 'Au revoir' to Monaco with my fourth F1 podium there was very pleasing.

It happened on a day when my former teammate Nico Rosberg emulated his famous dad, Keke, one of F1's greatest street-fighters, who won there in 1983 for Williams. Coincidentally I was behind Nico again when I finished second at Silverstone, my fifth F1 podium at another track which has always been kind to me, and I had one of my more enjoyable moments of the year when I went public with my decision to quit Grand Prix racing.

I had been to Austria two days earlier where I signed my Porsche contract and met with Mr Mateschitz at Hangar 7. I told him that I was going to announce my decision to move to endurance racing at a circuit, Silverstone, that had always felt like home to me. Typically, he had wished me well. In fact he gave me the impression he was disappointed, though maybe he felt that was the right thing to do, but he said he always felt sad when the gladiators dropped out of the sport. He liked having real men racing his cars.

Prior to making the announcement, Ann had checked my RBR contract with my lawyer, who confirmed that I was under no obligation to inform the team; I only had to notify them in the event of my switching to another F1 team. So on the Thursday morning, 10 minutes before Porsche issued their press release, I phoned Christian Horner and told him my F1 days were over. It was another crack in my relationship with Red Bull Racing but I was happy to wear that. I didn't want this to be done on anyone's terms but mine.

Another track that has been kind to me, the Nürburgring, had a nasty surprise in store this time. I felt, over the weekend, that this was a place where I could challenge for that elusive 10th Grand Prix victory – until lap 9 and my first pit stop. As I tried to accelerate away from the box, the right rear wheel came off my car. It bounced high and hit one of the FOM (Formula One Management) television cameramen on duty in pit lane. In comparison to what had happened to the poor man (who was not too seriously injured, as it turned out), the two-and-a-half minutes I lost in pit lane didn't matter. In the context of a race, though, they were terminal.

I made eight podium appearances in 2013 but unfortunately none of them came at another favourite place of mine, Spa-Francorchamps. Two practice starts on my way to the grid proved alarming and sure enough, the clutch bite point was all over the place and I bogged down at the start. I'd have loved to finish higher than fifth: driving a Formula 1 car round that great circuit is one of the things I miss about Grand Prix racing. The same applies, to a certain extent, to Monza, where I at last got on the podium for the first time in F1 alongside Vettel and Alonso. You see the fans hanging out of the trees in the royal park, you see full grandstands, you see kids with their grandparents – to me that's just wonderful.

Being on the podium again at Suzuka was brilliant, too – especially after the build-up! It began on the Sunday night post-race in Korea and ended with six Formula 1 drivers doing mock pit stops on taxis on the main streets of downtown Tokyo. Our bender involved me, Fernando, Lewis, Felipe, Jenson and Nico Rosberg. At some stage, as I recall, we also roped in DC and Martin Brundle. We'd started hooking into it on a private flight between the two venues. I confess that I've forgotten now exactly what it was we ended up drinking, but by the end we were stacking up the shot glasses and trying our damnedest to out-do each other. Alonso entered the fray late so we acted like stewards, deemed him to be two laps down and ordered him to neck a few to get himself back on the lead lap! The racing similarities got a bit out of hand – for example, I've no idea why Fernando told me at one point that he was coming in for a set of supersofts – but Webber was adjudged to have put it on pole. If you drank 15 of whatever we were drinking you got your name up on the wall so it's not hard to imagine six competitive guys getting right into it. I was up for another crack on the Tuesday and roped Nico and a few others into it with me! The photographs of us walking into the Suzuka paddock don't suggest that we're ready for the gunfight at the OK Corral . . .

But when we got back to real racing life I was on pole and the lap that put me there was one of my best ever. So much so that I did wonder if I should have taken off the pressure valve a bit more during my career, allowed myself the chance to let my hair down, but I was always thinking too much about the next day's fitness training session. I had to give best at the start to Romain Grosjean as he rocketed into the lead and it took a late switch from two to three stops to bring me back to second behind eventual winner Seb. I couldn't help feeling it was a chance gone begging and that in the end a 2.5-stop strategy might have done the job.

The next race was India, where we retained the Constructors' Championship but I retired from the race with an alternator failure, just as I did the year before when the team won the Constructors' title in Austin. Christian had shared with Ann and me that in a perfect world, Marko only really wanted a one-car team but the regulations prevented that. Judging by all the technical gremlins that had plagued my car for the last couple of years, it was hard to resist thinking that they'd effectively got their one-car team anyway. Ironically, Seb might have felt much the same after his 2014 season – in fact at one point I quipped, 'They've given him my car!'

With just three of my 215 Grands Prix remaining I was determined to finish as strongly as I could. So three straight podiums in Abu Dhabi, Austin and Brazil allowed me to feel that I was leaving at the right time: still driving well enough to keep company with the front-runners, still capable of putting the car on pole as I did in Abu Dhabi to equal Sir Jack's personal tally of 13, still quick enough to post fastest laps as I did on the 51st lap of my final race at Interlagos, matching Ayrton Senna in at least one stat department with my 19th fastest lap of my career!

Despite my differences with team management, a 1–2 finish in Brazil was a brilliant way to complete my seven-year stay at Red Bull Racing. I had said my personal goodbyes, in a sense, in Austin, a friendly, fun place, by inviting a group of people who had been with me throughout my single-seater racing career. People like Geoff Donohue, Spencer Martin and his son Matt, Jason Crump and his wife, Mel, Mum and Dad and the great friends I'd made in Austin, all of whom had been with us through thick and thin. We all had a sensational week, culminating in a post-race dinner at which even Dad got a bit teary. For me it was a nice closure, emotionally, on my career.

When we got to Brazil I was especially thrilled, looking back on it all, because the men beside me on the podium were Vettel and Alonso. I will always be proud to have raced alongside those two, arguably the fastest drivers of this generation, and being up there with them on my last day in F1 was another in a long list of very special moments. Sebastian said in our post-race debrief that we had had some very tough times but a huge percentage of the time we pushed each other very hard, and that he generally thrived having me in the other car. I thought his comments at that last race were pretty genuine.

I wouldn't say I'm a sentimental sort of bloke, but I will admit to being close to tears when I climbed into that car for my last race start. Before the race Dietrich sent me a text message:

> It's on my and Red Bull's part to thank you for all
> the years, your commitment and input! There will be
> nobody in F1 who won't miss you – and most we do.
> This is "your" race today, enjoy it! There are not many
> men and athletes like you in general – and not in F1 in
> particular. :) See you soon. Dietrich.

Dietrich is someone I continue to learn from and for whom I have the utmost respect. I'm absolutely honoured to have been able to continue with Red Bull in my own right, and proud to have the brand associated with me, considering what we went through, in my new life in sports-car racing with Porsche. I would have loved to have Adrian there with me too – I tried very hard to get him to join me at Porsche but instead he chose to go the route of America's Cup, which is understandable as it presents a whole new and fresh challenge for him.

Another emotional moment was taking off my helmet on the Interlagos slowing-down lap: it was something I wanted to do for the passionate Brazilian fans, to let them see the man beneath the mask. It was a different touch on a day when there had been a few of them, not least of all finding the Aussie flag draped across my cockpit on the grid, or seeing my crew wearing Aussie bush hats and sending me big 'Thank You' messages for the TV cameras to pick up.

Taking the crash hat off might have got me into trouble on any other day, but not when I was actually saying my good-byes to the sport and all its fans. Mind you, if the stewards had objected it would just have rounded off a season where I was up before the beaks on a few occasions. In fact, my fellow Red Bull athlete and skydiver Felix Baumgartner, who made world news in 2013 when he jumped to earth from a helium balloon in the stratosphere, sent me a text saying that he would personally pay my fine if I got hauled up in front of the stewards again!

I had already been 'pinged' three grid places for my alleged part in a Shanghai tussle with JEV, Jean-Éric Vergne; they reprimanded me again in Bahrain after Nico Rosberg and I came together; and they were on my case again most famously in Singapore. My race was over just before the scheduled finish because of an engine failure; I hitched a lift back to pit lane with Fernando, and official-dom took a dim view of that – they slapped a 10-place grid penalty on me for Korea.

You'd think an old-fashioned racer like Derek Warwick, who was the driver representative among the officials that Singapore weekend, might have taken a more lenient view. They claimed it was dangerous for Fernando to have stopped as Lewis Hamilton's Mercedes came past on the slow-down lap but Lewis was going slower at that point than the pit-lane speed limit! I was delighted, after that run-in with officialdom, to receive an email from Ferrari chairman Luca di Montezemolo. It was short and to the point:

> Dear Mark,
>
> I have seen the ridiculous penalty the FIA has inflicted you, exactly the contrary to what it should do to support a positive image of F1, as the public has shown to appreciate you hitching a ride on Fernando's car.
>
> Good luck for this end of F1 season and for the conclusion of your career in Formula 1, at the closing of which I would be very pleased to have you my guest in Maranello.
>
> Best regards,
>
> Luca di Montezemolo
>
> Chairman
>
> Ferrari

Tell it like it is! Unfortunately I never did get the opportunity to be a guest of Luca's at Maranello as he left Ferrari in the summer of 2014.

*

As the Brazilian curtain fell Ann was emotional too, but she was also relieved. After that final race she told me that the next day was the first day of the rest of my life. For almost 20 years we had been chasing and fulfilling a dream, under constant pressure to perform and deliver, but it was now time for me to start living my life.

Although I was about to embark on a fresh challenge with Porsche, the intensity and relentless scrutiny of everything you do and say, which goes hand-in-hand with F1, had been lifted. She told me that competing at the highest level for 12 years is an impressive stint by anyone's standards. Of my time in F1, Ann says, 'Of course I was disappointed he didn't win the championship in 2010 but ultimately I derived far greater satisfaction than any title could bring from the way Mark conducted himself as a true professional, rising above all the bullshit and being able to hold his head high.'

I began my story by confessing that I was an addict before I had reached the age of 10. I was reminded of that fact when I sat in the cockpit of RB9 on the grid at Interlagos at the end of 2013. People had been asking me all week long what I was going to miss most about being a Formula 1 driver. I hadn't been able to give a very convincing answer, I confess, probably because there was simply so much going through my mind: memories, moments, people met and places seen, chances missed and opportunities taken.

But suddenly I knew the answer.

I'm in the car on the starting grid and the guys all walk away; it's all down to me now; another race is about to unfold. That's a feeling I could never get anywhere else. It's the best legal drug you can get.

16

In Another Cockpit:
2014 and Beyond

IT'S A CLOSED WORLD.

But now the feeling of being shut in is totally different from what I knew in a Formula 1 car. There are two main reasons for that. The first is that I have a roof over my head. The second is that it's pitch dark outside.

For the first time since 1999 I am back in a sports car. No ordinary sports car, either: this is the Porsche 919 Hybrid, a radical sports prototype for the 21st century – but still a sports car with an enclosed cockpit.

Right now it's night-time in Portugal, in the European mid-winter. At the Portimão track in the Algarve, on the first of two days' testing, I am experiencing my first few laps in the Porsche 919.

I'm a little uneasy at first: have I made the right decision in quitting F1 and coming back to sports cars?

But I feel fantastic as well: I love driving at night in these cars. The headlights knife through the darkness; in the cockpit the atmosphere is unbelievable, with the glow from the instruments, the sense of being cocooned at the centre of things. It is very different from anything you could experience anywhere else.

You never experience the night-time in F1, not even in the Grands Prix like Singapore and Abu Dhabi, because the trackside lighting is so good that it's just like driving in daylight.

A few more laps in the car next day are all it takes to convince me. 'Pow!' The car feels taut and responsive, I love being back on Michelin tyres which I can 'feel' so well, the car is very high-tech – and it's quick. I know absolutely that the decision I announced at the 2013 British Grand Prix was right; I know I am going to enjoy the next chapter of my career.

Alex Wurz, often there or thereabouts at key moments in my racing life, hit the nail on the head when he described life as a sports-car racer: 'You are there simply to drive fast,' he said. 'That's all that matters. It's just 5 per cent politics versus 95 per cent racing.'

To me that sounded ideal: I wasn't ready to give up racing just yet, but it was the right time to leave 'that Formula 1 life' behind. I was tired of the travel, weary of all the goings-on in F1 paddocks around the world, and I was seriously over the politics. It got to the point where in the end many of my family and friends, Ann and Dad included, no longer felt like coming to see me race. They had grown weary of the way I was being treated. There was no point in wasting any more energy: nothing was ever going to change.

Maybe I'm too trusting by nature. I didn't think I needed to ask for an even-handed approach from my own team.

By mid-2010 I knew from some of the mechanics any even-handedness had gone. I started asking questions: did I have the best floor spec on my car, were all the micro-parts with the finest detail going to the other side of the garage? It saps your energy levels. Adrian was adamant that I did get the same parts, but there were just too many occasions when they were arriving late, so preparation of my car was compromised. In the end I wondered why Christian broke down in tears in the debrief after my last race in Brazil: was he feeling guilty, or was he just glad to see the back of me?

So in many ways the World Endurance Championship was perfect for me, especially as I had been offered a plum role with a marque whose Le Mans record is second to none. There is another crucial difference between being in the cockpit of a Grand Prix car and sitting in the Porsche: it's not all about me. In endurance racing you are genuinely a member of a team, inside the cockpit as well as outside.

Each race in the WEC is six hours long, with one exception. Each of the Porsche 919s has a team of three drivers. In Formula 1 you and your teammate are in the same livery – end of story. That teammate is the first driver whose times you look for at the end of a session: did you beat him? In the WEC your teammate is your brother: no secrets, no games, we are there to help each other at all times. It's not my car, it's ours. My teammates for 2014 were German Timo Bernhard and young New Zealander Brendon Hartley.

It's our car not only in spirit, but also in its physical make-up: I need to make sure that I am comfortable in the car – the seating position is a lot more upright than the 'lie-down' position in F1, so we use different muscles in the back, the stints in the car are long so you need to guard against numbness in the legs – but I also have to remember I am sharing the office with two other drivers, so compromise is essential to a degree. That was difficult to get used to, I must admit. I was taken aback at the first few test sessions when I saw drivers hanging around with time on their hands. It was very different from the pressure-cooker world of Formula 1, where we operated in a very narrow band, with data input coming from just two sources, each with his own car. Now it was coming from six drivers spread across two cars. It was frustrating at first not to be able to stamp my authority on the direction the car should take. It was tough, too, getting to know so many new people after seven years in the familiar environment of Red Bull Racing. The Porsche team was in its infancy; it would take time for 250 people to become a tight working group. It certainly wasn't all about me.

It *was* about Porsche's decision to return to the highest echelon of sports-car racing. It was also about the most famous race in the world: the Le Mans 24 Hours.

*

By the time I joined them, Porsche had won Le Mans a record 16 times. Their first success was in 1970; ironically, the last time they won there was in 1998, when I was among their opposition in the Mercedes-Benz. At Le Mans that year the two works Porsches came out on top, an outstanding way for Porsche to celebrate the 50th anniversary of the company's creation. But no sooner had they won Le Mans for the 16th time than they announced it would be the last. But times change, the world moves on, and for 2014 Porsche decided it was time to return to Le Mans.

They were ready to rise to the challenge of building a sports prototype – a car designed solely for track racing – in the era of hybrid power. The Porsche 919 would race in the LMP1 category, which is divided between the hybrid-powered machines (LMP1-H) and the conventional private entries (LMP1-L).

LMP1 is purely for full-time professional racing drivers. At 870 kilos the sports prototypes are almost 200 kilos heavier than a Grand Prix car. At Silverstone, where the opening WEC round was to take place, we could antici-pate being around 10 seconds a lap off F1 pace, but sports prototypes are definitely the closest cars in performance and handling to a Formula 1 machine.

If Porsche were keen to get back to grips with sports-car racing at the highest level, the same applied to their new driver. Yes, I had sworn in 1999 that I would never race in a car with a roof again. Yes, I felt then that I never wanted to see Le Mans again either. But this new breed of hybrid sports prototypes was an exciting alternative to F1. The lure of Porsche and their Le Mans history was immense. It was a challenge I just had to accept.

I was happy, too, not to have to be down at racing weight as early as February. With only eight races as compared to 18 or 20 in F1 the time-frame wasn't quite as demanding. In the later stages of my F1 career people asked if I was unwell because they thought I looked so gaunt – Dad said I looked 'as poor as wood' – but that was simply a result of keeping as much weight off my frame as humanly possible. It got so ridiculous that my race engineer Ciaron would ask before a race if I had managed a '#2' before getting into the car!

Physically, perhaps, the sports-car challenge would be a notch below the demands F1 places on the driver. But on the mental side I knew concentration levels would have to be consistently high to cope with the speed differential between the various classes of cars in endurance racing, to be on the ball when it came to passing back-markers and of course for driving through the night.

The Porsche team conducted a private endurance simulation to get the cars battle-ready for six-hour races at Silverstone and Spa to kick-start the WEC season, then the 919's first public airing came at a two-day test session at the end of March at the Le Castellet circuit in the south of France, a former F1 venue now used largely as a testing facility by other racing categories. People always read more into testing results than they perhaps should, but we were pleased with the way the car behaved: the #20 which I co-drove with Timo and Brendon was quickest overall.

Silverstone on the third weekend of April 2014 was an auspicious place to return to racing with a roof over my head. It was the scene of my first major international race win – in a sports car – back in 1998 when Bernd Schneider and I brought the Mercedes home. This time there were no real thoughts of victory: this was all about seeing whether the 919 was up to the task of six hours' high-speed racing on a quick, challenging circuit against world-class competition from Japan in the shape of Toyota and Germany's Audi team.

Qualifying sixth was no disgrace, especially as we were keeping an eye on preparation for the race itself rather than sheer one-lap speed, so we were doing a fair few set-up changes as the day went on. Claiming a podium for third place on Porsche's return to the international sports-car elite was a remarkable achievement. The race had to be red-flagged because of heavy rain, but we had 163 laps under our belts by then and while I still felt like a bit of a rookie in the class I was thrilled to have brought the car home.

It was a terrific learning experience too, especially when it came to threading the car through the back-markers, and getting through my first 'live' pit stop with the driver change routine. It's quite different from the F1 equivalent where you come in, hit your marks, 20 or more people swarm around your car and send you off again about three seconds later. In the Porsche, on the way in I was already running through the procedures: unplug the radio, disconnect the drink bottle, loosen the belts so I could exit quickly and let my teammate hop in. In endurance racing getting the crew bedded in to their own routines and responsibilities is a crucial factor; at Silverstone it went well and set us up nicely for the second round.

It took me back to a racetrack I love, Spa-Francorchamps in Belgium, on 3 May. Our sister car, #14, claimed Porsche's first pole position of their new era in sports-car racing while our #20 started fifth on the grid. Another landmark: despite some technical issues both cars made it to the race finish, one of the key early objectives for Porsche in this first season back. And so to Le Mans.

Going back to La Sarthe was a powerfully emotional experience. The last time I was there, I felt I could have died. Many people, in the media especially, were wondering how I would feel when I first took the 919 out onto the famous circuit. So was I. But as soon as I was on track the 1999 experiences felt as if they belonged to another lifetime.

Almost at once I realised I was really going to enjoy the challenge, especially as the 2014 event would give me the chance to complete my first racing laps of the 13.6-kilometre circuit.

Winning the 24 Hours was not uppermost in our minds at the Porsche team. Our professed aim was to get one of the 919s to the finish. We had done that at Silverstone, but after just a quarter of the Le Mans race time. We had proved our sheer speed with pole position in Belgium. Could we combine speed and durability for a 24-hour marathon? As for me, I simply wanted to leave La Sarthe with happier memories than I took away 15 years before.

At first it didn't look as if I would. Wednesday brought an early reminder of how badly Le Mans can bite you when free practice was red-flagged following a massive accident to Audi driver Loïc Duval. Happily he came out of it all right, though the medical people forbade him to take part in the race. It was a pleasant surprise when we ran in the top two positions on Wednesday, with the #20 leading the way, but once the Thursday evening session was finished we were second (#14) and fourth. One car on the front row, one on the second row: we had every reason to be pleased. I had only fired in two timed laps in the #20 but I was a lot more comfortable than I had felt at the pre-race test. I felt absolutely ready to race at Le Mans.

On Porsche's return to La Sarthe, Timo, Brendon and I led the race at the 22-hour mark but ultimately fell short when I had to retire the car with a powertrain problem. Nevertheless, it was a phenomenal effort by everyone involved. The team spirit was unbelievable all weekend – and not just in our camp. After the race Timo and I went to congratulate the winning Audi team and *we* received a standing

ovation from *them*, team and drivers alike. That camaraderie was something I had never experienced in my racing
life. I had genuinely good times at RBR and got on well with
the majority of the people there, so this is no reflection on
them. But in WEC racing there was an openness, a one-for-
all approach that I found very refreshing. After Le Mans,
my passion for endurance racing was fully reignited. It's the
toughest race in the endurance racing world; it's dangerous
because after all, you are racing at 350 kilometres an hour
in the night and the traffic. But the feeling you get when
it's all going well is irresistible. I would love to achieve an
outright win at Le Mans.

*

The WEC calendar is very different from the hectic F1
calendar. The races are a lot longer, but there are far fewer of
them. It wasn't until September that we went racing again.
There were five rounds remaining in the 2014 WEC season,
the first of them at the spectacular Circuit of the Americas
in Austin, Texas, always a favourite staging-post for Ann and
me. It was a dramatic weekend for weather, with massive
thunderstorms and the race red-flagged because of heavy
rain for 45 minutes. After qualifying second and third the
two 919s came home fourth and fifth.

At Fuji in Japan we qualified second and third, but this
time the #20 car secured another podium with third place
ahead of the #14 in fourth. Shanghai on the first weekend
in November saw the #14 claim another pole position while
we were just 24 thousandths of a second slower in third
place. Tyre damage saw us drop to sixth by the end but the
other three boys took our second successive podium and

our third for the season. Things were picking up nicely, and Bahrain, another track familiar to me from F1 days, brought another memorable moment for us: the two Porsches were on the podium together in second and third positions.

If Le Mans was the highlight for me in my first year back in the sports-car world, the lowest point was the crash that finished my race in the final WEC round in Brazil. It was the biggest crash of my entire career; I was incredibly lucky to come away relatively unscathed. Like a number of other big LMP1 accidents in recent years, mine involved one of the Ferrari GT cars. I wish there was more footage of it because to this day I don't fully understand how it happened. Judging by the point of impact with the wall, it would appear that I passed Matteo Cressoni on the inside of the last corner and he then made contact with the right rear of my car. The closing speeds of the prototypes and GT cars are astronomically different, so it's sometimes hard for those guys to judge how fast we are coming.

I don't remember anything of the accident itself. In fact I've lost 30 minutes from my memory. But instinct kicked in and I spoke to the guys on the radio, unplugged it and shut down the systems on my car. I asked the medics at the scene if I could get back in and finish the race! It was only once I had been transferred to the medivac helicopter that I came round. I recall Timo coming to see me and asking, 'What happened?' Funnily enough I asked him the same question! I may not remember that moment, but Annie certainly does. This is how she saw it.

'One of the reasons I remember it so well is that the day it happened, Sunday 30 November, was Luke's 23rd birthday. It was a rare weekend at home for Luke and me after I had decided to skip the final round of the WEC so I could spend time with him while he was home from university. Earlier in the day we had enjoyed a birthday breakfast at our local coffee shop with Mitch Evans, the young New Zealand driver we took under our wings when he came to the UK several years earlier and who lives close by.

'Meanwhile, almost 6000 miles away in São Paulo, Brazil, Mark was preparing for the six-hour WEC race. Later that afternoon Mitch, Luke and I settled down to watch it on a typically grey and dismal English winter's day. It was a highly entertaining race with plenty of battles throughout the order and it had started particularly well for Timo, Brendan and Mark in the #20 919. From pole position, Timo led and when he handed over to Mark for his first stint, they were leading by more than 20 seconds. However, it wasn't long after Mark handed over the driving duties to Brendon that he rang the house to say the car had lost power and the engineers were trying to recover the situation. As they dropped down the order, and knowing that they were fighting a losing battle with an underpowered car, we started to take our eye off the TV screen – Mitch left to meet a mate for dinner, Luke buried himself in his reference books and I was by myself, keeping one eye on what was happening on TV while reviewing sections of this very book's manuscript with the other.

'Somewhere, lurking in the back of my mind but never allowing it to intrude too much further, I had always wondered what it would be like not to be trackside in the event of Mark's having a bad crash. I was to find the answer that afternoon.

'Mark's had some big crashes over the years but Brazil 2014 was by far the worst he's ever suffered. I had been alerted to the fact there had been a nasty crash by the tone of the commentators, who had spotted the red flags. It got my attention and the cameras then picked up the mangled wreckage of a car in the middle of the track. It's bizarre the tricks your mind and eyes can play on you at moments like this: I thought I was seeing the obliterated remains of a single-seater car, not a sports car. There was nothing left of the car and there were flames licking around the area where a driver would or should be sitting in a single-seater. I've seen some terrible accidents and felt that whoever was in that one couldn't have survived.

'The TV identified it as a Porsche, then one of the LMP1 Porsches, which could only mean one of two cars – the #20 or the #14. Seconds later, they confirmed it was the #20 car of Mark Webber. I looked again, still seeing a single-seater car, and could see yellow – and the only yellow I could think of was the yellow on the top of Mark's race helmet. Knowing it was his car and it was him, I thought he had died. I couldn't watch any longer. I shouted to Luke that something terrible had happened. He said afterwards that he didn't think I was even watching the race at that stage and his first instinct was that something had happened to one of our dogs. But, when he got to me, he saw what was happening on TV. I sat on the floor in our hallway out of sight and sound of the TV with Luke doing his best to comfort and reassure me. He was terribly upset himself but he said he had to go back and watch what was happening so he would know.

'At first, the signs weren't encouraging – I remember him coming back to me saying, "It doesn't look good" Mum.'

But then a few seconds later I heard him yell that Mark had spoken on the radio and then that he had waved from the stretcher. The sense of relief was immense – we hugged and hugged one another. I returned to watch. The bigger and happily more positive picture began to emerge and when the accident was replayed, the penny dropped that what my mind had been telling me was a completely destroyed single-seater car was, in fact, only the back end of the Porsche 919. Had I stayed to watch the next bit of footage I would have seen the front of the car – the capsule where the drivers are cocooned – had done its job brilliantly as it was virtually intact.

'Further relief and reassurance was forthcoming within a few minutes when the Porsche team swung its crisis management procedure into action and made contact with me, asked where I was, asked if I had been watching and gave me the latest news which I could then relate to Alan and Di, who had been watching the race back home in Australia. Porsche handled everything supremely well and continued with regular updates over the phone for the next couple of hours until Mark was able to call me himself from hospital.

'He sounded drowsy and weak but it was a massive relief to hear his voice. He said he was fine but the concussion and losing 30 minutes of Sunday afternoon had shocked him: he said he didn't know how much more he wanted to keep putting himself through this. I told him that now wasn't the time to worry about that and we could talk about it later, knowing full well it was a decision that only he could make and one I wasn't going to influence.

'I am often asked how I bear watching Mark race and I suppose the simplest answer is that you know it's something they enjoy doing; it's what they get out of bed for every day. And actually it's not about you; you're not forced to sign up to be the partner or wife of a racing driver but if you do, you subscribe to living life on the edge. It can bring the highest of highs but it can also come at a price that you have to be prepared to accept.'

After the crash I was airlifted to the nearby Hospital Bandeirantes, where I was kept for further tests and overnight observation. The medical care I received was second to none and I was incredibly touched by the immediate response of the Brazilian motor sport community. People like Rubens Barrichello, Felipe Massa and Emerson Fittipaldi were among the first to get in touch. As word of my accident spread, I was inundated by messages from further afield: Gil de Ferran, Dario Franchitti, Michael Carrick (the Manchester United soccer player who has become a good mate), Pat Rafter, Dougie Lampkin, Jason Crump, Dan MacPherson, Lleyton Hewitt and so many of my current and former colleagues like Tom Kristensen, David Brabham, Fernando, JB, Seb, DC, Daniel Ricciardo, Adrian Newey, Christian Horner and Bernie Ecclestone. At times like these everything that's gone before is stripped away and becomes irrelevant. The sport becomes a sport again and the better side of human nature comes to the fore.

The crash was obviously a tough way to finish 2014. It was the biggest hit of my career and it took the longest time to recover from: I still wasn't in great shape six weeks after the accident. I was lucky only to sustain a few fractured ribs, a contusion of the left lung and pretty severe concussion. But I still trust myself, I trust the ultra-professional team I drive for and what happened to me in Brazil did not outweigh the positives from the rest of the year. At the time of writing I have completely recovered and I am totally committed to getting on with my racing career. Brazil was actually one of our strongest showings. We had qualified the #20 919 on pole and held a 20-second lead in the first part of the race. Three hours into the race we suffered a problem with the turbo and we lost power, but the sister car went on to win the race – and that was exactly what the doctor ordered for Porsche heading into 2015.

Epilogue

A LIFE IN SPORT

I HAVE ALWAYS BELIEVED I HAD A BIT OF THE OLD AUSSIE battler in me. When I think of my own Australian sporting heroes, past and present, such as Jack Brabham, Mick Doohan, Steve Waugh and Lleyton Hewitt, as well as talent they all had or have very similar traits: tenacity, the sheer guts and determination to go out there and achieve something that's pretty difficult to do – like competing at the highest level on the international stage. To me, that's always been a large part of our make-up in Australia.

Men like them share the same sporting qualities I'm most attracted to: integrity, humility and a sense of fair play. They don't constantly go on about what they've done or belittle their opposition, they show respect. They always bounce back and never give up.

In the world of F1, I'm still not sure to this day whether my Aussie battler mentality was the right one to take into the fray week in, week out. But I felt I performed better when I had my back to the wall: in a bizarre way I preferred to be chasing rather than leading. As much as I was encouraged by others from time to time to take a different stance, it was how I felt most comfortable in my own skin and that's all that really matters: being able to look yourself in the mirror.

There is a degree of selfishness involved: after all, you're the one in the cockpit trying to get the job done. Any elite athlete will admit to this side of his or her make-up. We're demanding, we have priorities, we want to focus on areas that are important to us, and nothing else matters. And being an elite athlete is no nine-to-five job: in fact it can come very close to consuming every waking moment, and that makes it particularly tough for those who have to live with you! Luke could certainly testify to that: with so much of our time and energy focused on my career, our home life took a back seat, certainly in the early years. At weekends Ann and I would be off racing somewhere in the UK or Europe, so Luke didn't have the same family life as his friends. With the help of a fantastic support network we did our best to ensure he had as normal a childhood as possible, but he still ribs us to this day about missing out on Sunday roasts and family holidays.

*

Looking at my racing heroes like Brabham and Doohan another way, I admit it's a shame that I haven't done all that they did. Yes, I'm a Grand Prix winner, yes, if I had won many more races it would have been nice, and what would be *really* nice would have been to go out as a World Champion. I didn't, but I gave it everything I had; my talent, my willingness to fly back to Australia in the early days for three frantic days to try to find a sponsor, full of cold sores, stressed out, on the phone crying – all those days are the capital we put in the bank. At times we thought I'd never even get to Formula 1. Once you reach that level you are constantly learning more about yourself. I would love to have achieved more but the man in the mirror looks back at me and tells me I did the best that I could. Ours may have been a different journey but we got there in the end.

You look at the sporting greats and ask *why* they got more out of their careers than you did – and I know *exactly* why. Men like Schumacher, Rossi, or rally champion Sébastien Loeb: I've been fortunate enough to watch all of them at close quarters. They get priorities and compromises right; they can slow things down mentally when they're operating on the limit. Mental recall is also a huge strength. A small example: I shared a KTM X-Bow car with Sébastien Loeb at a Red Bull event. The passenger had to operate a paintball machine-gun and hit targets while the driver navigated the course. When he got in the car, Loeb was very fussy over pedal positions, seat positions, making sure the seatbelts were sorted for the driver swap so we could win time there. He also ensured the gun was at a perfect height for most of our targets before we set off for the race. He wasn't doing it for fun either: our car won! It was all in the preparation.

I've been immensely impressed by how Valentino manages to keep finding drive and desire. Even more impressive is his ability to learn new techniques in the twilight of his career. In 2011, when he was at his lowest ebb in terms of results, he was involved in the accident that killed his great friend Marco Simoncelli in the Malaysian MotoGP. To recover from that tragedy, to rekindle the passion for winning when he could so easily have walked away, proved his enduring love of the sport.

Men like them had something extra in each column, or maybe there were some columns I hadn't covered at all. But I believe Aussie grit really helped me a lot; my preparation certainly helped me massively in getting to Formula 1 and surviving in that environment. I was tenacious; I think my bravery helped me as well; and as Lance Armstrong once said to me, I'm the most intense Australian he's ever met!

To let that intensity down a little I have always enjoyed watching other sports: Manchester United at Old Trafford, the Olympic Games in London, watching Mo Farah coming off the final bend in the 5000 metres – the veins standing out on his neck, a man on the absolute limit and in the loudest stadium I have ever been to in my life! True grit . . . Or the Isle of Man TT: the sheer courage involved in what a man on a motorcycle can do, just off-the-charts stuff – I never, ever take days like that for granted.

I've loved meeting some of the world's greatest sportspeople too: I once had 10 minutes with Pelé. It was just the great footballer, one other person and me in a room and he was such an amazing, friendly gentleman. Pelé changed a lot of people's lives: if he hadn't done what he did, so many others would never have had the opportunity to try to follow in his footsteps. I had a very small taste of that in Pelé's own backyard, and it simply whetted my appetite. Before my first victory in Brazil, in São Paulo in 2010, I visited a youth boxing club on the Wednesday: I said to Red Bull I wanted to go and see these youngsters and to their credit they helped me make that happen. And it was a great experience: you can see it in their eyes, this is their way to escape and it's just brilliant, I really enjoy seeing that spark. You can give them a chance, a bit of light in their lives, something to aspire to.

Some of that feeling spilled over into my decision to help my young fellow Aussie Will Power when he needed someone to give him wings of his own, racing in Europe before going on to really make the grade in the United States. More recently I've been taking a close interest in young New Zealander Mitch Evans as he finds his way in Europe. While they still need to possess that raw hunger, drive and determination, it seems only logical that young drivers should learn from what I achieved or how I coped with all those setbacks on the way through. David Campese, just to repeat the clearest example, was trying to give a young Aussie bloke wings when he helped me all those years ago. In motor racing and elsewhere I want to give something back in my own modest way in terms of helping people realise their potential. The word 'can't' is not really on: encouraging people to understand that, accept it and then act accordingly is a very rewarding thing to do and see.

In certain cases success comes only if you are prepared to put your reputation – your own self-respect – at risk. Think Michael Schumacher at La Rascasse back in 2006 when he deliberately 'parked' his car in qualifying for the Monaco GP after he messed up his own lap. More recently, Seb exposed a side of himself that was at odds with his cheerful, boyishly charming image with that egotistical, *Numero uno* forefinger gesture to the cameras after every pole, every victory. The public rarely see F1 drivers with their helmets off, which is why I removed mine on my slow-down lap at my final F1 race in Brazil. It's really only the men on the podium the fans get a good look at, and I thought Seb repeatedly shoving his finger in front of the camera could have a negative effect, not just on how he was perceived by the fans but, more importantly in my eyes, by other elite sportspeople. You want to earn their respect. You do that when you win with sincerity, style and grace, the way Roger Federer always has.

The finger gesture culminated in the booing after Malaysia 2013, but that was just one of several tricky podium situations with Seb when he was given a hostile reception, even as the Grand Prix winner. Monza in 2013 was the worst, with at least 25,000 spectators beneath the podium. John Surtees, the 1964 Ferrari World Champion, and Jean Alesi (another ex-Ferrari driver) were trying to conduct the podium ceremony; I could see John was having difficulty containing a crowd that was threatening to spoil the presentation of the trophies, so I asked Jean to try to bring the situation under control.

Passions were running high that day: neither of the local Milan soccer teams, Inter and AC, were playing that weekend so the F1 crowd was bigger and more vocal than usual. In the post-race press conference I said I thought the hostility shown towards Seb was too much on the day. At the same time I was disappointed to see Red Bull Racing doing a very good job of convincing themselves that the booing was because of how successful Seb had been. Everyone knew that wasn't the reason at all: the team could have done a lot more to help Seb manage his antics out of the car and the public's perception of him.

Going back to helmets, it was interesting that the FIA decided to ban changes to their colour-schemes in 2015. Seb was one of the biggest culprits when it came to changing his, and when he turned up at the 2010 British Grand Prix with a helmet design featuring mug-shots of 'his' boys, the members of his crew, we thought it was a tad inappropriate. Everyone heaped praise on him for showing how much he thought of them. Although it was a nice touch it left me in an awkward position with the boys on my car asking when I was going to do the same. I'm a no-nonsense sort of bloke so it never crossed my mind that I needed to show how much I valued the boys in such a public manner! The team didn't seem to be unduly concerned; in the end Seb satisfied everyone by putting the entire team on his helmet at the next British GP!

On another occasion, Seb showed just how far he was willing to go to when he crashed and damaged his front wing in practice at Suzuka in 2012. Christian told me Seb promptly forked out the money for a private plane to fly a new wing out from the Red Bull Racing factory with team personnel on board still working on it. It was probably a 300-grand exercise! Impressive – but it makes you wonder how the discussion to do just that first arose! It's an extreme length to go to but this is F1 and there are championships to be won!

I had difficult moments with Seb, but then the camaraderie with my fellow F1 drivers in general was never particularly strong. Maybe we've become rather blasé about the safety of our sport and we don't have the same level of respect for what we are doing against each other week in, week out as they did in the 1960s, '70s and '80s when fatalities were

more commonplace. You placed a lot more value on friendships when you feared they might be short-lived. The layout
of the paddock doesn't exactly encourage F1 fraternising
either. As the motor-homes became more palatial, you
would simply walk between those giant structures and the
cars in the garage, work with your team and go home. It was
quite rare to find a driver somewhere else in the paddock
chatting to another team or having dinner there.

But I always got on well with David Coulthard, Fernando
Alonso, Jenson Button and Robert Kubica. I first came
across Alonso in 2000 when I raced him in Formula 3000.
He was extremely young and had a lot of puppy-fat on board!
I think we naturally had a bit of respect for one another as
we were both driving for fairly average teams at the time and
winning races and scoring podiums. From what I know of
Fernando, his upbringing in rural Spain has similarities to
mine in Australia. It takes a long time to gain his trust. We
talked to each other at race weekends and sat together at
drivers' meetings – to be fair, the media probably portrayed
a stronger relationship than we actually had. We played a bit
of tennis when we were testing or at fly-away Grands Prix
where we might be staying in the same hotel for a week.
Our friendship and mutual respect grew more when we
started talking about me joining him at Ferrari and more
recently his desire to compete with Porsche at Le Mans in
2015. Neither story was ever leaked to the media – they
were always a good six months behind what was actually
happening! Fernando is a shy bloke and not super-confident
in himself out of the car but put him in a race car with
his heart rate up and you'd struggle to find a better racing
driver anywhere in the world.

I've known Jenson Button for a long time and we're from a similar generation. JB's had a phenomenal career; he's a tenacious bastard. It's funny how fitness was a chore and a challenge for him at the start of his F1 career but when he had a very uncompetitive car in 2008 he took up triathlon racing. I think it kept his hunger, self-drive and motivation going. We got a bit closer at the end of my career as we'd both grown up a bit and could see things differently. We spent a great few days in Tokyo between the 2013 South Korean and Japanese Grands Prix; I remember having breakfast the next morning with his dad, John, and whiling away a couple of hours talking about how the sport had changed and how JB and I had changed even within our own careers. Ann, Dad and I were shattered when John Button passed away at the start of 2014. The last thing he said to me at my final Grand Prix in Brazil was that he'd see me at Le Mans as he was planning to come to the race. I know Jenson has felt his dad's loss immensely but Ann and I have always admired the supportive, tightly knit group of family and friends around him, including his now wife Jessica and Mikey Collier, his trainer.

Like Fernando Alonso, Robert Kubica – the only Pole ever to win a Grand Prix, which he did in Canada in 2008 – was one of the few other drivers I felt I could relate to on a genuinely personal level. There were a lot of similarities between Robert and me. He got to F1 in the hardest possible way, and he had to leave his native country of Poland to do it. We were both tall, which brought problems in its wake in the car, and like me he had no time for any of the fun-fair stuff in the paddock, so we always had something to talk about.

Robert was – still is – a real warrior and he had an unbelievable talent. He was a tough prick, I have to say, and he deserved everything he got, except the shocking accident in February 2011 that nearly killed him and cut short his F1 career. It happened when Robert was rallying for fun on the Italian Riviera and it was staggering to realise how close he must have come to losing his life when a piece of guardrail pierced the entire length of his Skoda. We visited him in hospital, where he had endured seven hours of surgery on his hand and arm injuries, and it was horrible to see him in bed there. Of course I could relate to all of that, but he was so gaunt, so downcast – he broke down a little and it all affected Ann quite badly, seeing someone she knew looking so vulnerable and distraught. I remember having dinner with Robert at Monza earlier when he told me he was already disillusioned with F1 and how much he loved his rallying. He got some of his pace notes out and the passion in him was obvious. I believe he would have gone on to win the world title, in fact probably more than once, and I'm pretty sure looking at the man in the mirror would never have troubled Robert.

The new order of F1 is currently led by 2014 world champion Lewis Hamilton. While I might not have much in common with Lewis, we've always got on well and I think he is proving his worth as a world champion in and out of the car.

There is no doubt that in his early years Lewis's father Anthony played a massive part in shaping his career and getting him going. Anthony also drove some pretty heavy principles and disciplines into his son. Lewis was very quickly onto a rocket-ship and it was an almost vertical trip with McLaren. I think for Lewis's first few years there he was breathing, eating, drinking the team, living in Woking, no distractions, and that was evident by the incredible start to his F1 career. The media focus on him in the UK was massive and so was the pressure. Young sportspeople's biggest challenge is understanding themselves as human beings and steering clear of all the back-slappers. Lewis did go through some tough years as a person when there was a lean patch after his initial success. But he seems to be in a much better place now and more comfortable with who he is. He's a brave guy; put him in an environment where he has people believing in him and team harmony, and he's a very handy operator. I like his story, where he came from, and how he got to F1.

One of the young guns most likely to challenge Lewis for world titles in the future is Daniel Ricciardo and it's great to see the Aussie F1 tradition continuing in such a talented pair of hands. I remember just after he'd been announced as a Toro Rosso driver we invited Dan and his mum, Grace, out for dinner to celebrate Australia Day when we found out he was living fairly close to us and they would be on their own that night. Dan's from the big Italian community in Perth, Western Australia, and we had a big Ricciardo family dinner one night at the Stag, the pub-restaurant Ann used to own. Dan's father, Joe, has his own great story about how he came over to the UK and worked in the motor-sport industry as a mechanic for various junior formula teams, which sowed the seeds for Dan's racing career.

I arranged for my physio Roger Cleary to work with Dan in the lead-up to his first F1 test to ensure that he got through it in the best physical shape possible. Rog rang me up after the first day and said that Dan was smoked but although he was tired and sore they managed to get him through the second day. The cars back then were a lot more physically draining and harder to hang onto for a long period of time than they are now. Joe rang me up afterwards to say thank you. It was an important 48 hours for Dan to get through and to have a good little medical team there was only going to help him. It's all turned out very well for him, hasn't it? I was genuinely happy for Dan when he got the nod to move up to the senior Red Bull team for 2014. As another graduate of the Red Bull Junior Program, he fitted that team like a glove. What he went on to achieve during his first year there was sensational. Winning Grands Prix is not easy so to have three victories under his belt already bodes extremely well for his future. Not only does he have some old-fashioned qualities I'm a fan of, he is a breath of fresh air for F1.

So what makes a good Formula 1 driver? As with most sports it's down to mind management and composure under pressure. All drivers have the ability to operate in different conditions in a tight envelope of performance month after month, year after year. Consistency is a must, as is being able to concentrate on the task in hand for a long period of time. We're all competitive, but the top guys are intent on improving: they like the adrenaline, they get a buzz out of managing a dynamic environment and a rush from getting micro-decisions right. To some degree all drivers are arrogant and egotistical. But they're also proud of where they come from, especially when they are their country's sole representative. I always wanted my Australian qualities and values to come through and influence the people I was working with, not just something the media and the fans latched onto.

I think what frustrated some of the older-generation drivers (Michael Schumacher, DC, Fernando, JB, me and to a lesser extent, Lewis and Nico) was the huge shift with the new cars and tyres. Past, present or future, all we drivers want to do is go quicker. But after 2011 lap times took a huge drop, which was disappointing because the new regulations weren't testing us as we'd like. As an F1 competitor, a purist and huge fan of the sport I wanted a category so far ahead of any other that the drivers are intimidated and respectful of driving cars on the limit. We all felt the same, even Michael on his comeback, but we couldn't talk openly about not enjoying it as much. We would meet each other at the back of the trucks during pre-season testing and laugh about where the sport was going. It might be increasing the show but the stimulation for us was on the slide. It's good to hear that the powers-that-be are now looking to make the cars more demanding again for the 2017/18 season – the drivers will respond to that and relish the fresh challenges it throws at them.

As for me, I take great pride in what Bernie Ecclestone said when he learned there was a chance I would go to Ferrari. 'The old guy [meaning Enzo Ferrari himself] would have loved to have Mark in one of his cars.' Enzo Ferrari and Jack Brabham were two of the greatest figures in the early decades of the World Championship: self-made men, driven by ambition and self-belief, utterly determined to be the best. Jack gave me endless support and advice over the years and I know he took great pleasure in seeing me win some of our sport's most coveted Grands Prix. It was partly because of him that I decided not to join Ferrari. When he heard the rumours that I might be, he said he would be very disappointed: for him it was the absolute act of betrayal because they were his motivation – the ones he wanted to beat in his day. It was sad to learn of his death in May 2014.

As I found out when I got to know Bernie a bit more over the years, we share a passion for motorbikes and I love listening to some of his stories about the characters he's come across. He also has an amazing car collection, which not many people have seen, but Mr E, as he is often known, kindly allowed me to take Dad down for a look. It was a special day for us both. Typical Bernie though: he rang when I got there, said everything was for sale, would I care to make him an offer!

I've drawn inspiration from men like Jack Brabham and Steve Waugh for most of my life in sport. I once did, too, from Lance Armstrong. When I first came across him, Armstrong had two faces: one belonged to the multiple Tour de France-winning sports legend, the other to an individual who had faced and beaten the greatest challenge of all, the cancer that seemed certain to kill him.

I met him through a mutual friend, Morris Denton, and the three of us did various bike rides over the years, like the one in Monaco that ended so badly for Morris.

*

I didn't look at F1 as a means to seek fame and fortune. They are happy rewards of the journey I've been on, but all I ever wanted was to test myself against the best. For me it's about representing your country at the highest level and hearing your national anthem on the podium. It was about watching the Prosts, the Sennas and seeing if a kid from Queanbeyan could possibly make it to their level.

Life in the F1 bubble sat uncomfortably with me. As far as I'm concerned, I'm just a normal bloke doing a job that's a bit different. I've travelled the world and seen a lot of amazing places and met a lot of inspirational people. I've thoroughly enjoyed the privileges that come with my profession. But in the end it's the people who count most.

I was always very touched by the fans who came to support me. I'd see them at particular venues every year of my career without fail and they would always come with a birthday present or a good luck charm. I've been sent some incredible drawings and paintings and I appreciate it as the fans' way of demonstrating their own passion. Some people travelled a long way to see me compete. They'd wait outside our hotels and I'd enjoy hearing them explain their travels. They might give me a photo album they had put together of me competing and it meant something to me to see how passionate they were about the sport and following my career.

Mind you, there are days when you have more patience to deal with being in the public eye, and days when you don't. I've never forgotten Damon Hill telling me a story about his father, Graham, World Champion in 1962 and 1968, dutifully attending a signing session for fans at the British Grand Prix one year. Graham stayed far beyond the allotted time slot but when he finally stood up to leave the bloke who was next in line said to him, 'I always thought you were a pillock!'

But the Australian race fans were always brilliant and I'd try to accommodate them as much as I could, even if there were occasions in the last few years where I'd strike a deal with security at the end of a busy day: they'd let me out the far end of the paddock and into my waiting car! You might not know, if you haven't been to Melbourne, that adjacent to the F1 paddock is an enclosure where the die-hard fans assemble each year to get photos and autographs of F1 personnel as they head into the paddock. Woe betide any driver, team principal or celebrity who dares to ignore them: you won't get far before the booing and hissing starts. It's always very good-natured and generates a bit of banter among everyone. On the way to the circuit each morning, we used to mimic them calling out my name: 'MAARRKK, MAARKKK, MAARRK', it was a dead ringer for a murder of crows!

Sometimes it was murder trying to keep everyone else happy as well. Over the years, I was able to give other well-known sportspeople a glimpse of my life inside the F1 paddock and the intensity of the garage in the countdown to the race. Lleyton Hewitt, Michael Carrick, Fabien Barthez, Jason Crump, Ronnie O'Sullivan, Layne Beachley, Kevin Pietersen, Freddie Flintoff and numerous Australian cricketers and Rugby League players came to Grands Prix. They were always incredibly sensitive to my race preparations and cautious about invading my personal space, because they are only too familiar with the process themselves. What blew them away every single time was how visible and accessible the drivers are to everyone in the F1 paddock – I know it's something Bernie has always encouraged – and how we had to run the gauntlet every time we stepped out of our inner sanctum in the team's hospitality area to cross the paddock to the garages.

Sometimes, particularly at Monaco, where you walk among the public alongside the harbour to get to and from the pits, the drivers simply chose to stay in the garages or the engineer's room. What also blew my F1 guests away were the chaotic scenes on the grid with all the hangers-on, TV interviews moments before stepping into the car, and all the distractions we had to manage. I don't think there's any other sport where the participants are so much in the spotlight minutes before they get down to competitive business.

The team would always receive requests for TV interviews on the grid and I would generally say yes if it was someone like Martin Brundle or DC, as they've been there themselves and know what to ask, but the majority would be declined. Bernie and his entourage would always bring VIP guests onto the grid and introduce them to the drivers, but while we might smile and go through the motions, in reality we were a million miles away in our own little world.

The real world, the world I come from, is light years removed from all that. For all the travelling she has done to watch me race, for example, Mum is still happiest in her home environment in Queanbeyan. She likes nothing better than fussing over her loved ones and the family is her life, especially Leanne, Dean and their three children, who live locally. Mum enjoys coming over to Europe to see me but it's taken her a while to adjust to international travel and experiencing different cultures.

I know Mum trusted me when I was racing but she struggled to trust some of the other guys I was racing against. I think she was torn: knowing that I was so passionate and driven about my racing, something that had been on my mind since I was 14, she was undoubtedly proud of my focus towards it, but she didn't like the associated risks. I was quite insensitive to Mum's feelings about racing, in fact I never really thought about my family in terms of my risk-taking decisions in that environment. I was selfishly driven and arrogant in that sense but in my late thirties I became more attuned to how concerned Mum was by what I did for a living.

As for Dad, he has always been with me in spirit, and more often than not he's been right there beside me at the crucial turning-points in my career. He became a familiar and I believe a very popular figure in F1 paddocks around the world; to me it was always so reassuring to know he was around. He knew better than most what it had taken to get me there. His love of sport set me off on my own journey in life; the values he and Mum taught me stood me in good stead every step of the way. Being able to fly Dad up over the Australian coastline in a helicopter is certainly worth a couple of Grand Prix wins to me.

Nowadays my relationship with Leanne is the closest it's ever been. It's easier now I'm not in F1 because I'm not so distracted and can make the time for her and her family. While I was in F1, I may have been there physically but mentally I was still focusing on racing. I've always got on with my brother-in-law Dean and it's been great seeing their three kids developing their own interests and hobbies and starting to figure out what they want to do in life. It's terrific coming back to Australia for a break, but to come back and live is not a priority at the moment: we'll be juggling our time for a while to come.

I hope all those who have been a part of what we fondly call 'Team Webber' will also understand how much their support has meant along the way. I have been privileged to have good, solid people in my life, people I can trust, people who have put in the extra miles for me, people who will share the good times and the bad. Geoff Donohue down in Australia . . . Kerry Fenwick who once told Ann she needed her as her PA and has been with us ever since . . . I have drawn strength and inspiration from all of them.

In my private life my dogs Simba and Shadow have been, without exaggeration, a huge feature of my life. They keep me grounded: they don't care if I've just won Monaco or had the worst day in a cockpit I can ever remember, they just want me to stop messing about and take them out for a run. Their companionship is one of the central features of my life.

And of course Luke is like a younger brother to me. He was only a little tacker when we met. Sport brought Luke and me closer over time: he may be very academic but he's also very knowledgeable on the sporting front. He's a handy tennis player and a good runner. As he's got older we've been able to do more together and I've taken him to some big events like soccer matches at Old Trafford, one-day matches and Tests, Wimbledon and plenty of Grands Prix.

It would be wrong if I were to finish with any other name but Ann's. I don't much like saying 'Told you so', but I was right. Twenty years ago when I met her for the first time I said she must be somebody pretty important. Only she and I know just how important she has been in my life, and the focus, the discipline, the belief she invested in my career.

Together we started the fire and together we have come a long way.

Could we have done some things better? Probably.

Could we have made different decisions? Certainly.

Could we have tried harder to get where we wanted to be? No way.

There was no manual for what we were attempting to do. We used the skills we each had and then made it up as we went along, at least in the early days. Ann is a workaholic who seems to survive on no sleep. She is the most fiercely loyal person I have ever known; she has been unfailingly protective of me and what she sees as my best interests. She is the single most important presence in my life and my best friend. We have complete trust in one another; we are so finely attuned that we each instinctively know what the other is thinking. Ann has always kept me honest: with people like her to help, you don't have to work hard at being yourself.

'How the f#*k are *you* going to get to Formula 1 coming from Queanbeyan?' Together we faced that question so many times; together we answered it. F1 was a pinnacle for me. As I said when I rode up L'Alpe d'Huez with Alain Prost, who was such an inspiration to me, I have always liked ascending.

It's phenomenal to turn around, look back and see where you've come from.

Acknowledgements

Writing an autobiography is no five-minute job and mine has been a mammoth effort by those on the frontline, on and off over the past decade and more. First and foremost, my sincere thanks to my ghostwriter, Stuart Sykes, whose attention to detail has been impeccable. Stuart painstakingly trawled the archives and researched diligently to unearth family history I didn't even know about; he came up with every stat there was to know about my racing career, many of which I'd long forgotten. His biggest challenge of all, though, was deciphering what became known in the process of writing this book as 'Webberisms' for general reading consumption!

Stuart's work would surely have been even more laborious had it not been for the efforts of Chris Lambden, who started the task many years ago, when the idea of a book was first floated, with hours upon hours of early interviews.

Odd as it may seem now, the idea back then was for the book to conclude after my F1 debut at Melbourne in 2002. Happily F1 continued to dominate my life for a further 11 years and a lot more water has flowed under the bridge during that time.

My thanks and admiration to my partner, Ann, for her unwavering commitment to the book, which has consumed a large part of her life over the past two years, and to her son Luke, who was always available to cast an educated eye over numerous drafts and help with the editing process.

Last but not least, thank you to Pan Macmillan, in particular Angus Fontaine and Samantha Sainsbury, for believing I had a worthwhile story to tell. Their patience, guidance and gentle persuasion in encouraging me to share the world I was part of with a wider audience was challenging at times. But I'm thankful to Pan Macmillan for allowing the final decisions to rest with me and I hope between us we've struck a happy balance for the reader.

Of course my career, and therefore my story, would not have been possible without all those people who provided inspiration, support, guidance, insight and friendship. It would take up too many pages to acknowledge them individually, so I hope they will forgive me if I provide an alphabetical list. Each of them knows what their backing meant to me along the way: Valerie Aguer, Dave and Jackie Aldridge, Arai Helmets, Arlene Bansal, Layne Beachley, the Brabham family, Flavio Briatore, Bob Butler, David Campese, John Cavill, the Christensen family, Roger Cleary, Rich Connor, Bob Copp, Morris Denton and family, Alan Docking, Geoff Donohue, Mick Doohan, Kerry Fenwick, Michael Foreman, David Furner, Harry Galloway, Don and

Sue Gatherer, Judith Griggs, David Hahn, John Harnden, Nick Harris, Wolfgang Hatz, Norbert Haug, Bob and Nancy Johnson (and thanks for the cool front-cover shot, Nancy!), and Peter Larner.

Andy Lawson, Spencer Martin, Dietrich Mateschitz, Rod McLean, Dan McPherson, Gordon Message, Bruno Michel, David Moffatt, Chris Morris and family, Adrian Newey, Trevor O'Hoy, Tim and Debbie Parker, Barbara Proske, Dick Puxty, Mike and Pam Reese, Bernd Schneider, Rick Scully, Bernie Shrosbree, Eva Sobonova, Simon Sostaric, Sir Jackie and Lady Stewart and family, Paul Stoddart, Chris Styring, Simon Taylor, Gerhard Ungar, Ron Walker and Danny Wallis.

My sincere thanks to all of them – and to you – for sharing my journey.

Index